St. George's School

Sapientia Utriusque Vitæ Lumen

Presented by

Samuel Nash Vautier Golding
Class of '02

For St. George's School,

I wrote this book because I was following the Xbox from the beginning. The justification for doing it (the box) was to turn games into an art form and to turn the craft of making games into a profession as legitimate as making movies or writing books. That dream is chronicled herein. If you share in it, read on.

Dean Takahashi

OPENING THE
XBOX

Inside Microsoft's Plan to Unleash an Entertainment Revolution

DEAN TAKAHASHI

PRIMA PUBLISHING

Published by Prima Publishing, Roseville, California. Member of the Crown Publishing Group, a division of Random House, Inc.

PRIMA PUBLISHING and colophon are trademarks of Random House, Inc., registered with the United States Patent and Trademark Office.

Library of Congress Cataloging-in-Publication Data on File

ISBN 0-7615-3708-2

02 03 04 05 HH 10 9 8 7 6 5 4 3 2 1
Printed in the United States of America

First Edition

Visit us online at www.primapublishing.com

For Q, QT, and QD

Failure is an intrinsic step toward success.

—CLAYTON CHRISTENSEN,
THE INNOVATOR'S DILEMMA

CONTENTS

FOREWORD

IT IS A RARE AND REMARKABLE experience indeed to be able to take part from the very beginning in something that touches so many people, that inspires and excites the imaginations of so many people, and that in the end changes the lives of so many people as Xbox has.

Xbox was conceived of and championed by a small group of passionate, creative individuals who were so driven and convinced by the power of their idea that even the setbacks that rose in their path served only to strengthen their conviction. It was a simple idea that seems manifestly obvious now—that games could be more, that by creating a platform, a tool really, designed explicitly for game artists, we could give them the opportunity to take their medium to the next level.

Not to overstate it—it is after all, a game console—but consider what a bold undertaking it has been. Consider the skepticism of an entire industry, of analysts, of journalists, of consumers. Consider the risks undertaken by Microsoft not only to design and produce millions of units of hardware, but an entire entertainment business.

And now consider that Microsoft, the great giant, allowed itself to be drawn into this project by a group of relatively junior employees. In the pages that follow, I hope you can get a feeling for what it was like to start with nothing more than three friends and a slide presentation and end up with a multi-billion dollar business and one of the most recognized consumer brands in the world.

Let me take a moment here, before I get too full of myself, to tell you about one of my early encounters with Dean Takahashi, and how I found out that he was writing this book.

The morning of the much-anticipated Xbox announcement at the 2000 Game Developers Conference was easily the most stressful of my young life. Aside from the fact that to most people back then the idea of Microsoft successfully making a game console still seemed genuinely crazy, and the fact that I was laying it all on the line right there on stage next to maximum leader Bill Gates, the hardware itself was so new that nobody was 100 percent sure that it would actually run when the time came.

You see, inside the giant silver X that Bill and I were about to uncover, inside that beautiful solid piece of billet aluminum that I and the embryonic Xbox team had lovingly carved and polished to a blinding shine (I think Horace to this day has metal polish under his nails), was one of the first Nvidia NV15 chips ever to be produced, sitting on one of the most advanced chipsets ever to be coaxed into full speed, powered by barely tested new versions of its drivers, running demo software that was some of the first ever to use the new features of the hardware. It was literally the bleeding edge, and—as an added bonus—if you left it on too long, it would overheat, underheat, or who knew what, and become embarrassingly unstable.

All this in front of the most important people in the world as far as Xbox was concerned—the people who make the games that would, in the end, determine the success or failure of this crazy project. Not to mention that these were also my friends and peers, the people I hoped to be working with for many happy years. If everything worked, we would be heroes—Xbox would be the first console ever to show honest, real technology up front, the first console to announce to, and emphatically celebrate the importance of, the people who make the games. If it didn't work, well, let's just say it was one of those moments that causes you to think, "What the hell am I doing here?"

I will never forget the feeling of walking offstage after the announcement. It had the surreal quality that comes only from major life events, from the culmination of incredible hard work, stress, luck, and a lot of dreaming. Of course, everything had worked out fine, and after the obligatory, exhausting afternoon of press interviews (one every hour, no breaks, repeat until collapse), we were more than ready to have a good stiff drink. Remember that we'd been working basically 24 hours a day for weeks on end to get ready for the announcement, so when some brilliant, benevolent Xbox staffer arranged for us to have dinner and blow off some steam at a local restaurant we jumped, literally, at the chance.

I won't go into detail; however, it suffices to say that at the end of the evening we somehow all ended up, as a group, having an uncommanded yet highly entertaining ride in the restaurant's elevator as it slid for several floors out of control. We laughed, swore one another to secrecy, and chalked it up to a bonding experience.

The next morning, one of the reporters I had talked to the day before approached me, holding an open notebook, pen at the ready. "Tell me about elevator," he said, completely deadpan. "Huh?" I cleverly replied. But my face most likely said it all. I basically ran away from him at that point, remembering that he was from a pretty big newspaper or maybe a magazine.

Later that day he returned, this time with one of our stern-looking Xbox PR people in tow. "Seamus, this is Dean Takahashi of the *Wall Street Journal*. He has a question for you." Dean, notebook open, pen to paper, once again commanded, "Tell me about elevator, I think I know the whole story."

"Um, a team that doesn't have fun can't make a fun product." Not my best spin-doctoring, but at the time I thought it was enough to make the "elevator incident" into a non-story.

Two days later, my Dad called. "Nice piece in the *Journal*, son," he quipped, in the voice reserved for truly galactic screwups. It turned out that Dean had not only been undeterred by my lame response, he had actually published it in the *Wall Street Journal*, along with a sprightly little piece about how I almost killed the entire Xbox project in one stroke by jumping, ostensibly drunk, into a full elevator just as the doors were closing.

So you can imagine my delight when Dean told me he was going to apply those same dogged research skills to write an entire book on Xbox.

A lot of great people at Microsoft and at our partner companies throughout the world have worked incredibly hard to bring Xbox to life. I came to Microsoft to learn about the discipline of software production, and instead learned about a company that would take big risks based on the passion of its employees, a company full of people ready to take on any challenge no matter how tough, a company that values self-questioning and reality checking above all else; a truly great company. I met a group of people who challenged me, supported me, and changed my life. And if you think it takes courage to propose something like Xbox, imagine the courage it takes to volunteer to leave a successful career on an established, profitable product to come work with the crazies on an untested, expensive dream. I hope someday to have the intestinal fortitude of guys like Robbie Bach and Ed Fries, who did exactly that.

The story of Xbox is a great one, full of great ideas, great challenges, and ultimately—I pray—great victory. It has certainly been one of the greatest learning experiences in my life; it has made me feel humbled many more times than it has made me feel like a hero. I sincerely hope you enjoy reading about this thing that forever changed all of our lives, and that it gives you some insight into what it was like to embark on this journey—one I didn't realize the magnitude of until it was too late to turn back!

—*Seamus Blackley*

P.S. If Dean's descriptions of all of us on the Xbox team seem in any way unflattering, please remember that Dean is a rather short, pudgy, bespectacled man who nobody could mistake for anything other than a journalist. Conversely, if Dean's descriptions seem flattering, he's a brilliant, hard-hitting, unrelenting journalist, unafraid to go where others fear to tread.

ACKNOWLEDGMENTS

I NEVER THOUGHT I WOULD GET the energy to write a book. The two hours of free time in a day (after family time—gotta say that to please my wife) were best used playing games. Better to conquer entire worlds than wrestle with words. The latter was my day job. This book started as a suggestion in July 2000 during a visit to Redmond. Xbox public relations officers David Hufford and Carrie Cowan asked if I was interested in doing an Xbox book. I told them yes, particularly if it was an independent journalistic effort without the official stamp of endorsement from Microsoft. I worked up a proposal and began collecting material for the book. As the Xbox gathered momentum, I waited for Microsoft's response. I dreamed about having the same level of access that Tracy Kidder had for *The Soul of a New Machine,* which was the model for the "you are there" feeling I wanted to create with the book. When could I go up to Redmond and watch some super-secret meetings in progress? I waited. And waited. And waited. Robbie Bach approved the idea in principal, but it took a backseat to getting the Xbox out the door. I finally remembered I was a journalist and that I could find my own way into the story. I found insiders willing to help. The Xbox team felt like they were making history, and they wanted someone to record it despite the absence of a 100 percent official PR blessing. Were it not for this unofficial help, I would never have finished on time nor would I have gotten a flavor for the events behind closed doors. I owe those sources my gratitude, but I can't thank them by name because they didn't get clearance to talk to me. Official interviews with Microsoft were tardy, but for arranging them I thank Jen Martin of Edelman PR and James Bernard. I appreciated the official interview time I got from Mike Abrash, J Allard, Drew Angeloff, Robbie Bach, Kevin Bachus, Seamus Blackley, Tim Bucher, John Connors, Don Coyner, Jon DeVaan, Cameron Ferroni, Ed Fries, Jeff Henshaw, Todd Holmdahl, Jason Jones, Horace Luke, John O'Rourke, and Rick Rashid. Bill Gates provided some help in an e-mail while I was at the *Wall Street Journal* and I caught him again later in a short interview.

Many people outside of Microsoft at Nintendo, Sony, Sega, analyst firms, and a multitude of game publishers and developers also filled in key pieces of the story. Derek Perez, Jen-Hsun Huang, David Kirk, Chris Malachowsky, Phil Carmack, Dan Vivoli, and the rest of the crew at Nvidia were especially helpful. George Haber of GigaPixel shared his tale openly. David Wu, Bobby Kotick, Bruno Bonnell, Brian Farrell, Peter Moore, Lorne Lanning, Sherry McKenna, Tim Miller, Tim Sweeney, John Carmack, Alan Yu, Doug Lowenstein, Alex St. John, John Inada, Dan Duncalf, Julian Eggebrecht, Jason Rubin, Jim Sacherman, and Kirk James generously shared their stories. Family members helped me fill in the blanks on many of the characters.

I want to thank the *Red Herring* editors for generously allowing me to work on the book in between magazine stories. I owe a great deal to top editors Jason Pontin and Blaise Zerega. My former boss at the *Red Herring,* David Diamond, was also a big help early on as I struggled to propose the book and find a publisher and an agent. I borrowed heavily from pieces that I wrote for the *Red Herring* and the *Wall Street Journal.* In particular, chapters three and five include much material that ran first in the *Red Herring.* Matt Jarrette of Prima and Dierdre Hussey of the *Red Herring* helped with promotion. I received excellent editing advice from former *Red Herring* staffers Debbie Gravitz and Vinnee Tong. Geoff Keighley supplied invaluable writing and reporting tips as I was wrapping up my draft. Mark Williams gave me good writing tips. My editors at Prima, David Richardson and Andrew Vallas, put up with my endless messages and gave good editing feedback. Hilary Powers did an excellent copyedit. My nephew Brett Tjader kept me posted on games. I thank my tireless agent, Danielle Jatlow, of Waterside Productions. I got help from experienced journalists like Steven Kent, Marc Saltzman, Van Burnham, Mike Salmon, Tom Ham, Joe Funk, Alex Pham, Ben Seto, and Tom Russo. Mom provided great proofreading, and many friends and family were generous with writer-sustaining praise. And thanks to readers like Hiko Ikeda, who provide me with the feedback from the real world. Finally, my wife and two children put up with this obsession of mine for 18 months and I can't thank them enough for their love and support. They're the reason I had the energy to do this book.

CHAPTER 1

SHADOW OF THE PAST

BILL GATES WAS SHOWING OFF his new baby at the Game Developers Conference in early 2000. Thousands of people packed the room, and the event was on TV all over the world. Standing on a dark, cavernous stage, Gates talked about the future of gaming as he got ready to unveil what he coyly called a "secret, a very deep secret." Thanks to months of rumors, everyone was in the know: The secret was the Xbox, Microsoft's new video game console. He pulled a black shroud off a table and there was the machine, a shiny chrome-finished device in the shape of a letter X, with a big green jewel at its center.

1

"The modest tag line here is the future of console gaming," he said.

To demonstrate the Xbox, Gates invited one of its instigators, Jonathan "Seamus" Blackley, to come onto the stage with him. Blackley draped a leather jacket emblazoned with the Xbox logo over Gates's shoulders and then proceeded to wow the audience by showing on a big screen what the Xbox could do. He offered 3-D animations that looked real, ranging from ping pong balls bouncing around a room to a computer-animated woman practicing martial arts maneuvers in perfect unison with a 16-foot-tall robot. Blackley got a roar of applause. The Xbox was Microsoft's weapon to take on the Japanese in the video game business and make gaming the premiere entertainment medium. And, more than the words of the world's richest man, it was the eye-popping demos that made this proposition credible.

"We've put quite a budget behind this one, and we're going to break through in a very big way," Gates concluded.

Few people outside the industry knew much about Blackley, a seasoned game developer who only a year ago had shipped one of the industry's biggest lemons—a failed dinosaur game called *Trespasser*. Now he was sharing the limelight with the world's richest man, making lemonade that game fanatics were drinking with delight. He and his friends had persuaded Bill Gates to pour money into the Xbox. Just who was this Blackley guy?

This was not the first time Blackley had rubbed shoulders with someone so famous. A few years earlier, he toiled on *Trespasser* for filmmaker Steven Spielberg. Spielberg's DreamWorks movie studio in Los Angeles had hired Blackley to help it break into the computer games business, and Blackley aimed to make a great game out of the big DreamWorks hit, *Jurassic Park: The Lost World*. It was a hip job for someone who believed that making video games was more than a technological feat: It was an artistic enterprise, like the craft of making a movie. The association with Spielberg gave Blackley cachet, validating his passion for the emerging art form of interactive entertainment.

Though he'd worked in other fields, gaming was his real love. He says, "[I was always] burning to get this emotion out of me and put it into the people playing the games."

Blackley was not your typical Hollywood smoothie. His cheeks hung wider than the rest of his face, giving him a kind of chipmunk look. His grin was impish and his voice high-pitched. He had close-shorn brownish red hair that made it easier to spot the stud piercing his earlobe. He stood 6'2" and weighed about 190 pounds; he had the build of a linebacker. He spoke a mile a minute and could match wits with the brightest. Besides games, he had mastered an eclectic mix of topics including cars, physics, jazz, and history. He dressed in daring fashions, combining Nehru-style jackets and black sock hats. His flair set him apart from the typically conservative tech crowd. One of his friends described him as "one of the first cool people I met among the geeks" in the games business.

Blackley's knack for talking was one of the things that got him into trouble when he was at DreamWorks. He had built up the hype machine for a new game that would have realistic physics—a world where the laws of everyday life would apply. If you threw a stone in the water, it would splash. Game magazines predicted it would be a monster success. W. J. "Jerry" Sanders III, CEO of Advanced Micro Devices, showed it off in the hope that it would sell more of his microprocessors for personal computers. And Bill Gates himself saw a demo and e-mailed Blackley's boss, saying that Blackley was "brilliant."

Blackley had tried to make his game so real that gamers would lose themselves in an artificial world of an island full of dangerous dinosaurs. He wanted the game world to be as real as the movie. Instead, gamers found that the game was slow-paced, buggy, and riddled with inconsistencies; they could shoot at a realistic dinosaur with a realistic rifle, but they couldn't predict whether the monster would be hurt or even annoyed. Instead, it was so numbingly realistic it was boring. *Trespasser* was expected to sell a million units, but when it debuted in the fall of 1998, only 60,000 units sold. It generated about $2.4 million in revenue in the United States, a fraction of its estimated $8 million costs. Blackley's flame-out was spectacular. He had been a modern-day Icarus burning his wings by flying too close to the sun. This man, who liked to soar in the clouds in his own glider, had been in his dream job. With melted wings he fell into the sea. He quit the job at Dream-Works and sought out a place to salve his wounds in anonymity. As it all came crashing down, Blackley assumed his career in games was finished.

"I figured no one would trust me to make a game again because I fucked up," he recalls. "It was an emotional disaster."

It was all the more crushing because Blackley felt he had let Spielberg down. People aimed their darts at the moviemaker, saying he had no business being in games. Blackley was disappointed in himself because he had given up a career as a theoretical physicist—atom-smashing work he felt was akin to "staring at the face of God"—to fulfill his lifelong passion of creating compelling games. He had been very good at game development. One of his titles, *Flight Unlimited,* sold 780,000 units, and he had grown so confident at creating games that he trusted his own intuition. He was in for a huge surprise. He was trying to move games closer to film, and instead he had set games back.

"*Trespasser* was a victim of overambition, of trying to achieve way too much innovation," says Austin Grossman, a designer and writer who had worked with Blackley on *Trespasser.* "But that was Seamus. He wasn't there to do a job. He was there to make his mark."

Monica Singh, another producer at DreamWorks and a close friend, says Blackley took the reviews as if they were personal attacks against him.

As Singh tried to console Blackley, she watched him "descend into his darkest time." He moved out of the office he shared with another producer and began working in an office by himself away from the rest of the team. He didn't goof around like he once did. He visited his parents in New Mexico but was too fidgety to relax. He broke up with the girlfriend he had been seeing for eight years.

Blackley kept thinking about what might have been. He still says, "I believe *Trespasser* could have been a magnificent game if I had figured out how to pull the team out of the mistakes I had led them into." But at that point, no amount of agonizing would undo the problems.

Blackley felt he had to get away. He took off on a vacation through Europe and toured a bunch of World War II battlefields and castles. In England, he checked out the historic sites of the war-era code breakers like Alan Turing, whose work became the foundation of computer science. He braved the spiders and looked through the gun emplacements at Point du Hoc, where U.S. Army Rangers scaled the cliffs to take out German artillery on D-Day. He walked on Omaha Beach where soldiers died by the hundreds as they crawled and staggered up the beach in the face of withering machine gun fire. Here, he could forget about work and contemplate heroism in another time. When he returned from his trip, he gathered his belongings and left Hollywood for Redmond, a suburb of Seattle.

On February 5, 1999, Blackley showed up at Microsoft feeling like a failure. It was his first day as an employee of the Gates empire. Rain had so drenched the lawn of the corporate housing where he stayed that it was inundated with standing water. He was homesick for his sunny Hollywood. He sat through the required orientation to get his company identification badge. Then he went to his office. No window views. Every new employee at Microsoft started out with the same kind of windowless nine-by twelve-foot office and worked their way up to window views. He knew it shouldn't matter, but, irrationally, he was pissed and depressed. Yet he liked the anonymity. "I was going to be just a regular guy," he recalled. "Just do my work and go home by 5:30 P.M. and hang out with the dog." That was just what he felt he needed to exorcise his personal demons and rehabilitate his spirit. At the time, he was 30 years old.

The sprawling campus was a congenial place—at least when the rain wasn't pouring. It was sprinkled with low-rise white buildings with green-tinted glass. A creek wound its way through stands of evergreen trees. The dozens of buildings provided nearly 5 million square feet of office space. Well stocked with beverage dispensers, volleyball courts, soccer fields, and other perks, Microsoft had all the trappings of a hugely successful company. At the time Blackley joined it, Microsoft was on its way to reporting $19.75 billion in annual revenue and astounding profits of $7.7 billion. The campus was populated with multiple tiers of employees. About 73.6 percent of them were male, and the average age was 34.1 years—but their fortunes differed sharply depending on how long they'd been with the company. In the parking lots, employee cars illustrated the stratified work environment. Sleek Porsches and BMWs glistened in the sunshine next to dinged-up 1972 Toyota Corollas and their cousins. Far from rich himself, Blackley had a few friends on campus in this super-rich fraternity. It was an insular neighborhood, where people belonged to the cult of Bill Gates. Microsoft was viewed with considerable disrespect from the outside as a bunch of copycats and hegemonists. But inside, Softies believed that they were misunderstood innovators. They had an ability to execute ruthlessly. The attitude was fiercely antigovernment because of the recent antitrust case. One division even had a piñata in the image of U.S. Attorney General Janet Reno, filled with bitter chocolate.

Not long after he started at Microsoft, Blackley attended the March 1999 Game Developers Conference in San Jose, California. As the conference ended, Blackley met with Johnny Wilson, editor-in-chief of *Computer Gaming World,* a game review magazine. The gray-bearded Wilson was a kind of elder statesman among game critics and he had done much to build the hype around *Trespasser,* which graced the cover of *CGW* more than a year before its release. Wilson saw Blackley as an ambitious genius who tried to break new ground. Yet his magazine was one of those that panned the game. Wilson and Blackley sat atop the Microsoft booth at the end of the show, as workers were busy dismantling the exhibits. Blackley was mentally packing away his dreams. Wilson stretched out his hands to Blackley and told him in a kindly voice, "Seamus, keep making games." The moment was too much for Blackley. He broke down in tears.

At Microsoft, Blackley settled into a job as a graphics program manager working for one of the company's multimedia executives. There, in the shadow of the Cascade Mountains, he figured he could always get rich from Microsoft's lucrative stock options (if the stock performed miracles) and do some good coding.

"I wanted to keep my head down and focus on good old-fashioned technology," Blackley recalls.

It was an opportunity to escape the embarrassment that awaited him from chance encounters with fellow game developers. Stripped of the things that gave him confidence, he had to start rebuilding his sense of self. Blackley's trip to Redmond might have achieved his aim of technical grace and anonymity. But Blackley wasn't meant to be a bystander. Once, he interceded when a pit bull seized the throat of a Labrador retriever that a little boy was walking through a friend's neighborhood. A crowd of bystanders just stood by and watched or yelled, "Do something!" Blackley moved between the dogs and began pulling the pit bull off the helpless retriever. He wrapped his huge bulk around the pit bull, which hung on to its prey. He began pounding the dog with his fists. Finally, the pit bull yelped and let go. Blackley had saved the Labrador's life, while very clearly risking his own, according to witnesses on the scene. He got up, walked into his friend's house and began crying, thinking, "That dog was just doing what it was bred to do. It didn't know any better. It just doesn't make you feel good hitting a dog like that."

Just days into the job at Microsoft, Blackley steered off course. Sony announced the details of its PlayStation 2 game console. It was such a big event in the history of games that Blackley felt weird sitting on the sidelines. A friend of his, Otto Berkes, had already been contemplating how to take on Sony. He got Blackley to think about Microsoft's response. And Jay Torborg, one of Blackley's overseers, asked him to write an analysis comparing the graphics of the PlayStation 2 to those of the PC. Blackley took the assignment on the road. His former girlfriend had recently moved to Boston. He visited her, and on the trip back he started thinking about his assignment. He thought of how *Trespasser* could have been a magnificent game if the current technology had been available when he started. So much had moved forward on the PC. The graphics chip makers were hitting their stride with 3-D animation hardware. The Windows 98 operating system was fully capable of running games without constantly crashing. There was a growing base of fans and a community of dedicated game developers.

"You realize that you're at a tipping point for things to happen," Blackley recalled. "That occurred to me on the plane. It switched on in my head, and I became driven. It was like taking on a new mission: What if we could make a game console at Microsoft?"

Blackley might not have had such a hard time with *Trespasser* if the PC weren't such a pain to program. He had needed more horsepower to do his game right, but he also had to make sure it ran on the slowest of game computers as well as the fastest. That had always been the curse of doing PC games. Computer gamers owned a mishmash of hardware that had been made by different companies with a wide array of configurations. It was a miracle that most computers were even remotely close to compatible with the Microsoft and Intel standards. The only way to make sure a game would run on all machines was to shoot for the lowest common denominator. And the technology kept changing. Even seasoned game developers fretted, as Blackley discovered on *Trespasser,* that "it's like we have to recreate the camera every time we want to do a new film." That was a contrast to video game consoles, which were stable, predictable platforms because they were all uniform and because they changed technology only once every five years or so.

Working at Microsoft in the division focused on graphics, Blackley had been exposed to the latest graphics chip technologies, the ones that were still in the labs. Blackley made his technical comparisons. It dawned on him, "we could smoke the PlayStation 2." He knew that DirectX had better tools than the PlayStation 2. So he thought, "What if there were a game console that was easy to program?" What if that console could take advantage of the best of PC technologies without taking on the complexity of having to support dozens of different combinations of user hardware, with incompatible sound cards or graphics components? It was not a brilliant thought. It was obvious. It was also obvious to most people that it couldn't be done. The PC always had these tradeoffs, and video game consoles had others, such as early technological obsolescence. Nothing would ever change that. But Blackley persisted in experimenting with this what-if exercise.

"I realized we could make a superdooper bad-ass game console," he says. "The hardware didn't have to be the limiting factor anymore. It could be like the canvas that allowed the artist to express his true intentions without so many compromises."

Upon his return to Redmond, he began sharing this "bullshit idea" among his friends at work. There was so much activity already going on that it was never clear if he started the project or joined an existing one. Even before he began recruiting, three others were already working on the same idea. Ted Hase, a manager in the Developer Relations Group who promoted game technology; Kevin Bachus, a product marketing manager for DirectX who had an encyclopedic knowledge of the games industry; and Otto Berkes, a DirectX graphics programming whiz who had begun work on a "Windows entertainment platform." They could all relate because they too had complained for years about the PC. They all wanted Microsoft to create a console. The friends exchanged some e-mail and decided to call the machine the Xbox, named after the DirectX technology that allowed games to run on Microsoft's Windows software.

One by one, coworkers signed on board. Blackley met with Bill Gates and Microsoft President Steve Ballmer more times than most other first-year Microsoft employees could ever hope. The two men replaced Spielberg as Blackley's business idols. Again, he happily played the role of their gregarious acolyte. By the end of the planning he had persuaded one of the world's biggest technology giants to commit billions of dollars over five years to what would be the manifestation of the "war for the eyeballs" predicted years earlier by Intel Chairman Andrew Grove, who felt that an all-out battle for consumers was about to bring the PC industry into conflict with consumer electronics makers. Planting a virus that reshaped the company, Blackley and his friends instigated the largest start-up in Microsoft's history. He inaugurated a world war between the hegemonies of Microsoft, Sony, and Nintendo. A year after the idea sprouted, Gates and Blackley told the world about the Xbox at the Game Developers Conference, and 20 months after that Microsoft unleashed the Xbox on gamers and vowed to sell tens of millions of units.

Blackley had recovered from failure. He dove back into the fray and set himself up for either a glorious comeback or an even more gargantuan crash. He felt the depths of despair and the elation of victory. He became the little guy people in the games industry rooted for—even though he was part of a giant, much-vilified company. This is the story of how he and his cohorts convinced Bill Gates to enter the video game business, pitting technology based on the PC against the established consoles of Sony, Nintendo, and (for a time) Sega—in what would be no less than a worldwide battle for control of entertainment in the living room. Time will tell if Microsoft will take over the video game business and control the future of entertainment in the same way that it has absorbed so many other high-tech markets. Brilliant or stupid. Fast or slow. Does Microsoft really get it? People would wonder that throughout the entire Xbox project. But one lesson was surprisingly clear to Blackley: "It turned out that fucking up was a really good experience."

CHAPTER 2

DO SOMETHING!

BLACKLEY'S PROPOSAL CAUGHT TRACTION because the enthusiasm for games trickled down from the top of Microsoft. It was on the mind of Chairman Bill Gates, who wanted to get into the living room. He had a lock on the PC and he needed the TV. Getting his software into a game console was one way. This, however, was easier said than done.

His company had failed several times in the games business. The company's PC games business was growing but had not been profitable. Flagship offerings like *Microsoft Flight Simulator* and the newer *Age of Empires* sold millions of copies, but the consoles were another story. In 1983, the company had teamed up with consumer electronics companies (including Sony) to launch its own hybrid PC-console, dubbed MSX, in Asian markets. For lack of good games, it never took off. In the mid-1990s, Microsoft's game division contemplated doing games for the original Sony PlayStation but could never come to terms in signing the nondisclosure agreement. Gates' DirectX minions had succeeded in convincing Japan's Sega Enterprises, the third-ranked console maker, to put Microsoft's Windows CE operating system into the Sega Dreamcast console. But that console drew big yawns as Sega ran out of cash to promote it. Dragon, the version of CE that Microsoft developed for the Dreamcast, was slow, partly because Sega's graphics vendor changed the details of the hardware five times before it was done. Most game developers skipped Dragon and used Sega's tools for creating games for the Dreamcast. The Dreamcast grabbed barely 15 percent of the market in its U.S. launch. Over time the share sank, and the console was scuttled in 2001. Game developers who heard about these Microsoft blunders just shook their heads.

"Microsoft has tried to do this before and you have to wonder about their level of commitment to the games industry," said Trip Hawkins, CEO of 3DO, a game publisher that had also had its dreams of creating an American-designed game console in the early 1990s.

But Gates hadn't given up. He approached Sony's CEO, Nobuyuki Idei, well before the PS 2 announcement in 1999. Gates wanted Idei to use Microsoft's programming tools, which Gates argued would make it easy to make games for the upcoming PlayStation 2. Idei turned Gates down. According to Idei, Gates flew into a rage since Sony had rebuffed him in other areas, too. Idei was surprised at how personally Gates took these affronts, whereas most other CEOs of global companies understood that their peers would be both rivals and allies in different markets.

"With Microsoft, open architecture means Microsoft architecture," Idei said in an interview with Ken Auletta of the *New Yorker* magazine.[1]

Gates came back from meetings with Sony and told his people that he knew that Sony wanted to compete with Microsoft and that the PlayStation 2 was going to be more than a TV set-top or a game box. It was going to be a threat to the PC. From Gates' account, Microsoft executives thought the meetings were amiable encounters in contrast to Idei.

Of course, it was easy for Sony to turn Microsoft away. Everyone knew the lesson of the IBM personal computer. In 1981, IBM was in such a rush to get a PC to the market that it patched together a machine using a Microsoft operating system and a chip from Intel, rather than making those pieces itself. That wedge was all those companies needed. Soon enough, IBM lost its proprietary edge. The key chokeholds belonged to Intel and Microsoft. Both were able to reap monopoly profits because everyone had to be compatible with them to run the software that consumers and businesses wanted. The lesson was not lost: Use Microsoft's software at your own peril. John Malone, the powerful chairman of TCI, then the nation's biggest cable TV operator, said he didn't want to be beholden to Microsoft. He was reluctant to allow it inside cable set-top boxes.[2] Gerald Levin, CEO of Time Warner, said in a speech several years before he sold his company to America Online that he expected Intel and Microsoft to leverage their dominant positions in technology into footholds in media. Disney CEO Michael Eisner said, "The common wisdom right now is the person to worry about the most right now is Bill Gates."[3] It was as if the world had adopted a containment policy against the Microsoft menace, the same way the United States tried to contain the Soviet Union. Microsoft's peace offerings and partnership pledges wouldn't work anymore. Everyone could see its real intentions, given the company's past history of aggression. The corporate track record was becoming evident day by day with the progress of the antitrust trial. With the weight of history against an alliance, Microsoft and Sony walked away without an agreement. "We didn't think Microsoft was serious about games," said Kunitake Ando, Sony's president and chief operating officer.

Sony proceeded to announce the details of its gigantic project, the PlayStation 2, on March 2, 1999. Sony's Ken Kutaragi and his team had worked on the new console for five years. Perhaps the Sony executives should have remembered why they got into the games business in the first place. Before it began work on the PlayStation, Sony had a manufacturing alliance with Nintendo. But in 1991, Kyoto-based Nintendo decided to betray Sony by striking a manufacturing alliance with Philips Electronics. Chastened, Kutaragi, the creator of the Play-Station, proposed to make his own console. Seeking revenge, Norio Ohga, then Sony's CEO, approved the venture in a rage, waving his arms and shouting, "Do it!" during a contentious product pitch meeting. Likewise, many years later, a spurned Bill Gates could be expected to take his revenge on Sony.[4]

But why should these new rulers of the games universe have cared about Bill Gates? Sony had emerged as the victor of the last console war. Sony captured 47 percent of the worldwide video game console market from 1995 to 2000, according to market researcher Cahners In-Stat. Nintendo had 28 percent, Sega had 23 percent, and others like 3DO were left with 2 percent. Nintendo had its stronghold in well-known brands such as Mario and a grip on the market for kids under 12. It had defined video games in the mid-1980s as it took leadership away from Atari and other early leaders. Sega had a moment in the sun in the early 1990s with its Genesis console, but it was focused on the rebellious lot of hardcore gamers and had failed with its follow-up generations of Saturn and Dreamcast consoles.

Sony had achieved broad market penetration with its Play-Station by targeting the 18- to 34-year-old males whose opinions were key. They influenced those younger than them.

Nintendo, on the other hand, was constantly dogged by the question: Do you really want to play games on your little brother's machine? Sony had also figured out that the CD-ROM, the compact disc that could be deciphered with laser beams, was far cheaper to mass produce than Nintendo's cartridges, which used pricey semiconductor memory. Whereas games for the Nintendo 64 often sold for $50 to $60, Sony could make a profit on games that sold for $40. Over five years, Sony drove its hardware costs from $450 down to $80. And while Nintendo had heavily restricted who could make games on its platform, Sony welcomed almost all comers. As a result, it covered all the bases more quickly in terms of consumer preferences. It was easy to find several games in each category, whether baseball, football, fantasy role-playing, fighting, or racing games. By 1999, the Sony console penetrated a third of U.S. homes, with customers spread from kids to adults 55 and older. While Nintendo had Mario, Sony's minions came up with *Crash Bandicoot,* which sold more than 22 million copies counting all of its sequels. Nintendo had once owned 95 percent of the market. But with over 80 million PlayStation unit sales worldwide, Sony was the company to beat.

Sony was confident its reign would continue because it had the jump on the next generation. The PS 2 would have unprecedented powers and would even be classified as a supercomputer under Japan's export control laws. It would be a "revolutionary computer entertainment system set to reinvent the nature of video games," according to Sony. The machine sported a 128-bit microprocessor dubbed the Emotion Engine for its purported ability to create emotional responses in gamers through realistic depictions of humans—the goal that had eluded Seamus Blackley at DreamWorks.

Because computer images consist of simple polygons that are strung together in complex meshes, the quality of computer graphics is often measured in how many polygons the machine can draw in a second. The PlayStation 2 could process a theoretical maximum of 66 million polygons per second, about 183 times faster than the 360,000 polygons per second for the original PlayStation launched in 1994, and about 10 to 15 times faster than the Sega Dreamcast launched in 1998. The performance of the $299 PS 2 would be many times more than the fastest $1 million Silicon Graphics Reality Engine supercomputers of the early 1990s. This translated to some real visual differences. Instead of just 400 polygons, cars in the *Gran Turismo 3* racing game could be built from 4,000 polygons. That was akin to painting a picture with a finer paintbrush, allowing for richer details like reflections, shadows, and bumpy surfaces.

Sony planned to surpass the 80 million unit sales for its original box by selling 100 million to 150 million PS 2s by 2004, Sony's Ando said. The new box would offer the value of backward compatibility, a feature lifted from the PC. A gamer's entire library of original PlayStation games would play on the PS 2. Sony planned to break down all the sales barriers in the games industry, adding consumers who had never felt the urge to blast away at digital bits. Since the machine doubled as a digital video disc player and could be configured to connect to the Internet, it was more than just a video game console.

3DO's Trip Hawkins said at a games summit at the Massachusetts Institute of Technology that the Sony box was a "Trojan Horse," purchased as a game machine but used as an entertainment hub that usurps the roles of the TV set-top box and personal computer. Hawkins had said as much when he launched the 3DO Real Multiplayer in 1993, which became an early failure. From Hawkins' perspective, Sony's Trojan Horse stood a better chance at replacing the personal computer as the home's entertainment box.

Sony spared no expense on the machine. Sony had committed to building its own $1 billion chip factory to make its graphics chip and it hired Toshiba to jointly build its Emotion Engine microprocessor. Over time, Sony would begin to make money by driving manufacturing costs down. It could do so by shrinking the size of its chips so that they were more manufacturable and took less material to build. Every couple of years, semiconductor technology advanced to the next level, with chip makers building chips with finer and finer circuitry. And, with the razor-and-razor-blades model, Sony could afford to lose money for a time on the hardware sales as long as it generated high margins with software royalties from third-party game publishers and sales of its own software. Still, the initial costs were staggering. Keith Diefendorff, then editor-in-chief of the *Microprocessor Report,* estimated that the Emotion Engine and the graphics chip were so large that they each carried a manufacturing cost of $100. Asked about the cost estimates, Sony engineer Hidetoka Magoshi said, "We don't care how much it costs."

Sony had incorporated into its plans a chip-industry truism known as Moore's Law. Formulated by Intel Chairman Gordon Moore in 1965, Moore's Law predicted that chips would double performance every 18 months. That was because every 18 months the chip miniaturization technology would advance so that the circuitry could be drawn with finer and finer lines. Circuits could be closer together, and they would become faster because the electrons flowing through them had less distance to travel. As a result, designers would be able to put twice as many transistors on the same size chip to boost the chip's performance (PC makers used this approach to cram new technology into new boxes every six months or so), or they could choose to halve the size of the chip and lower its manufacturing costs (console makers used this approach).

As a result, Sony priced its first PlayStation machines at $300 or more and then brought the price down to about $99 by the end of the five years. This approach also had the advantage of giving developers a stable platform to target. With the PC, the platform was always a moving target while the price stayed relatively constant.

Sony also spent several hundred million dollars on marketing and advertising. Most of the hardcore gamers were certain to buy the machine at the outset as they had done with the Sega Dreamcast, but Sony also wanted to advertise the PS 2 brand in a way that would help expand the overall market for games. Sony made sure that gamers would buy this box. But so would just about everyone else who owned a television set. It was not just the future of video game entertainment, but the future of entertainment, period, crowed Kazuo Hirai, president of Sony's U.S. game hardware unit.

"Our goals are much different from our competition's," said Andrew House, senior vice president of marketing at Sony's U.S. unit, during an interview at Sony's magnificent Metreon entertainment complex in San Francisco. "We're trying to reach a broader audience. If it is just a game console, then we've failed."

Without Microsoft software in it, this Sony machine wasn't quite "bad-ass" enough for Blackley, or for Gates. Blackley had noticed, like many other game developers, that the Sony box would be a nightmare to program. It used parallel processors, four of them operating simultaneously and in a way that made it hard to balance the work load between the central processing unit and the graphics processors. Most PC and game-console programmers were used to dealing with just one main processor and one graphics processor that weren't as hard to keep busy. They didn't like the task of dividing their software up so that it could keep all those multiple processors busy, particularly if there was no suite of development tools that could make it easy for them to do so. For years, companies had attempted to introduce parallel processing machines, like Sega's Saturn console. And, each time, machines that were simpler to program won the hearts of developers.

"Parallel processing has never taken off because it's so damn hard for people to think about," says Mark Pesce, a graphics expert and author of *The Playful World*. "The learning curve is horrendous, with maybe 18 to 36 months for people to learn how to program it."

Winning over developers was the first step to winning over consumers. Blackley knew that the PC processing model, which focused on a single central processing unit, a single graphics chip, and easier software-writing tools would be far easier for game developers.

THE RETREAT

Shortly after the Sony announcement, Microsoft's top executives met at the inn at Resort Semiahmoo, a waterside retreat that sits at the tip of a mile-long peninsula jutting into Puget Sound near Blaine in Washington State, not far from the Canadian border and about two hours' drive from Seattle. For three days, March 18 through 20, they reviewed business strategy in light of the company's 25th anniversary. It so happened that a five-week recess had just begun in the Microsoft antitrust trial, allowing Gates to focus on business.

"Steve [Ballmer] and I were in the process of redefining Microsoft's vision for the first time in 25 years," Gates said in an e-mail interview. "And as part of that process we had been discussing how to add value in the home beyond the work we've always done on the PC. In our reviews over the years, we've always talked about how gamers are the early adopters of technology in the home and we've discussed ways to better serve them."[5]

In attendance were Robbie Bach, general manager of the consumer software division that made everything from games to Office productivity software; Rick Thompson, vice president of the hardware group that made joysticks and mice; Craig Mundie, a strategist who ran non-PC consumer businesses and who specialized in strategies that involved more than one division; Rick Rashid, senior vice president of research; David Cole, vice president of the consumer Windows operating systems; and Jon DeVaan, a senior vice president of consumer products who was in charge of the WebTV group, which made a set-top box that combined Internet browsing with the TV.

These men rarely lost any battles that Bill Gates had ordered them to win. With the Sony announcement fresh in their heads, Gates's group proposed to start a business that would allow Microsoft to capture a bigger share of the games market, and not just by expanding the PC games business.

No one at Microsoft needed reminders about Sony. On March 7, 1999, the *New York Times* ran a long story by veteran technology journalist John Markoff about the coming battle between Microsoft and Sony. He predicted that PC technology would invade consumer electronics as the age of digital electronics progressed.[6]

There was plenty of dissatisfaction in the executive ranks about the PC and its ability to move into the living room. All previous attempts to do living-room computers had been dismal failures. The press was now talking about a "post-PC era" of devices known as information appliances. These simple, stripped-down devices would excel at just a few things, like running a browser for Web cruising—and they didn't need to use Microsoft software.

Microsoft itself had recognized this threat and had created its Windows CE operating system. The stripped-down Windows CE software could be the brains of devices like handheld computers. Called PocketPCs, these computers couldn't run word processors, but they could do things like play music files, run calendars and address books, and download e-mail via a wireless connection. For years, these devices had been over-hyped, but they were starting to gain some traction. So the top brass at Microsoft was already aware of a possible shift away from a PC-centric world, and they were planning contingencies in case the non-PC devices took off quickly. Furthermore, the company bought WebTV Networks in August 1997 for $425 million. Microsoft was in the midst of putting Windows CE into that product. But Windows CE wasn't making much headway because it required a lot of memory and therefore more expensive hardware to run.

Why did Microsoft think it could beat Sony in video games? The answer goes back to the PC. Sony was a vertical market player, making many of its own components in its own food chain. Microsoft could assault the market with a horizontal strategy, providing its software to sit atop an amalgam of hardware components each made by a specialist that could drive the costs down faster. Whereas Sony, to some degree, was compelled to use much of its own technology, Microsoft could cherry-pick the best technologies and come up with a better game console. The task was like a replay of using best-of-breed components to put together a low-cost PC.

In addition, Sony's competitive posture was like waving a red flag in front of the Microsoft bull. The company's executives were bragging that they had set the standards in games, that Windows just didn't matter in the entertainment market, and that you really needed specialized hardware designed for entertainment. Games were the No. 2 application used on home computers, behind word processing. But PC gaming was clearly on the defensive versus console gaming. Smart publishers—like Electronic Arts, which reaped two-thirds of its revenues from consoles—were shifting to the consoles from the PC. Only one of the top 30 game titles in 1998 was a PC title, and the rest were all console games. And console hardware, priced much lower than a PC, had been outselling the home computer for several years on a unit basis. Sony's PlayStation all by itself was beginning to come close to surpassing home computer sales, and PlayStation unit sales were larger than the sales of the top five home computer makers combined. In Sony's 1998 fiscal year, when manufacturing costs had dropped considerably on the consoles, PlayStation business accounted for 44 percent of the company's operating profits.

Observers believed Microsoft would tread slowly because of legal scrutiny and because it wasn't a hardware company. Gates knew that the antitrust case against IBM in the 1970s caused the behemoth to lose its grip on the computer industry by making IBM move slowly. Microsoft wouldn't bog down in a legal quagmire that Gates called "IBM disease."[7] In addition, Gates had written in both of his business books that Microsoft's goal was to do what no other technology company had ever accomplished: to successfully bridge the transition from one era of technology to another. And, for once, here was a market where Gates could charge in and be considered a good guy rescuing the industry.

At Gates's urging, the executive group at Resort Semiahmoo concluded Microsoft had a chance to expand its role in gaming and that it needed to come up with an answer to the PlayStation 2. The renegades knew that Gates was having the big retreat, but they hadn't yet briefed him or anyone else about their plans.

"We didn't know about the Xbox at the time," said executive Robbie Bach.

It was a coincidence that the Xbox bubbled up from the bottom as Gates showed interest in games, but that was just a measure of how worrisome Sony had become to Microsoft. Everyone was worried. Rick Thompson raised an alarm at the retreat.

"If Sony, America Online, and AT&T ever got together, they could put a game box out that would be subsidized by your telephone, Internet, or cable TV bill and give it away for free at the local Safeway," Thompson said.

The thought was very frightening, for it showed how an alliance of rivals could gang up to break Microsoft's hold on consumers using the PC. Thompson was noting a change in selling hardware: Give away the hardware and make money with software or services. It was much like the business model for cellular phones, which were selling in far higher numbers than PCs. From Thompson's point of view, this wasn't necessarily a threat to the PC, which was primarily a productivity tool. The TV would most likely demand different devices, and Thompson thought that Microsoft should address both of them. The executives themselves had no clear plan. "For them to say let's do a game console would have been like me saying, 'I'm going to build a nuclear weapon in my garage,'" Blackley said later.[8]

But Bill Gates asked Craig Mundie, the man who had been responsible for the WebTV acquisition, to take the raw ideas for a games business and organize a cross-divisional initiative within Microsoft. Upon returning to Microsoft, Mundie put out the word that people should attend a meeting on March 31 to consider the games business strategy. Gates knew that the window of opportunity for Microsoft to establish a presence in the living room was closing; he had to act fast.

So the idea filtering down from the top was inadvertently set up to meet with the Xbox proposal that bubbled up from the bottom at roughly the same time. The renegades would soon be legit. But they faced huge hurdles as Microsoft tried to rationalize its diverse product lines, making sure that the company's products were consistent to the degree possible. This rationalization cost the Xbox entrepreneurs vital weeks. Veterans among Microsoft's ranks called this the "strategy tax."[9]

Meanwhile, Sony was poised to launch in Japan in March 2000. And Nintendo had been working on its next-generation console since 1998.

CHAPTER 3

HIGH TIDE FOR THE GAMES INDUSTRY

BLACKLEY AND THE OTHERS knew they were getting into something big. Video games were crossing the chasm between the addicts and the mainstream.[1]

With the PlayStation 2, Sony believed it had begun a new era in entertainment. The launch, scheduled for spring 2000 in Japan and fall 2000 in the United States, was just the beginning of the next-generation wave. Nintendo was sure to follow its Nintendo 64 with a new box and it looked like Microsoft would introduce its Xbox as well. Added to that was Nintendo's GameBoy Advance, the latest version of its handheld game player, which would debut in the summer of

2001. Sega's Dreamcast had tried to start the new era, but the company pulled the plug after selling only 8 million consoles worldwide. Sony would carry on the assault on the larger entertainment industry.

As they marched to market, each of the remaining companies planned a big ad blitz, and their combined budgets called for more than $1.5 billion in advertising for the new consoles— all aimed at making gaming seem like the coolest activity on earth, not just a pastime for nerds. Microsoft's game group chief, Ed Fries, believed the console competition would work like the space race between the United States and the Soviet Union, in this case advancing innovation in games and driving their mass-market acceptance.

The contenders were out to grab a bigger share of entertainment dollars and a longer slice of leisure time, and to dispel their negative images in popular culture. In the years ahead, the pundits predicted, games would unify into a single mass market—as online consoles and computers would allow players to meet together in cyberspace. That contrasted with the prevailing trend in entertainment, which, particularly with TV, was splintering.

In the game industry's master plan, games would become an inescapable part of mainstream culture. People would play games everywhere, in bars and restaurants, at work during breaks on computer networks, on the go with handhelds and cell phones, and at home with their computers and consoles. Graphics on the PlayStation 2 was 600 times better than the original PlayStation's, allowing for new kinds of special effects and virtual worlds. Games could still create cartoon animations for kids, but now they were also creating the fanciful special effects and realism that could appeal to older fans as well. It was expected that this kind of entertainment technology would appeal to all cultures. A case in point came from John Barbour, chief executive officer of Toysrus.com, who was taken aback on on getting an e-mail from a boy on Bora Bora, a remote Pacific island in French Polynesia, asking for a PlayStation 2.

"That says something about gaming, and its reach," says Barbour.

On the surface it seemed that the world already belonged to the game industry. Most industry people knew that video game sales were closing in on movie box-office receipts in the United States. But, that comparison didn't tell the whole story. At the turn of the century, there were still some obstacles to Planet Game. Worldwide, the video game business—including peripherals, game rentals, game sales, portables, and console hardware—added up to about $20 billion. Additional revenues from PC games, cell phones, set-top boxes, and online games could conceivably push the number to $30 billion. Cahners Instat estimated the business would double between 2000 and 2005. Forrester Research predicted the games industry would triple in the same time frame, while International Data Corp. predicted that the percentage of households with game consoles would double to 70 percent. But estimates of all movie-related revenues from pay-per-view to DVD rentals and sales—not to mention TV revenues—far exceeded the size of the games industry. Adams Media Research estimated the movie-TV combination could be many times as large as the games industry.

Many adults had outgrown gaming and complained that games had become too hard to learn. They didn't have the time to waste 50 hours before they discovered the secrets of *The Legend of Zelda* or became good enough to beat their kids. Gaming also seemed likely to be thwarted until more people were using high-speed Internet connections, which had reached only 8 percent of United States households as of 2001. Women and girls were often left out of the target audience, limiting the breakout opportunities for blockbuster games. And few people said they got as big an emotional charge out of games as they did from movies.

"We have a long way to go," said Peter Molyneux, president of Lionhead Studios in Guildford, England, and one of the most-celebrated game designers in the industry. "We are just getting out of the circus tent and into the cinema. But we're not even in the talkies yet."

Gaming had a history of failed attempts to go mainstream. Gamers had distant memories of failed companies like 3DO and Rocket Science, the decline of arcades, and the failures of Hollywood's investments in gaming that left investors scarred. 3DO launched in 1993 with a box that touted the CD-ROM but cost too much and didn't have enough games. Rocket Science tried to use Hollywood talent to create games but it folded in the mid-1990s. And numerous movie studios started game divisions only to shut them down. Thanks in no small part to the failure of *Trespasser,* Spielberg's DreamWorks movie studio sold off its game division to Electronic Arts.

One growing obstacle for gaming was intangible: a widespread perception that games were too violent. Political opponents of violent games such as U.S. Senator Joseph Lieberman (D-Conn.), received a boost in media attention after the high school shootings in Littleton, Colorado, in the spring of 1999. The teenage shooters, who killed a dozen students and one teacher before turning the guns on themselves, were big fans of the violent computer game *Doom.* Every subsequent school shooting prompted more outrage and even lawsuits against the games industry, which indignantly said it was a scapegoat. Reacting to Littleton, the Federal Trade Commission reported in September 2000 that the games industry, like movies and music, targeted violent entertainment at kids. The FTC studied advertisements in youth-oriented media, looked at internal company marketing plans, and even ran undercover operations to show how easy it was for kids to buy mature-rated games. These critics made people wonder if games were breeding grounds for antisocial geeks, weirdos, mass murderers, and addicts. For many, gaming was a source of cultural pollution.

Not all parents were swayed by the concerns about violence, and blazing guns haven't hurt the marketability of movies, but many wondered about how games affect their children. Since adults bought 90 percent of games sold, parental disapproval remained an obstacle to the manifest destiny of games.

Beyond the violence issue, "parents worried about the socialization of their children," said Brenda Laurel, an entertainment researcher and former developer of games for girls. "They fear their children, especially young boys, are disappearing into these worlds of games and are forgoing social interaction."

Henry Jenkins, a professor of comparative media studies at the Massachusetts Institute of Technology, fretted at a games conference in 1999 that games might get stuck in the same cultural ghetto as comic books, which despite their diversity never expanded their audience after increased regulation—banning things such as positive depictions of illicit drug experiences—in the 1960s. Jenkins traced the negative attitude toward games to the "American Puritanical ethic that holds play as suspicious." This attitude has greeted each new form of entertainment, be it novels, radio, TV, or comics. By comparison, game playing was far more readily accepted in places such as Japan, which is a smaller market for games than the United States but has more gaming per capita.

"Gaming is a pawn in the debate, a part of a much larger culture war aimed at discrediting the entertainment industry," Jenkins said. "But there's a shift in who's playing games and that's having an enormous cultural impact."

It wasn't just young male teenage delinquents playing games anymore. The resistance to gaming was futile in a lot of ways, like trying to halt the advance of the Borg in *Star Trek* or the spread of Disney worldwide. Nolan Bushnell, founder of Atari and chief executive officer of uWink, a Los Angeles–based maker of game terminals for public places, said that games are the latest evolution of play, which serves a fundamental purpose for the human species.

"The power of play is to engage in simulations that people can't do in real life because of the consequences that happen in real life," he said. "There are people who say we should just work and sleep, but most will agree that entertainment balances life out. Creativity comes from fantasy, and you get some of that from movies, some from games, and a whole panoply of experiences."

Over time, the economic success of gaming and its growing diversity of subject matter will likely silence its cultural enemies. History shows that gaming doubles its revenues with each product generation, or once every five years. Edward Williams, a game stock analyst at Gerard Klauer Mattison, predicted that more than 200 million next-generation consoles would be sold between 2000 and 2005, compared to about 125 million for the previous generation of consoles.

Throughout the 1990s, the game industry was on the offensive in the battle over its image, and it was no surprise that every game advertisement showed how cool it was to play games and belong to a hip crowd of insiders. The Interactive Digital Software Association, the game industry's trade group, tried to overcome the perception of games as geeky toys by trotting out an impressive load of statistics during conferences in 1999 and 2000.

Indeed, for those who remembered games as child's play, it was time to revisit the scenery. About 61 percent of game players are adults and the average player is 28, according to the IDSA. The biggest categories of games are strategy and role-playing, followed closely by action, sports, and racing, while the violent shooting and fighting games are about 15 percent of the market. Females are 43 percent of the audience. Players over 50 are 13 percent of the audience. About 145 million Americans, more than half of the population, said they played games.

Outside the United States, markets like Japan, Korea, and the United Kingdom were embracing gaming in huge numbers.

(Sony noted there were 2,800 games created for the Play-Station in Japan, versus only 800 in the United States.) In South Korea, about 25,000 new Internet cafes sprouted and quickly filled with people playing online multiplayer PC games like *Starcraft*, a real-time science-fiction strategy game. In a country with only 50 million people, an estimated 20 percent were hooked on games.

At the turn of the century, movies and television still had the bigger celebrities and audiences that crossed over many different geographies. That's why the film *Titanic* raked in $1.8 billion in box-office receipts worldwide, and why the *Survivor* reality TV show drew an audience of 40 million in an evening.

But game publishers were taking a page from Hollywood's book in cross-selling. Nintendo's *Pokemon* is an example of how games can be considered an entertainment property similar to Disney's *The Lion King*. Nintendo sold more than 65 million *Pokemon* games worldwide, generating revenues of billions of dollars. It also revived sales of its 10-year-old handheld Game-Boy and set the stage for the launch of its GameBoy Advance. Including licensed revenues from products like trading cards, cartoons, movies, and merchandise, cumulative *Pokemon* revenues surpassed $14 billion worldwide in 2001.

"In our case, the game is bigger than the [*Pokemon*] movie," said Minoru Arakawa, president of Nintendo of America in Redmond, Washington.

The game makers were even making runs at movie-like games with movie-like budgets. Square Co., a Tokyo-based gaming giant, tripped up on its *Final Fantasy: The Spirits Within*. The company spent $137 million on the animated film based on its popular game series, but it only achieved $35 million in United States box-office sales. But the movie-game convergence wasn't just a Japanese phenomenon. The digital gunslinging game character Lara Croft sold more than 20 million units worldwide for publisher Eidos Interactive, and in the summer of 2001 a *Tomb*

Raider movie hit the big screen, produced by Paramount Pictures. The movie grossed $131 million in the United States, and it finally ended any doubt that a popular game could be made into a blockbuster movie. About 100 games were being considered as the basis for movies, according to the IDSA. Judging by all the celebrity endorsements in games, from Tiger Woods to the rock group Kiss, entertainers had figured out where the money was. And, in turn, those celebrities helped parents become more comfortable with the subject matter of games.

The key piece in the gaming master plan was supposed to be the Internet, as next-generation consoles move players to the Web, according to "Pervasive Gaming," a report by former analyst Jeremy Schwartz at Forrester Research. Interacting with other people engaged in the same game, not just watching an event, seems inherently more entertaining, giving games an advantage over passive entertainment, said Schwartz. He believes that Internet-based consoles will eventually transform entertainment by blending TV programming with games, leading to content that resembles *Who Wants to Be a Millionaire?* rather than the trigger-happy offspring of *Doom*. Games where social interaction was key were attracting grandmothers and others who weren't hardcore gamers, and that was drawing advertisers. Microsoft's MSN Gaming Zone grew to 18 million registered users, many of whom played games such as *Spades* for free. Yet the Zone got revenues from ads, such as a truck driving game sponsored by Toyota, and from subscriptions for premium games. Over time, Schwartz believed that product placements in games would eventually grab ad dollars away from the traditional media.

Demographic change will also deliver bigger audiences for games. The baby boom echo, the cohort of kids born to baby boomers between 1977 and 1997, has become the biggest generation of youths in United States history. This generation—numbering about 80 million and roughly 30 percent of all Americans—grew up "bathed in bits," says author Donald

Tapscott. They've been wired from an early age and are far more comfortable with interactive entertainment than with passive TV viewing.

"When these kids play games, they're developing in new ways," says Tapscott, author of *Growing Up Digital*. "They're learning about characters, storytelling, communicating. They're actors instead of recipients."[2]

For this generation, the rites of passage are not about beating Dad on the basketball court but about beating Dad in *Twisted Metal Black* or *Madden NFL 2002*. The tradition of trash-talking rivals in the mall arcades moved to Internet play, where raking your competitor over the coals and then bragging about it was becoming a tradition. With this generation in mind, it isn't surprising that surveys showed that a third of the population viewed playing electronic games as the most fun entertainment, according to a 2000 survey by the IDSA.

Certainly younger crowds were playing games more—about 80 percent of kids ages 8 to 12 are gamers—but the kids who grew up with *Pong* and *Pac-Man* are now pushing 40. Some older gamers have outgrown games, but many are sticking with their old hobby, whether that means renting Nintendo games at the video store for their own kids or playing online against old college friends. The habit could be much like listening to rock music, says David Cole, an analyst at DFC Intelligence in La Jolla, California. As baby boomers age, they continue to listen to new kinds of rock, not just the songs that they grew up with. Over time, the adult gamers have shifted attitudes about who plays games and whether gaming is socially acceptable.

"Gaming relieves stress," says Jim Downey, a 34-year-old network consultant in Howell, New Jersey, and a married father of two. "It's something that takes you out of your everyday mindset. I play it on my own, with my friends, or with my five-year-old. I even love *Spades* online because I used to play it with my grandmother all the time after school. It's all legitimate entertainment."

Girls may flock to the machines as long as the content draws them. Ever since Mattel introduced its first Barbie computer game in 1996 and Purple Moon launched its intellectual games for girls, the market for girls' games has grown. Other companies are following in their footsteps, and women have begun flocking to game Web sites that offer "family games" such as Uproar.com's *Family Feud*. Then there are women who play to silence the trash-talking males in games like *Quake*.

Crossover titles, which use a known brand made famous in another medium, can also hit huge numbers if the game itself is a good one. Nintendo and its key developer Rare Ltd. scored a gigantic hit with the James Bond license for its *Goldeneye* game, and Electronic Arts expects to score well with *James Bond* for the PlayStation 2. Parents are comfortable buying these kinds of branded games, and players like them because they are easy to learn. That's one reason that Electronic Arts paid tens of millions of dollars for the rights to create games based on the popular *Harry Potter* novels. Sony's online fantasy role-playing game *EverQuest* is a big hit, but observers believe that such a game based on *The Lord of the Rings* or *Star Wars* would be much bigger. Taking the cue, EA and Sierra Studios signed up to make *Lord of the Rings* games, and LucasArts planned to make a massively multiplayer game called *Star Wars Galaxies*. Such a movie tie-in, of course, was the hope of Blackley's ill-fated dinosaur game. Sports franchises were also quite popular, with sports stars like Tiger Woods crossing over to lift sales of normally lackluster golf games.

It is because of sports and crossover games that many of the top 10 hits in video games are the same in Europe, Japan, and the United States. Of course, many in the games industry would prefer that a universal hit on the scale of the movie *Titanic* emerge from the brands that are homegrown within games. And a few franchises that have gathered momentum over the years show some promise.

The Sims has sold more than 10 million units worldwide and generated more than $300 million in revenues for Electronic Arts in the past several years. It's an example of the growing variety of games that appeal to the mass market player. The game, which allows people to simulate the life of a family or neighborhood, is a hit among all ages and genders. Hardcore gamers like its novelty, and non-gamers enjoy the fact that social interaction, not violence, is the main object of the game. As if playing with dolls, players can create make-believe situations like first dates with their game characters and watch how the events might unfold in real life.

Will Wright created *The Sims* as part of a seven-year intellectual effort to dive deeper into the behavior of cities and to sort out the behavior of individual people and neighborhoods. Wright's research took him from the study of architecture and the economics of everyday things to the psychological theories of Abraham Maslow.

The popularity of *The Sims* represents a rare union of the hardcore gamers, who number around 9 million in the United States, and the casual game fans, who number about 30 million. The casual gamers are having the most dramatic impact on the bestseller lists by buying titles that are accessible to just about everyone, like *Frogger* and *Rollercoaster Tycoon*.

The lesson of *The Sims* was that fans reward fresh thinking, not just tired sequels. To broaden their appeal, games of the future have to be "less about elves, orcs, and aliens" and more about topics that "are accessible to normal human beings," says Warren Spector, a seasoned game designer at Eidos' Ion Storm division in Austin.

The thinkers of the games industry hold out hope that homegrown games, which don't borrow creative assets from another medium, will ultimately trigger "emotional responses" from audiences, the feelings of joy or sorrow that the best movies evoke. Artistic minded critics like Jenkins are training the new game development talent to think this way, but it takes much experimentation, an unappealing proposition for a risk-averse industry that stays with tried-and-true formulas like Hollywood does.

"The holy grail is to make the game that can make someone cry," says Warren Spector. "Emotion is key. Imagine if you said something funny and a game character laughed. Maybe you get them angry and then you're forced to back off before shooting."

It isn't too hard to imagine such games as a new kind of art, the kind deserving of academic study and Oscars. The IDSA's Doug Lowenstein says that games are the only medium that combines many different types of art in one package. "Interactive games are the ultimate synthesis of artistic forms," he says. "You are taking story ideas, scripts, storyboards, graphics design, original sound, artists and animators, design documents—all the elements of artistic expression are there in a single product."

Ultimately, artistic titles will give the fans of gaming their best ammunition in the battle with cultural warriors who believe that gaming has no redeeming value, says Jenkins. The artistic, creative games could bridge high art and pop culture, mass market and hardcore game fans.

Jenkins likes to trot out a comparison in the birth of other art forms. He writes, "In 1925, the leading literary and arts critic Gilbert Seldes took a radical approach to the aesthetics of popular culture in a treatise titled *The Seven Lively Arts*. Adopting what was then a controversial position, Seldes argued that America's primary contributions to artistic expression had come through emerging forms of popular culture such as jazz, the Broadway musical, the Hollywood cinema, and the comic strip. While these arts have gained cultural respectability over the past 75 years, each was disreputable when Seldes staked out his position." Computer games, Jenkins concludes, "are art—a popular art, an emerging art, a largely unrecognized art, but an art nevertheless."[3]

CHAPTER 4

THE BOOMERANG GAME

THE STAKES IN THE GAMES BUSINESS weren't just financial. They had cultural significance—and even a bearing on what would be considered art in the digital age. Bill Gates himself probably wasn't thinking about this as he contemplated diving into games. But these broader issues meant more to Blackley and his cohorts as the Xbox gathered momentum within Microsoft. He wanted gaming to be considered a high art, and he wanted to give artists the ultimate machine for the purpose.

"I hope the Xbox will be a petri dish for great things where artists gain control of what games are all about," he said. "And the technology will be good enough so people can bring their visions to life."

Blackley was no stranger to gaming. He was one of those people whose life was a big arc. He tried to escape the dreams of his adolescence and move into serious work, only to be drawn back to his first love.

He was born in New Mexico in 1968. Blackley's father, Fred, was a radiologist who grew up in Colorado Springs. Alice, his future wife, was a Minnesotan who moved to Colorado to suppress her allergies and go to school. They met in college. The family bounced around from city to city, in part just to find better jobs but also because Fred Blackley encountered the occasional corrupt hospital radiology department, where employees would steal the silver halide residue from the X rays and secretly sell it. When Fred Blackley opposed these practices, he didn't last long in his job.

"We moved all around the West as he moved from job to job," Seamus Blackley recalled. "We lived in Casper, Wyoming; Las Vegas; Phoenix; Long Beach."

Every year, Blackley went to a different school until the fifth grade. In Albuquerque, the elder Blackley made a stand, exposing the silver-stealing practice. Blackley remembers his father receiving death threats over the phone in the middle of the night. The calls terrified the young boy and his mother. But Blackley's father prevailed and was appointed chairman of the department. His father would later dismiss his son's admiration for this moral stance, but young Blackley considered his dad a real-life hero.

Of course, some moves were just to find better jobs. At last, the family settled into a four-bedroom house in a crime-free neighborhood in Albuquerque. The parents enrolled their son in a prep school, the Albuquerque Academy, where the boy scored well on tests—getting one of the highest entry test scores—and proceeded to do horribly on his grades.

Blackley went through a phase of making Mercury gas bombs. His mother told him to put the bombs in the garage, not in the house—a reflection of more innocent times than today.

"Back then, we had no reason to think he would blow the house up," Alice Blackley said.

Of course, she didn't know what kind of explosives these were. Blackley and his friends put the bombs—which exploded upon contact—on the tips of rockets. As Blackley drove around town in his Jeep, he would launch the rockets at billboards; the bombs would rip huge holes in the signs. Blackley played pranks on his sister Amanda, like booby-trapping the family bathroom with alarms. Though perhaps misguided, the boy was bright. "I was a computer guy before anyone knew what a floppy disk was," he says. "I won awards for artistic things. I played in band, piano, lighting in theater, built go-carts. I liked to have projects. I did a lot of that but was massively fucked up."

Blackley's affinity for non-academic subjects didn't make it easy for him to fit into the academic school. When he was about 10 years old, he discovered the joys of computing with the school's Digital Equipment Corp. PDP-11 minicomputer. With his friends, he started creating crude animations and zany computer games with titles like "Marble Madness." While arcade games were becoming common, computer games were still so rare that Blackley had to create them on his own. The fourth bedroom of the house became a computer room.

"We wrote programs as a contest to see who could write cooler stuff," Blackley recalls. "We'd jealously guard our tools. I had a blitting engine for the Apple II and could move color characters around the screen. My friend Chris couldn't. We traded tools around."

To Blackley, the finest game ever made was *Robotron: 2084,* which he describes as akin to *The Great Gatsby.* The game debuted in arcades in 1982, when Blackley was still in high school. The object was to save the last human family and kill anything or anyone that got in the way. Two joysticks were used to play, one for moving and the other for firing. The enemies in the game were called Robotrons. The game was one of those unwinnable contests that made you hot and sweaty by the end of the fighting.[1] The screen got so busy with enemies that it was impossible to win. Blackley loved the split-second choices he had to make: defend against the enemies or rescue the humans. Years later, Blackley was in heaven when he met Eugene Jarvis, the creator of *Robotron: 2084*.

He continued to do poorly in high school, getting a grade point average of about 2.3. Blackley would go home and read books on electronics rather than do his homework. Radio Shack was his favorite store. He was always building gadgets. But a physics teacher, Bill Kleyboecher, made an impression on Blackley. Kleyboecher made physics fun. He set off explosions during experiments to catch students' attention, always with some kind of lesson in mind. He became a role model for Blackley; the two became close enough as friends to dine together. Years later, Blackley would think of Kleyboecher as one of the heroes of his life.

By the time college approached, he wanted to get away. He applied for and was admitted to Tufts University near Boston. He went there with "no skills for survival." He quickly became bored with his classes and formed a jazz quartet that played in hotels around Boston. In his sophomore year, he opened a recording studio that created radio commercials. After two years at school, he had no credits toward graduation. His parents asked him if he wanted to transfer back to a school closer to home. Then he met a girl and became close to someone who could understand him. He made money tutoring students in the sciences. The jazz performances gave him a lift. Jazz helped him conquer a lingering fear of performing in public, and he treasured the experience of driving around in Boston late at night while his Jamaican band members smoked pot in the back of the van.

He returned to New Mexico and got a summer job at a research foundation in his father's hospital. There, he became an apprentice to a physicist named Eiichi Fukushima, and something snapped into place. Blackley applied himself and managed to publish a paper in the *Journal of Magnetic Resonance* on "magnetic resonance flow imaging," the technology that improves upon X rays for seeing inside the human body. Energized by the experience of writing a paper, he became a different student. He returned to school in Boston and loaded up on medical physics classes, earning enough credits to graduate within two years.

"Something just clicked," he says. "And I busted my ass. I went from total dickhead to the Dean's list."

Because he was good at physics, Blackley let the momentum carry him into further graduate studies at the Fermi National Accelerator Laboratory, a federal lab outside Chicago that was named after one of the inventors of the atomic bomb. He studied particle physics and obscure physical curiosities like kaons, giving up music entirely. About this time he picked up a habit of flying gliders and got his pilot's license. But his first love remained physics, even though it was only earning him a student's stipend of about $11,000 a year, before taxes. He embraced the sacrifices of a poor man's life. He recalled that he couldn't buy a can of Coke whenever he wanted to, because he had to keep track of his loose change. The memory of being so poor would haunt him for years.

He stayed with physics until his adviser crashed and burned in a highly political dispute within the Fermi Labs. His adviser and another theorist had figured out how to search for the "top quark," a subatomic particle that is one of the fundamental building blocks of nature, without the need to use expensive new equipment. That equipment had already been paid for, and government bureaucrats were not amused by the findings. As a result, Blackley's adviser was ostracized. Blackley said the experience was disillusioning. Almost overnight, he no longer wanted to pour hours into work that could become so petty and politicized. Funding for particle accelerators was deteriorating until, finally, in 1993, Congress decided to kill the proposal to create the $11 billion Superconducting Supercollider, a particle accelerator that Blackley would eventually need to do his job. It was like staring at the face of God and being told to look somewhere else. He decided to abandon his career smashing atoms and agreed to design aerobatic airplanes, the kind used in stunt flying.

But before he started that job, Blackley's life boomeranged back to games. To get back with his girlfriend in Boston, Blackley answered a want ad placed by Ned Lerner, the founder of a computer game company in Cambridge, called Looking Glass Technologies. It was 1992, Blackley was 24 years old, and he became the physics weenie at Looking Glass, in charge of making the company's games look and feel more realistic. It was the perfect place and job for him—and not just because it had a *Robotron: 2084* game on its premises.

Ned Lerner's credits included a top-selling Chuck Yeager combat flight simulator that had sold more than a million copies, and Blackley admired it so much he quizzed Lerner about it for hours. Lerner needed a programmer who could write a physics model for a car-racing game. The simulated cars in the game needed to behave like real-world cars, moving with the right bounce, aerodynamics, and collisions. These weren't simple matters to simulate, but it was easy for Blackley, who got a kick out of creating a world where he determined the rules of physics.

"I realized how cool it was to do physics in games," he said. "I'd do demos on how marbles should fall."

He became just as passionate about physics in games as he was about particle physics. That came naturally at Looking Glass, where the goal was to create the "literature of games." Games weren't some lower-class form of entertainment for the bright MIT grads at Looking Glass. Looking Glass games weren't meant just to entertain little boys who wanted to blow things up; they were art, and Blackley found it easy to buy into the belief that games could be as exalted as movies, books, and paintings.

Blackley again felt like he had found his calling. He worked on the car game (which couldn't be modified in time to use his work) and then he created the physics characteristics for the hit science-fiction game *System Shock*. Next, he headed his own team creating a game called *Flight Unlimited*, where his pilot's license, physics knowledge, and gliding experience came in handy. In the game, Blackley created realistic flight dynamics that calculated a plane's position depending on how it was affected by weight, wind resistance, angle of descent, and a host of other factors. And he did so without bogging down the relatively weak computers of the day with excessive number-crunching. The first version of the game sold more than 780,000 copies, a surprising number for a niche product.

"Pilots told me they really liked how the planes handled and I was really proudest of that," he said. "I started to try to spread the word on physics throughout the game community."

But the job had its tensions. The core group at Looking Glass included a group of MIT graduates who lived in Deco Morono, otherwise known as "the House of Ten Dumb Guys," whereas Blackley was an outsider as a graduate of Tufts who didn't live in that house. Blackley was held in high regard among his colleagues, but some looked down on his goal of making games that appealed to mainstream people. Other colleagues, including Doug Church, wanted to make cool games nerds could really appreciate, like the *Ultima Underworld* role-playing game. But Blackley appreciated the intellectual environment at Looking Glass. "There were so many people who knew what they were doing there that they could call bullshit on you," he said.

As he learned management skills as the leader of *Flight Unlimited,* Blackley worked hard to inspire his team. In contrast to other Looking Glass managers, he didn't take over tasks and make others feel stupid, says James Dollar, a former artist at Looking Glass. Yet there were negatives to his style. Blackley wasn't ultra-organized. His idea of good management was to invite someone over for a gourmet dinner and have a casual conversation about work.

Blackley picked up a variety of hobbies to satisfy his intellectual curiosity. He frequently went to watch "aerobatic" stunt plane shows, he took up gliding again, and he often talked about creating a company to send rockets into space. He bought a BMW 2002 and spent hours souping it up.

He worked on more games until he encountered a new manager who "ripped the guts out of Looking Glass" and argued with Blackley at just about every turn. Blackley wanted to do a combat flight simulator, but the manager, installed by venture capitalists who wanted a more professional management team, wanted Blackley to work on a sequel to *Flight Unlimited.* When he refused, the manager told Blackley to leave immediately. His colleagues were shocked. Lerner and Blackley both cried as the finality sunk in. One friend helped Blackley take his things out to the car, rolling a creaking cart past the manager's office as slowly as possible on each trip outside, just as a way to give the manager a guilt trip.

TRESPASSER

So Blackley took off once more, this time winding up with Steven Spielberg at DreamWorks. He had the games bug and was willing to put up with a lot to pursue it. He had gotten into the games industry by accident, the same way most game developers did.

At DreamWorks, he was on a first-name basis with Spielberg. A natural extrovert, Blackley carried himself confidently. He was good at putting people at ease. He made time to play while working for his film idol. Once, he and the famed director raced electric golf carts with actor Jeff Goldblum through the Universal Studios movie lot. Their carts came within 15 feet of a tourist tram, but none of the tourists noticed. The job in the showbiz unreality of Los Angeles promised to show off the young man's prowess as a game designer. It would make use of all those cold winters he spent mastering high-energy physics as a student in Chicago and Boston. Although he was hired to do research on gaming technology, he saw a greater opportunity. He moved into managing the dinosaur game project when the shooting schedule for *Jurassic Park: The Lost World* moved ahead a year. So much for research. He was now a man with a schedule and a budget. Starting in 1995, he led a team of 40 people in an effort to design one of the most ambitious computer games. The project had everything going for it. It had the backing of cash-rich DreamWorks, a license made hot by the successful prior *Jurassic Park* film, and a plot that just screamed to be made into a game. The right game designer could make it a monster hit.

Blackley, blinded by the bright lights of the *Jurassic Park* franchise, had wanted the world of the game to be as real as the movie. In the world of video games, players are typically tied into the predefined environments of the game, able to move only where the programmer allows. Game corridors may have many doors, but it will turn out that only one of them is unlocked, a pretty big clue that the universe is deterministic. A script of programmed code might force something interesting to happen, like a collision between two cars. But it couldn't happen by sheer serendipity. Blackley had something more in mind. He believed a player should be able to wander around an island full of dinosaurs and enjoy complete freedom to use the terrain for game strategy. The game characters wouldn't just ape a predetermined script that threw them into conflict with dinosaurs. Game characters would exhibit what artificial intelligence experts call "emergent behavior," meaning that an artificial consciousness could emerge and engage in independent behavior. Blackley and his programmers would plant the seeds, define how things would grow in the world, and then things would just start happening. It was a physics geek's dream, and no surprise coming from someone who loved reading textbooks like *Foundations of Quantum Chromodynamics*. The *Trespasser* world would be physically accurate. It would encompass as much as 15 square kilometers of an island cast in 3-D space.

Unaware he was setting himself up for a fall, Blackley proudly showed off his game's features to game reviewers. Jerry Sanders of AMD had Blackley show the game to guests such as Michael Dell, the thirty-something multibillionaire founder of computer maker Dell Computer Corp. But Blackley had tried to be creative on too many fronts. The project fell behind schedule. His first mistake: trying to program the physics engine for the game and manage the team at the same time. Commissioned in 1996, the game was supposed to appear in mid-1997. But Blackley fell behind on the engine because it was so hard to cram all the physics rules into compact code that quickly displayed graphics on a computer screen. The delays pushed the game's launch into late 1998. Blackley got visits from DreamWorks cofounder and animation king Jeffrey Katzenberg, who wanted to know how the game was progressing and why it needed a bigger budget. The pressure mounted. Fellow producers at DreamWorks called him. They let him know that the future of the game division was hanging on his project and their budgets were drying up because so much money was pouring into *Trespasser*. He was digging himself a hole, just like any other doomed programmer with a project beyond rescue by all-night jam sessions.

By 1998, costs spiraled to several times the original budget. For all of Sanders's boasting, the computers of the day were relatively weak. On top of that, Blackley took so much time creating the physics engine—the software under the hood of the game that would choreograph interactions and render the characters and scenery—that his designers had to move ahead without him. That meant they would not have the benefit of designing the game first, then tweaking the physics engine later. Blackley had no time to modify the physics engine, which was a little buggy, to suit the game.

Gamers saw flaws too. When the game debuted, they decided it wasn't fun. There was little immediate gratification. When you shot at the dinosaurs with a gun, you never knew if you would kill them, or just annoy them. It took too long to find interesting things to do. Some critics complained they had too much freedom as they wandered around the island in search of action. Worse, Blackley's game didn't take advantage of 3-D hardware; it was designed for older computers.

Rob Wyatt, a coworker who handled the graphics programming, said, "Everything about the game was Seamus Seamus Seamus from the start. He had this vision for what it would be. We kept telling him things wouldn't work. Then it flopped. We said we did exactly what you told us to do. So when it came time for the blame, it was Seamus Seamus Seamus."

After he quit DreamWorks, Blackley interviewed at Microsoft. He said goodbye to his home in Hollywood. He packed up his things, shipped his yellow Ferrari 348 Spyder by truck to Seattle. Then he flew up with his dog, Paco, to take the job at Microsoft. He moved into a corporate apartment and cooked himself some comfort food: enchiladas with red chili sauce that reminded him of New Mexico. It proceeded to rain for 100 days straight.

Microsoft had just struck an alliance with Silicon Graphics Inc., the maker of graphics supercomputers based in Mountain View, California. SGI was seeking to expand the reach of its technology. The mission of the project, code-named Fahrenheit, was to enable gee-whiz animations on regular desktop computers running Microsoft Windows. It wasn't glamorous, but it was still a soldierly mission in the empire of Bill Gates.

Shortly after Blackley started his job, SGI had quietly begun pulling the plug on Fahrenheit. Silicon Graphics was hemorrhaging money and it was cutting back on its expenses. In the world at large, the media was focused on the Microsoft antitrust trial, where the government was finishing its work grilling Microsoft executives who were the company's witnesses. The trial was going badly, and most observers noted that Microsoft's witnesses were slowly having their credibility eviscerated by the government's lead lawyer, David Boies. On March 2, 1999, Sony announced the details of the PlayStation 2.

Blackley went to the 1999 Game Developers Conference to see the demo of the new machine. Masking his feelings, he spoke on a panel about physics in games with his friends Chris Hecker and David Wu. They were all brothers in the physics-geek fraternity, and they were in their element at the geek-chic conference. Blackley seemed chipper enough as he, Hecker, and Wu conducted an interview about game physics with a reporter from the *Wall Street Journal.*

Blackley seemed genuinely excited that physics was now a topic of discussion in the games industry. He even high-fived Wu and Hecker after the newspaper interview. But he later confided, "That interview was like shoving a hot poker into my eye." He was feeling low despite the strides the game had made toward realism.

As the men sat at a round table in the conference hallway, several of Blackley's game developer friends interrupted the conversation just to say hello.

"Amongst developers, people respected him for what he tried to do," said Alan Yu, director of the GDC and a close friend of Blackley's. "He took the kind of risks you have to do to make our industry better."

They admired Blackley for his almost-epic game, even after his failure. Few knew that Blackley had begun work on something even more epic.

CHAPTER **5**

PC GAMES GROW UP

LUCKILY FOR BLACKLEY, he wasn't the only renegade at Microsoft. Nor was he the only gamer. His crusade became possible only because Microsoft had been investing in games for more than a decade, and a host of seemingly happenstance developments came together at the right time.

Back in Microsoft's early days (in the 1980s), graphics were so primitive that a track-and-field game had to be lettered with the words "foam pit" because it wasn't obvious that the box on the screen was supposed to represent something real. The games made little beeping sounds for music.

The company's games ran under the Microsoft Disk Operating System (MS-DOS) and gradually evolved into simulations with better graphics. One of the biggest hits was Microsoft's *Flight Simulator.* The game allowed wannabe-pilots to take control of an airplane, using keyboard commands to control every event from take-off to landing. The series debuted in 1983, and, with constant revisions, it eventually sold more than 15 million copies. Revenues from *Flight Simulator* funded a steady increase in the games business every year, even though Seamus Blackley's *Flight Unlimited* eclipsed it for a time.

In 1985, Microsoft tried to fend off competition from Apple's Macintosh with the first version of Windows, which gave users a graphical user interface that simplified computing so that anyone with a mouse could click on pull-down menus to issue commands, rather than type in some arcane codes à la DOS.

But Windows 1.0 wasn't built for multimedia, and most game developers ignored it, writing code for DOS that ran underneath the Windows software. Windows was fine at business software, but atrocious when it came to games, in part because it consumed so much memory. Working with DOS, some programmers began to create some spectacular games.

The market exploded again with games like *Wing Commander,* a sci-fi combat flight simulator, and *Myst,* an adult-oriented mystery with graphics that were sophisticated for the time. The game appeared first on the Macintosh and was the first to use its CD-ROM, or compact disc read-only memory. On the Windows PC, the game sold millions, with the total sales hitting 7 million units—making it the biggest single-title PC blockbuster ever.

The next game to bust the PC market open was id Software's *Doom,* published in 1993 and one of the first games released over the Internet to reach widespread audiences. *Doom* pioneered high-quality 3-D graphics and featured a "first-person" perspective. Devoid of a storyline, the game gave the player the visual perspective of a gunman, and it forced the player to shoot everything in sight. The game introduced the concept of multiplayer combat—called death matches—over networks, and it became a cult hit that circulated in the millions worldwide.

Also, as multimedia became a hot ticket in personal computers and Intel launched its Pentium family of microprocessors in 1993, computers became powerful enough to run nifty graphics like those in *Doom*. Taking advantage of the hardware, Microsoft planned a major upgrade that made game developers take notice. With Windows 95, Microsoft finally eliminated DOS and brought multimedia capabilities to its core Windows software. Games like id's next blockbuster, *Quake*, released in 1996, could run directly on top of Windows 95.

And for the first time, prices for personal computers were dipping below $1,000. Some hit $500, and a few ill-fated computer makers gave their machines away for free, hoping to make money on Internet services. The PC was no longer outlandishly priced compared to the $200 or $300 video game consoles.

With sales of PCs topping 100 million units a year worldwide in both business and consumer markets, the leaders of the PC industry started to feel cocky. Andrew Grove, CEO of Intel, which made the microprocessor chips in three-fourths of the world's PCs, gave the keynote speech at the Electronic Entertainment Expo in Atlanta in 1997. Grove, author of a book called *Only the Paranoid Survive*, trotted out a historical example that he felt would be instructive for the video games industry. He noted that Intel crossed a "strategic inflection point," or a major discontinuity in a business where an industry player must either shift gears or face a perpetual decline. By shifting into PC microprocessors and getting out of commodity memory chips, Intel correctly sensed the times and traded a bad market for one of the world's greatest monopolies. A more familiar example: The railroads failed to realize they were in the transportation business, not the railroad business. When airplanes and truck transportation came along, the railroads failed to adapt and lost out.

Likewise, Grove said in his speech, the time was at hand for video game companies to realize that they would soon be overtaken by the PC entertainment industry. After all, Grove said, home PC sales were overtaking game console sales, and the PC had a much wider demographic reach than the games industry, which Grove said hit 8- to 17-year-old males.

"The video games industry is not in trouble at all; in fact, it is doing well," Grove said. "But, a bit like we were building microprocessors, even as our memory business was prospering, something is gradually sneaking up on the world. That something is personal computers and increasingly high-powered personal computers in the home."

It was time, Grove warned, for video game makers to jump on the PC bandwagon. PC technologies were advancing rapidly with every spin of Moore's Law. The Internet was exploding, and connected entertainment would become crucial in the future. Grove predicted that "the competition for leisure time is, in fact, for eyeball hours." TV was very well entrenched, but interactive entertainment on the PC was going to challenge the TV for those eyeballs.

"I think the definition of the industry that says we are in the business of building and selling video games is too restrictive," Grove said. "We need to open it to a new definition that says our business is to create and sell interactive entertainment."

Yet for all of the reach of personal computers, which were present in far more U.S. households than video game consoles, PC gaming was still less lucrative than consoles as a business. By 1997, PC games were a $1.3 billion business, about half the size of the console market, according to NPD Funworld. By 2000, PC gaming had grown only slightly to $1.6 billion. Top games industry executives like Larry Probst, CEO of Electronic Arts, just weren't impressed with the PC market, since video games were accounting for two thirds of EA's revenues while the PC was about a third of revenues. PC games were just too hard to develop because the platform was a moving target, and

PC games crashed too often. Grove, who had proved a seer of the technological future many times over, was wrong about this one. The PC wasn't taking over. But it would get some help from a few geeks who were in love with multimedia.

THE BEASTIE BOYS

Just as the first Sony PlayStation arrived on the scene in 1994 and began to pose a threat to gaming on the PC, the computer got reinforcements of its own. Alex St. John and his colleagues Eric Engstrom and Craig Eisler stepped into the picture at Microsoft with DirectX.

The three Microsoft coders had been nicknamed the "Beastie Boys" not only because of their sheer size—the baby-faced St. John weighed in at over 300 pounds and the others came close—but because of their outrageous behavior. They were renegades who didn't care about corporate rules.

When they wanted something done, they just did it. St. John was the ringleader, like John Belushi in a Microsoft version of *Animal House*. They were tolerated to a degree because Microsoft wasn't a formal company. It was cofounded by a young punk who liked people with "bandwidth," or natural intelligence.

Alex St. John was forged into an instrument of higher causes by none other than Bill Gates himself. St. John had been a kind of wandering pilgrim before he joined Microsoft. Born in 1967 in Berkeley, California, he was raised by his parents in Alaska, where his father was a professor of linguistics and physics and his mother was an elementary school teacher. He was homeschooled and would sometimes spend hours reading books or playing computer games at the college where his father taught.

He scored a perfect 1600 on his SAT, but decided to drop out of college after two years. He took a job as a programmer at Hell Graphics—a division of a German company—in Woburn, Massachusetts. There, he would deliberately annoy his colleagues by goose-stepping and raising Hitler salutes. This kind of character, obnoxious but technically brilliant and articulate, was welcome among the eclectic ranks at Microsoft, which came calling for his expertise in graphics and printing technologies in 1992.

St. John made clear from the start his inclination for being outrageous. In his job interview at the Microsoft Empire, he flippantly summed up what drew him to Microsoft.

"Bill [Gates] kicks ass," he said, according to the book that chronicles St. John's achievements, *Renegades of the Empire* by Michael Drummond.[1] "I like kicking ass. I enjoy the feeling of killing competitors and dominating markets."

Gates was a hero to St. John because he was upsetting IBM's choke-hold on computing. Many shared that attitude at Microsoft. Because he could charm as well as code, St. John was hired aboard as a technical evangelist, a senior job for a 25-year-old. His job was to stir religious fervor for Microsoft's products. He took the job to heart—too much so. Just a couple of months after he started, he angered Gates by criticizing Microsoft's own printer software in the press, pointing out it was slow and featureless compared to Apple Computer's better technology that allowed it to dominate desktop publishing. Gates shot him an e-mail nastygram, and St. John figured he'd be fired. Unaware that Gates often challenged employees just to test their mettle, St. John stewed and then he mailed a reply explaining why Gates was wrong, stirring up a political firestorm but eventually winning his point.

The experience made him bold. "From that point on," St. John says, "I acted as if I didn't care about whether I would be fired."

As he grew more influential, St. John became even bolder. While working out at the gym, St. John and his fellow engineers, Eric Engstrom and Craig Eisler, hatched a plot to take over the games business.

DirectX was a collection of applications programming interfaces, or APIs, that enabled software developers to write code to exploit any type of PC hardware. The technology was crucial to the games business because it allowed software developers to write games in a standard way: They wrote the software so that it was compatible with the APIs. Then the API software layer would consult the rest of the hardware to see what resources were available to execute the program. The API would then make use of the particular 3-D hardware or sound system in the user's PC.

They drafted their proposal on November 18, 1994, and submitted it shortly thereafter. But Microsoft was a mass of warring camps. Many different research projects were under way, from interactive television boxes to other methods for enhancing entertainment on the PC. St. John succeeded in getting other projects derailed, but that didn't mean the company jumped all over the DirectX proposal. The legitimate proposal got ignored, and so the Beastie Boys—pirates out to get their own way at any cost—were born.

"We had to do it the crazy way, stealing resources, getting caught, and then stealing resources again," says St. John, who became so obsessed with the project that he allowed his marriage to fall apart.

Each of the men had the authority to spend a limited amount of money before triggering their bosses' attention, and so they began assembling the team of engineers to get the work done.

They believed in their mission. DirectX was crucial to the PC because it allowed game developers to make use of all the add-in gear that computers had gained without worrying about a particular mix. Whatever 3-D hardware, sound card, video player, and music program a user had could be tapped because of the unifying standards cobbled together in DirectX.

Before DirectX, Windows was too slow at playing back video or painting graphics on the screen. Microsoft's partner on the PC, Intel, had long chafed at the primitive multimedia capabilities of Windows. To speed up development of the platform, the Intel Architecture Labs in Portland, Oregon, dreamed up a layer of multimedia-friendly software that would work with Microsoft's Windows 3.1 operating system. Andrew Grove of Intel announced the "native signal processing" initiative at the Comdex trade show in Las Vegas in November 1994, about the same time that the Beastie Boys were getting started.

But NSP fell flat for a variety of reasons. Other chip vendors felt NSP was an unrealistic power grab by Intel to control all processing within the computer, extending its grasp from the central processing unit to sound, video, and graphics processing as well. NSP also was geared to debut on Windows 3.1 just as Microsoft was preparing the software community to shift to Windows 95. Many software vendors complained that it didn't work and that they were hearing different views from Microsoft. Others, including the Department of Justice, saw more sinister reasons for NSP's failure. The feds believed that Microsoft used its monopoly clout to intimidate Intel and its PC allies into dropping NSP, a charge which Microsoft denied. The lingering effect of the dispute was that it set a tone of mistrust between Microsoft and Intel in entertainment. St. John was acutely aware of the politics behind Intel's attempted power grab, and his own internal efforts took on a higher priority as part of Microsoft's attempt to fend off Intel.

"The pressure generated by Intel . . . gave us the internal mandate for us to build our own solution," St. John said.

With DirectX, PC game developers could be certain that their games would be somewhat stable and make use of the hardware on a PC, and that allowed the PC to race ahead of the consoles in terms of graphics quality. The Sony PlayStation was stuck with 1994 technology, and the Nintendo 64's hardware was fixed upon launch in 1996.

"If it weren't for DirectX, the PC would have fallen behind the consoles," says Jon Peddie, a longtime graphics industry analyst.

THE COMPANY MAN

Once DirectX was established, it was up to game creators to take up the cause and make games that made use of it. Microsoft's own games division embraced DirectX. Ed Fries, a manager in Microsoft's highly successful Office division, moved over in 1995 to become general manager of the internal PC games business, which had little to show for itself other than the perennial bestseller *Flight Simulator* games. If St. John was a renegade, Fries was a company man.

Fries, a "painfully thin" man with wavy brown hair, was a Microsoft lifer. He grew up in Bellevue, Washington, where he raced motorcycles around the fields that eventually became Microsoft's corporate headquarters.

The first personal computers appeared in the 1970s when Fries was in high school. He made his own game based on the popular *Frogger* title. He put his name, "Eddy Fries," into the code. A company called Romox saw it posted on a bulletin board, then tracked him down and hired him to revise it. They paid Fries several thousand dollars to publish the game, which was renamed *Princess and Frog* to avoid a copyright lawsuit. He made a couple more games for Romox before he decided to do some serious system administration work. He got a degree in computer science from the New Mexico Institute of Mining and Technology.

In the summer of 1985, Microsoft hired him as an intern, responsible for upgrading the software used to create and display online tutorials. Fries got a reputation as a hot programmer, and so the next year he was hired permanently and assigned to write code for Microsoft's Excel spreadsheet for Windows 2.0, which he did for 18 months. He then began moving up the management chain within the Excel group.

At the end of five years, he was managing the Excel technical team, and then, to fill an opening, he was put in charge of development of Microsoft's word processing program, Microsoft Word. He managed that group for another five years, shipping three versions of the program during that time. The work was exciting because it was another of Microsoft's holy wars. Thanks to the strategy of bundling its productivity programs in Office, Microsoft eventually won the war against IBM and others.

Microsoft had gone public in March 1986, and its generous stock options yielded a jackpot payoff. An employee who came on board as early as Fries had to have stock holdings valued in the millions of dollars, according to estimates by friends. He used some of the money to buy a home on a one-acre plot on the shore of Lake Washington. His wife raised a variety of farm animals on their estate, but his new riches didn't make him feel like retiring. Rather, Fries said the wealth made him a better worker.

"I work at Microsoft because I choose to be here," he said. "I can say what I think and I don't have that worry about how I have to keep my job to feed my family."

Fries chose to stay at Microsoft and return to his first love, games. So, in 1995, he was named head of the games group. At the time, Microsoft had about four game development teams with a total of 150 people, including contractors. Fries began an ambitious push to develop more games inside Microsoft, and to hire third-party developers who would make games that would be published under the Microsoft brand name. He hooked up with a small company in Dallas—Ensemble Studios—which was led by veteran game designers Bruce Shelley and Rick Goodman. The men were working on a "real-time strategy" game involving warfare and empire-building in ancient times. Shelley said "the big plus we saw in Ed Fries was that he played games and thus was knowledgeable about them."

With funding from his friend Tony Goodman, Shelley and his team had been working on the game since the beginning of 1995. They began showing it to potential publishers in December 1995 and cut a publishing deal with Fries in the spring of

1996. But the project became bigger and bigger. Bruce Shelley found he had to ask Fries for more time and a second round of money. Fries took a look at the work in progress and decided to OK the funds.

One of the biggest fights in the game development process was whether Microsoft would allow Ensemble's game to feature blood splotches when soldiers were killed. Tasteful or not, the advocates of blood prevailed, and some, like St. John, said that the decision told them that Microsoft was beginning to understand games. Fries argued that Microsoft would indeed publish edgy games that gamers could relate to, but it would refrain from the mature-rated titles that got game publishers into trouble with parents' groups and politicians. In comparison to St. John, who wanted Microsoft to do bloody chain-saw hacking horror games, Fries seemed like a moderate and that helped his standing with his superiors. When Microsoft published *Age of Empires* in October 1997, it became an instant success, selling a million copies by mid-1998. It also became a vehicle for Fries to continue expanding Microsoft's games business.

"*Age of Empires* helped us finance our growth, but what's been good about the growth was that it was mostly organic," Fries said.

In November 1998, he cut a publishing deal with Digital Anvil in Austin, Texas, a studio owned by Chris and Erin Roberts, the brothers who had created *Wing Commander* in 1990. In January 1999, Microsoft acquired Fasa Interactive, a Chicago game developer that made robot games. And in April 1999, it bought Access Software, a maker of golf games. That deal was a step up because Microsoft dispensed with its policy of requiring its acquired companies to relocate their employees to Redmond. Now Microsoft was big enough to ally itself with the rock stars of gaming. It was on schedule to produce 30 games a year, and the division was generating about $200 million in sales a year. That wasn't enough to frighten market leaders like Electronic Arts, whose CEO often said he didn't consider Microsoft competition.

Age of Empires finally allowed Microsoft to earn some respect among hardcore gamers and developers, who had viewed the Microsoft brand with a certain amount of disdain. Games like *Flight Simulator* weren't considered "cool," and that image had hurt the company's ability to attract the top talent in game development. Fries's unit wasn't always profitable, largely because the big hits had to make up for a bunch of duds such as the investment in Digital Anvil, which chewed up tens of millions of dollars for little return. But the division was pretty much able to fund its own expansion plans, since its sales growth, while somewhat erratic year to year depending on the release schedules for big games, continued to expand.

Once Fries had some hits, he focused on extending the brands with sequels. He also expanded Microsoft's online presence with the MSN Gaming Zone, which drew millions of players a month. Without this strong games division, Microsoft would not have been in a position to challenge either Nintendo or Sony in game software. *Age of Empires* was also one of the myriad PC games that helped DirectX take off and allowed the PC to maintain a technical superiority over the newest game consoles.

Once DirectX found its footing, St. John spared no expense to get software developers to adopt it. He threw big parties with themes like "Pax Romana," complete with "slave girls," bodybuilders in togas, and a couple of live lions in a cage. A Playboy Playmate auctioned off guests who were deemed "slaves" to the audience. Those who got the thumbs-down were thrown into a pseudo lion pit. The events made him a controversial figure, with developers winding up either appalled or enthralled with him. St. John considered the parties, which became more elaborate each year, well worth the expense since thousands of game developers came and heard Microsoft preach about DirectX.

Inside Microsoft, St. John grew more and more belligerent. He admits now that he "burned a lot of bridges without thinking about consequences."

"If you disagreed with him, he would just inundate you with five times as much e-mail text as you could write," says one former Microsoft colleague who battled with St. John. "You just had to give in to him because you couldn't type fast enough."

Blackley met St. John while working at Looking Glass, and again as DirectX was being launched. St. John invited Blackley and another young programmer named Tim Sweeney of Epic Games to give a presentation of cool game technology to Bill Gates and others at Microsoft. Blackley was nervous and asked what he should say to Gates. St. John said not to worry and that he would make sure that Blackley got to sit next to Gates. (Gates accidentally drank Blackley's Coke). Blackley gave a superb demo of the realistic physics in *Trespasser.* He had an animated discussion with Gates. Sweeney, who had never met Blackley before, was amused to see how Blackley had talked himself into being the center of attention. Gates later sent a complimentary e-mail note about Blackley's brilliance to his boss at DreamWorks.

"All Seamus had to do on his part was to tell Bill Gates that he liked DirectX," St. John said. "He performed admirably" and thereby helped St. John justify his own job in the eyes of Gates.

Blackley would later remember this lesson well: Game developers were the air cover that St. John needed to show Gates that DirectX was capturing important mind share. Gates and St. John had a minor disagreement on one point, and St. John ribbed Gates by saying, "Perhaps I should just be your janitor instead," as he went through the motions of emptying the garbage cans in the conference room. Gates tolerated St. John's clowning, and that made Blackley think it might be cool to work at Microsoft.

Like a character out of Dungeons and Dragons, St. John would stalk the halls of the company sporting a long beard and swinging a fake battle-ax at his colleagues. His geeky know-how and humor allowed him to get away with almost anything, like bursting into rooms and spraying silly string at people he didn't know.

But then he was assigned to a new boss and got into hot water over his next big DirectX promotion: the alien space-ship. For a DirectX marketing party in November 1996, St. John hired Swiss designer H. R. Giger—creator of the spaceship for the film *Alien*—to create another faux spaceship. St. John planned to lead thousands of developers and press through the spacecraft into a warehouse, whereupon they would discover they were being "abducted" by an alien disguised as . . . Bill Gates. St. John had already spent $2 million on the project when his new boss canceled it two weeks before it was to be held, resulting in $2 million more in cancellation penalties.

One of St. John's last acts on the DirectX team was to recruit a product marketing manager named Kevin Bachus, a publisher of games at Mindscape who had complained about Microsoft's failure to support the game publishing community with marketing programs similar to those offered by consoles. St. John invited him aboard to market Windows as a cool games platform. Bachus was one of the people who kept telling St. John to get Microsoft's act together on games by doing a console.

The next year, St. John moved on to another renegade project, a 3-D multimedia browser called Chromeffects. The technology wasn't as popular as DirectX and was eventually canceled. In June 1997, St. John again battled with his managers over why DirectX was losing ground to the competition in the graphic race and was ordered to apologize. But his e-mail apology was so sarcastic that they fired him for insubordination, causing him to lose out on more than $5 million in unvested stock options. After he left, St. John formed a new business called WildTangent to create 3-D animations on Web pages, and he wound up hiring about half of the original DirectX team.

DirectX went on to great success, allowing the U.S. PC games business to grow from about $1.3 billion in 1997 to $1.6 billion in 2000. That growth rate wasn't spectacular, but games on the PC might otherwise have disappeared altogether because of console game sales growth.

Some of St. John's colleagues, including some of the people on the emerging Xbox team, regretted his departure. Were it not for Alex St. John and his DirectX, the Xbox itself could never have been born, and the key people on the Xbox project recognized his importance. Blackley and his cohort Kevin Bachus could look to St. John's rebellious antics as a precedent for getting things done at Microsoft.

J Allard, a kindred renegade who would become a key player on the Xbox, never met St. John, but he had heard many of his stories. He said, "I feel like there's a little bit of Alex in every Xbox that we're going to make."

CHAPTER 6

THE BOY IN THE APPLE TREE

THE PC NEEDED MORE REINFORCEMENTS than just the Beastie Boys.

At the same time that Windows 95 was being released and DirectX was coming into its own, a small company in Silicon Valley called Nvidia was planning on changing the world of computer animation with a piece of hardware. Oddly enough, much like Blackley himself, this company would also emerge stronger from one of business history's fierce Darwinian struggles.

In 1995, 3-D animation was the stuff of Silicon Graphics supercomputers, the $100,000 machines that had been used to create the dinosaurs in Steven Spielberg's blockbuster movie *Jurassic Park*. The SGI machines were bargains compared to the $1 million simulators of the 1980s that the military used to train soldiers and pilots. Jen-Hsun Huang, Chris Malachowsky, and Curtis Priem wanted to bring that technology to the personal computer.

The trio of engineers had founded Nvidia in Sunnyvale, California, in January 1993. Huang had held senior engineering and marketing jobs at chip makers LSI Logic and Advanced Micro Devices. He was the ringleader of the threesome and became CEO. Malachowsky and Priem had worked at workstation maker Sun Microsystems. Between them they had dozens of patents on graphics technology. The Taiwan-born Huang had been toughened for business. When he was nine, his parents sent him and his older brother to the United States to be educated. Unfortunately, they didn't realize that the place they had chosen was a school for troubled children in, of all places, Oneida, Kentucky. Huang didn't figure out that it was a reform school. But he managed to survive in the school for 18 months. He kept thinking "what a great country" as he discovered places like McDonald's restaurants. And he had an apple tree just outside his bedroom window—a real luxury, as apples were a rarity at home and his mother used to make a big deal when she served them.

"I would steal the saltshaker from the cafeteria and go climb the apple tree," Huang said. "I would sit there for hours putting salt on apples and eating them."

He proceeded to get serious about school. He picked up engineering degrees at Oregon State University and Stanford University. Upon founding Nvidia, he was a seasoned engineering veteran.

But 1993 was very early to be talking about making 3-D graphics for personal computers. The trio used their own money to get started and bought a desktop computer with an Intel 486DX2 microprocessor that ran at 66 megahertz. They all proceeded to learn how to use Microsoft's Windows operating system.

"This isn't as bad as I thought," Huang recalled thinking. "Then one of our engineers asked me how to save a file. Then I thought, oh shit, we're dead. We're dead." If the engineers couldn't save a file, how would they ever finish an extremely complicated graphics chip?

They spent two years working on a 3-D graphics chip dubbed the NV1. The chip was the first to target a market of 3-D games for ordinary consumers. It would allow people to put a graphics add-on board in their computers and, for a few hundred dollars, enjoy special effects like the ability to move in three dimensions.

The product launched in May 1995 and—like Blackley's overly ambitious game—it promptly flopped. Nobody in computer gaming knew how to easily create 3-D animations, and, worse yet, Nvidia used a technique called "quadratic curved surfaces" to assemble images instead of the traditional polygons most 3-D programmers and game developers were used to. It was great hardware with no software. But the chip accomplished a couple of things: It enabled Huang to raise his first round of funding from Sequoia Capital and Sierra Ventures, a couple of seasoned Silicon Valley venture capital companies. It also drew the attention of Japan's Sega Enterprises, one of the biggest video game makers, which had briefly unseated Nintendo with its Genesis console.

Sega was planning to replace its ailing Saturn game machine with a new one. The Saturn had a weak combination of 3-D and 2-D, so Sega commissioned a new machine that could handle 3-D better. Shoichiro Irimajiri, CEO of Sega, liked Huang's pitch about quadratic curved surfaces because they appeared to create realistic images more quickly. For graphics, Sega wanted to rely on Nvidia. Huang signed up to design a new graphics chip, the NV2, which would be manufactured by Japan's Hitachi. The project stretched out. Irimajiri's people discovered the NV2 had a weakness: When images were viewed up close, they were distorted in comparison to normal polygon-based art.

"We were struggling to develop software that could use those curves, but we gave up," Irimajiri said.

Huang realized that his company didn't have the resources to focus on both the Sega deal and the PC market. He decided that the PC market was more important, and he saw that Sega was having problems of its own. So he pleaded with Sega's executives to be released from the contract. Fortunately, Irimajiri graciously let Huang out of the contract and even paid him for his services. "We made a special deal to ease the pain for both sides," Irimajiri said.

Huang, in turn, devoted one employee to finishing a prototype for Sega, which accepted it and moved on to its next project.

Nvidia might have died a quick death with these two staggering setbacks. But Huang got another chance. He laid off dozens of people—more than half the company—in 1996, but managed to get more funding from his venture capitalists, Sierra and Sequoia. He knew that Moore's Law about the progress of chip technology was on his side. As chips became more powerful, they could be made correspondingly smaller and thus cheaper to make. Huang had to bide his time. He commanded his team to design a chip for the next cycle when more developers would have software ready to make use of his chips. He put his engineers on a death march.

Meanwhile, S3, a Santa Clara, California, graphics chip maker, stormed the market for 3-D graphics chips in 1995 with an evolutionary approach that allowed developers to add 3-D graphics to their machines for the same cost as 2-D graphics. These chips weren't as powerful as Nvidia's, but they delivered "3-D for free," that is, for the same price as a 2-D chip and the company trounced Nvidia in the market. Starting with games like id Software's *Quake,* developers came around to programming 3-D games. Other graphics companies like 3Dfx Interactive made a splash in the market, and soon there were as many as 50 companies making 3-D chips, including giants like Intel. Venture capitalists smelled profits, and they stampeded to find companies to fund.

S3 became a victim of its own success. It expanded into new areas like audio and frittered away its engineering resources in customer support projects. It chose to support the wrong form of memory, and it suffered some management upheaval. Then, in late 1995 and 1996, memory chip prices collapsed. For most chip makers, the crash was a horrible event. But because 3-D animations consumed so much memory, cheap memory suddenly made the prospect of cheaper and more powerful 3-D graphics a practical reality. This meant there was a new opportunity for companies that shot for the high end.

"Our fortunes rose and fell with the price of memory," Huang said.

The public was starting to get hooked on 3-D. 3Dfx Interactive, founded by several former Silicon Graphics employees and venture capitalist Gordon Campbell, hooked gamers with its Voodoo and Voodoo 2 chip sets and a proprietary graphics technology called GLIDE. For graphics chip makers, the hazards were many; most collapsed within a couple of years, with less than ten surviving a few years after the market began. Life was perilous at the start-ups, but the overall industry was thriving. Since new products launched every six months, the king of the hill changed regularly. S3 eventually lost out to a Canadian company, ATI Technologies, based near Toronto. Intel entered the market in 1997, but it found that it couldn't stay on the treadmill and retreated to low-end graphics chips. 3Dfx likewise fell off the treadmill.

The tenacity of Huang kept Nvidia alive. He often inspired his troops by saying they could be 30 days from going out of business. "Some of the time, it was true," said Michael Hara, who was then a corporate marketing vice president. Huang didn't feel frustrated or scared.[1] He knew that the 3-D market was only beginning to take off. The opportunity was still there. But he had to drive his engineers to think about the market, not just technology. This time, Nvidia stuck with graphics standards supported by Intel and Microsoft (especially Microsoft's Direct3D standard) as well as the familiar polygon style of graphics rendering. The troops had to deliver on time. They had to stop adding new features and settle quickly on a design. That allowed them to play again in the next round, and add the features they missed into the next chip on the product road map.

"I learned you can change the culture of a company slightly in good times, but dramatically in bad times," Huang said. "What made it easy was our old strategy wasn't working. We had to make strong decisions."

Huang had found that his partnership with its contract chip manufacturer, SGS-Thompson (later called ST Microelectronics), wasn't working out. He negotiated better terms with a Taiwanese contract chip manufacturer. But the shift meant a cash crunch. Huang rallied his troops to get the bugs out of their newest chip. They did so and shipped the designs off to Taiwan. The company began shipping the chips to customers with only a dozen or so days of cash left. Launched in April 1997, Nvidia's Riva 128 became a big hit. It could process graphics as fast as the market leader at the time, 3Dfx, but it only used one chip instead of two. Within eight months, the company sold more than a million chips. That rebound was all Huang needed.

With time, Malachowsky, the head of engineering, had multiple teams of engineers working concurrently. Even though it took a year and a half to finish a chip, Nvidia could still launch a chip every six months or so. Soon enough, analysts who had written off Nvidia were calling it the company that executed flawlessly. In January 1999, Nvidia went public, and Huang's share of the stock was valued at $20 million. In May 1999, Nvidia shipped its ten millionth graphics chip.

Nvidia was well on its way toward taking control of the graphics industry, even though it only held about a 20 percent market share overall. In August 1999, Nvidia launched the GeForce 256, which blew everyone else away with its high-resolution graphics. With 23 million transistors, the chip had more than 40 times the transistor count of the company's first chip in 1995. Nvidia expanded into one graphics market after another, until it spanned everything from laptop chips to powerful scientific workstations. Huang's goal of becoming the most powerful company in computer graphics was within sight, just four years after the company's doom was predicted. One day, perhaps in 10 years, Huang said that his company could become more important than Sony.

And why not? Huang's business paranoia had allowed him to beat gigantic rivals like Intel in the computer graphics business. His company controlled the pace of innovation in digital entertainment. Graphics chips, clearly, were becoming more valuable in a gamer's computer than the much more expensive microprocessor.

"Sony's threat is goodness for Nvidia," Huang said in the summer of 1999. "It is a wonderful challenge. It will galvanize us to make our technology much more affordable."

With such ambitions, it was inevitable that Huang would hook up with Seamus Blackley on the Xbox project. Microsoft had no choice but to deal with Huang, or so it seemed.

CHAPTER 7

THE NEW RENEGADES

THE INGREDIENTS WERE READY. DirectX was in place. PC gaming had evolved and 3-D graphics was improving at an exponential rate. The Microsoft culture of tolerating rebellious renegades, within limits, was well established. The company's own games business had developed enough so that it wasn't a staggering shift for the entertainment business unit to make console games. Microsoft was in a position to embrace the ideas of Blackley and his cohorts.

But the decision to make a game console was so far out of Microsoft's territory in software that it was a major undertaking. The Xbox renegades had to convince cohorts to go along one by one. In a company of 30,000 employees (at the time), the task intimidated Blackley. He felt like the oddball game developer lost among a sea of productivity and operating system software programmers.

But Blackley wasn't the only one leading the charge; the Xbox was a group effort. Other key characters had ideas to do a Microsoft game console long before Blackley ever got there. Otto Berkes was one of them. In early 1999, he was a graphics specialist who managed dozens of engineers in the 200-person DirectX division of Microsoft. For several months, he had been contemplating how to create a version of Windows for entertainment. Berkes, who had a black beard and a piercing stare, was a programmer who headed the development of graphics APIs in DirectX. He was the son of a Hungarian physician who immigrated to the United States when Berkes was still a child. Berkes's father didn't want his sons growing up in a repressive society. Calling in favors from patients who worked for the government, he arranged for the entire family to visit Austria. At the time, in 1969, it was a matter of policy that families were not allowed to cross the border because of the risk of defection. The Berkes family showed up at a border checkpoint. Had they been stopped and had their papers questioned, they would have been arrested. They crossed safely and lived near some Austrian relatives for 18 months. Then they moved to the United States.

"My parents gave up everything because they valued freedom," Berkes recalled.

Berkes grew up on the eastern seaboard, bouncing from town to town and settling for the most part in Florida. Berkes gained an affinity for technical things in the early days of the PC. He studied physics and computer science and eventually made his way to software. In 1992 he got tangled in a trade-secret theft case between Vermont Microsystems and Autodesk Inc. Berkes had switched jobs and developed graphics software for Autodesk that was similar to what he had already written while at Vermont Microsystems, a creator of one of the first graphics processors. Berkes created different code compared to his Vermont Microsystems software, but Autodesk lost the case. At the time, Berkes only felt he was solving a familiar problem using his own methodology, intuition, and expertise. It taught him to be a skeptic.

At Microsoft, Berkes put the lawsuit behind him and became one of the most respected people in computer graphics. He grew rich enough with stock options to support his family's passion for equestrian sports and earned his share of nasty spills in learning to ride himself. With their three horses and a pony, he and his family competed in horse shows with jumping events. He worked to develop the graphics technology that was part of DirectX, and he already knew Blackley well as a game developer. Blackley liked Berkes because he was smart, cynical, and dark. Berkes had given up a job slot among his group of engineers so that Blackley could be hired at Microsoft to work for another manager. Few knew the innards of the technology better. Early on, Blackley socialized with Berkes, going over to his house for dinner.

Ted Hase was also an instigator. He was in charge of evangelism for Windows games in the Developer Relations Group, which had the task of getting software developers to write programs to run on Microsoft's operating systems. A former Army sergeant who taught troops how to use computers, Hase was a flashy man with a bodybuilder's physique and long diamond earrings. He was a fast-talking evangelist on a par with predecessors like Alex St. John, but he was more politically savvy. Roughly 10 people reported to Hase, including a product marketing manager named Kevin Bachus. Hase inspired great loyalty in his people. He gave them the freedom to propose ideas and take credit for them when they succeeded. When word surfaced about the PlayStation 2 on Japanese Web sites in late 1998, Hase saw it as a threat to Windows gaming. It was so much more capable than past consoles that it was a computer in itself, able to connect to the Internet or run non-game software.

Hase had already been concerned about the way PC game developers were failing like crazy—and defecting to the original PlayStation. To him, they were the dead canaries in the coal mine—the first sign of a serious threat brewing. The miners (that is, the top successes in the business) were still breathing, but the air was going bad.

"I don't think many people inside the company understood that well at the time," said Morris Beton, who was Hase's boss in the developer relations group.

Over time, the threat became more obvious. If Sony was offering a better return on the investment required to develop a game, Microsoft was in the middle of a big gas leak. Hase brought his concerns up with Beton. "Why don't you do a better PS 2 than the PS 2," Beton replied.

Hase and Beton decided that the way to get developers back was to pitch them on a new kind of hardware platform. It would be a low-cost computer with everything stripped out of its operating system except what was needed to run games. It was, Beton recalled, "a way to reprice the operating system for a lower target." He added, "Ted took the idea and ran with it."

Hase approached Berkes and shared his thoughts. Like Hase, Berkes believed that Windows could be fixed. He didn't believe it should be tossed out as a gaming platform. They believed that the PC had a huge advantage as an open platform, where developers could design whatever they wanted without paying royalties to anyone. People often faulted the PC for being the medium for junk software, but Hase noted that no one ever complained about the movie or music industries producing too much product. Hase wanted to head off the PS 2 and get maybe 20 percent of the PlayStation fans to switch to the PC instead of upgrading to the PS 2. It was urgent to catch the competition when it was vulnerable, especially during a product upgrade.

"The PS 2 was a huge motivator," Hase said. "But we saw the PC as a creativity platform that could be made economically more attractive."

Berkes was trying to figure out the obstacles to gaming on PCs and how to overcome them. Blackley came on board with his own ideas, which were oriented more toward making an ideal machine for game developers. (It was never completely clear who came up with the Xbox idea first.) In meetings at their offices, the two men told each other what they thought. Together the coconspirators drafted a proposal to push Microsoft to create a Windows game machine. At the time, they thought that the machine, dubbed the Windows Entertainment Platform, could run a future version of the Windows 98 operating system for consumer PCs. They didn't think Microsoft would actually make this machine because they figured PC makers would do the job much better. Rather, Microsoft could supply the software and describe the hardware. Microsoft would license the design to personal computer makers, who would sell consoles to consumers.

Based on the thinking at the time, this game machine could use DirectX to run games designed for the PC with very little rewriting. While tools for the game consoles kept changing and were hard to learn, the tools for creating DirectX games were well known and easy to use. Theoretically, someone would be able to play a game written for DirectX on either the game machine or a PC. This thinking would later change, but for the time being it was useful since it encouraged other Microsoft managers to sign aboard. If the game machine supported Windows, then it wasn't a threat to the core franchise. That was extremely important within the internal politics of Microsoft.

The Xbox would be like marrying the best of the PC with the best of video game consoles. It would be a stable platform, meaning it would have uniform hardware that wouldn't change. That would make it easy for game developers to make games, in contrast to the PC, where the wide variety of hardware options—from sound cards to graphics cards—made the PC a moving target. And if the Xbox had uniform hardware, games running on it would be easier to play and less likely to crash. Also, PC graphics were doubling in performance every six months thanks to companies like Nvidia, and they were about to leap ahead of the PS 2. If the Xbox consisted of PC components, it could take advantage of economies of scale, since many PC parts were manufactured in the tens of millions. These parts could migrate down a cost curve faster than components for a console made by a single vendor.

Berkes believed the Windows Entertainment Platform would form the heart of "a PC imbued with the attributes of a console." His enthusiasm came as a relief to Blackley, who was nervous about putting forth such a brash plan. Berkes, in turn, saw Blackley as "a very good internal marketing person because he was so passionate." Everyone had heard for years from game developers that Microsoft should do a console because it had all the right technology. Now it was time. Hase drafted Kevin Bachus, who had also wanted Microsoft to do a console. As a project, the Xbox got going in the middle of March 1999.

The foursome met for one of their first strategy sessions on March 30, 1999, in conference room No. 2095 of Building 5 on the Microsoft campus. It was just outside Hase's office, and a marketing assistant made sure there were plenty of Jelly Bellies available to eat. (Blackley kept picking out the red ones.) The four men were very different in a lot of ways. Hase and Berkes had become rich from Microsoft stock options, while Bachus and Blackley were newcomers. Hase and Blackley were outgoing, while Bachus and Berkes were introspective. Blackley and Berkes were technical, while Bachus and Hase were strategists. Even so, it was like a huddle of the Four Musketeers, Bachus recalled. They didn't identify a boss. But Blackley was so loud and overbearing that he became a primary rabble-rouser and the chief contact with game developers, the crucial supporters who could provide air cover—that is, a kind of intellectual justification for the reasons behind the Xbox. Hase focused on the strategy of selling the idea within Microsoft because he had the authority, connections, and experience to do so. Berkes was the technical guru. And Bachus brought perspectives on the plan's business aspects. Each took part in every decision. It was the most united moment the Xbox would ever know.

"It was the best time in my life," Blackley said.

Perhaps it was a coincidence, but when Blackley came on board at Microsoft, things finally started to happen that drove Microsoft to create a console. Blackley believed that those who thought about the console before him needed the impetus and passion to carry out their ideas. For sure, the Xbox was by no means a one-man show.

The team was cohesive because the men all passionately believed in the technology they were creating. They shared the same dream. They all had experience in game development or game technology. People on the outside believed that Microsoft was such a powerful company that it could do anything it wanted. It could have bought every single company in the games industry with its cash hoard. But inside, the Xbox team ran up against walls of intellectual arrogance. They had to deal with others who thought they knew better about business models and teams and new technologies. These four believed in their ideas so much that they were willing to go up against an ocean of skepticism day after day.

"Nobody believed we could pull it off," Bachus said.

They were renegades doing a side project, but, then again, they each had considerable authority within the company. Hase and Berkes could assign employees to work on special projects. Hase had told Morris Beton about his new project. Beton blessed it but told Hase and Bachus they still had to do their day jobs. Berkes theoretically reported to Jay Torborg, whose health problems had led him to disengage from work, leaving Berkes a lot of leeway. He knew he had to deliver DirectX, version 7, so he was going out on a limb by adding the new project. He took further advantage of his lack of supervision by asking two engineers, Drew Bliss and Colin McCartney, to work on software for the Xbox. He told no one else about his side project.

It was in the little conference room around a circular table that these renegades hatched what Blackley and Bachus would later call Project Midway. Blackley liked the name because the box was going to be midway between a PC and a game console—and because it conjured up images of the Battle of Midway in World War II, when Americans used subterfuge and intelligence to deal a staggering blow to the Japanese Imperial Navy. Here, an American company was going up against the Japanese empires of Sony, Sega, and Nintendo. Needless to say, it was a politically incorrect code name in an industry where Microsoft would have to rely on Japanese developers and publishers. The group wanted the box to be a console played on the TV set with a controller. But they also wanted the machine to have the benefits of being a Windows PC, and that made their proposal palatable to Microsoft executives.

Bachus believed gaming on the PC was huge but underappreciated within Microsoft and by the general public. It was a great market, but Microsoft and Windows got no credit for bringing it to life. Consumers didn't see the PC as the only place where they could play games like *Quake* or *Unreal*. That was a contrast to game consoles. People instantly associated Mario with Nintendo's consoles. Bachus believed Microsoft should launch the new platform as if it were launching a console.

"When I saw the proposal from the other three, I refocused it," Bachus said. "They were very technology focused. I said, 'Let's think about what kind of consumers we're building this for, and how to get the game publishers on board.'"

While Berkes and Hase agreed to help get the Xbox off the ground, Bachus signed up with Blackley for the long haul. Hase and Berkes wanted to focus on improving the PC, rather than on creating a new appliance that had little to do with Windows technology. Bachus had always wanted to enable game developers to dazzle people with cool technology. He saw that Xbox was the way to do it.

"It was all built around this dream," Bachus said. "To make developing games on the PC more consistent and to make developers' lives easier by giving them a console that was really easy to program."

Blackley and Bachus became inseparable for the next two years. Cool-headed and quiet, Bachus was harder to get to know. He was analytical and not very personable at first. He took a long time to warm up to people. He had a dry sense of humor. Blackley thought that Bachus was in fact the funniest person he had ever met. He didn't mind conversations that were one-sided or that had long pauses in them. He stayed silent until he had something to say.

"He was the yin to Seamus's yang," said Alan Yu, the Game Developers Conference program director (and later overall director), who was friends with both men. "Kevin was a universally misunderstood person. People saw him as standoffish. He is quiet, but a really good guy."

Chanel Summers, who later joined the Xbox team working for Blackley, saw a friendship develop between Bachus and Blackley, whom she affectionately dubbed Laurel and Hardy.

"They have two brains, but they make up this one large alien creature," she said.

THE OTHER DREAMER

Kevin Bachus was born a few months after Blackley in 1968 in Wichita, Kansas. His mother was an accounting professor who took time off to have four children, and his father owned a surplus and salvage store as well as a couple of other low-tech businesses such as supplying office furniture to the Wal-Mart chain. Bachus was the oldest of the four kids. At the age of two, he learned how to pick out songs on the piano. His mother wanted to encourage him with piano lessons, but she couldn't find anyone willing to teach such a young student. Over time, he continued with the piano and then switched to a synthesizer. But Bachus never tried to compete or pursue the concert life.

"Kevin would compose and write compositions," said Nancy Foran, his mother. (His parents split when he was a teenager and his mother later remarried). "His thing was not playing Mozart perfectly. He would practice until he could play a song and know how it sounded. That would be enough for him."

Bachus also learned to type by age three and was typing letters to his grandmother before he could write. Like his fellow renegades, Bachus grew up with gadgets. While his younger brother, Dan, liked sports of all kinds, Kevin did not. Together they played with all the video game consoles in the room they shared as they were growing up. They watched a lot of *Star Trek* and Kevin adopted his father's habit of reading science fiction. "I remember Kevin was always playing with flying games," Dan Bachus said. "And he read a lot."

At age 12, Bachus ordered a Heathkit computer, a hobbyist's machine that required the user to assemble it himself. It was a kind of solitary enterprise since the IBM PC hadn't been created yet. Bachus created text-based games and kept at it. One game he created was an early stab at 3-D graphics on a computer, putting a player in a vehicle driving through a maze. It resembled the game of *Pac-Man,* but from Pac-Man's point of view. At the same time, young Kevin grew fond of writing. He bought a modem, set up an e-mail account, and put together an e-mail newsletter in the days when few people had e-mail. He wrote his views about PC games and circulated them among a small network of gamers. His favorite game was *TRACON,* a PC game that simulated air traffic control and was addictive in a way similar to *Tetris* because the player had to juggle tasks simultaneously. As his parents began using computers for work, Bachus would help them figure out how to use them. He was a good student in high school but didn't move in the most popular circles. Unlike his brother Dan, Kevin enjoyed the company of just a few friends that he saw frequently.

Everyone figured young Kevin would go into electronics, but he was a rebel.

"I resisted going into computers because it was expected of me, so I went in the opposite direction into film instead," he said.

He attended the film school at the University of Southern California and began writing screenplays. He filmed a documentary about fans such as "Trekkies" who became obsessed with shows like *Star Trek*. The work brought him into contact with the actors and writers who put the science-fiction series together. He concluded in the thesis that, "if you have something that people really believe in, they will go to great lengths to define their identity around it and build their community around it." He took time out to take flying lessons and became a licensed pilot. He figured the Los Angeles air space was so complicated it would be a good place to learn how to master a small plane.

While at USC, he met Chanel Summers, who was a year younger than he was. She was studying biomedical engineering but later switched to classics and philosophy. She was working on a robotic arm when she met Bachus. "It was love at first sight," she says. They began dating. For a while, Hollywood was fun. While Bachus was researching a documentary, Bachus and Summers dressed up and sneaked into the Emmys. They snapped pictures and sent them home to family.

Bachus soured on Hollywood as he struggled to get work. "The film industry was such a social industry, where it depended not on how good you were but on whether you had friends who wanted to work with you," Bachus recalled. "That was too unpredictable for me."

So instead, Bachus flirted briefly with the idea of becoming a technology journalist. The couple moved together to San Francisco. He took a job as a technical editor for a magazine called *Corporate Computing*. That venture went bust and Bachus freelanced for a few publications. Then Bachus took a 45-degree turn into the games industry.

"Until that point, I had resisted making a job out of my hobby," Bachus said.

He took a job in corporate communications at Software Toolworks, a games and education software company based in Novato, California. Summers was already working there producing and developing games. Bachus moved throughout the company until he ended up working with the company's software developers in Europe. By this time, Software Toolworks changed its name to Mindscape and began focusing more on games. Bachus moved over to run business development for Mindscape's entertainment division. He found that, even more than he liked games, he liked working out business deals that enabled the game developers to show off the best of what they could do. This was an industry in its infancy, Bachus thought, like film in the time of the Lumière brothers who invented film cameras. It needed solid businesspeople who could help the visionaries create real businesses.

Bachus followed trends closely on the PC. When Microsoft published its Windows 95 operating system, Bachus got Mindscape to throw its resources into Windows games. That's how he met Alex St. John, the DirectX evangelist at Microsoft. Bachus admired the big man's ability to woo developers to his cause. St. John says that Bachus kept nagging him to create a much bigger marketing campaign to show how Windows was the ideal brand that enabled cool new games.

"When you thought of Windows, you didn't think of how it enabled great technology like the best games," Bachus said. "It was far different from the PlayStation brand, where everyone knew that it meant great games. That's what I wanted to change at Microsoft."

St. John believed that Bachus had the same passion and Jedi-like powers of persuasion as himself. He turned the tables on Bachus. If you really want to get Microsoft to change, St. John said, why not join Microsoft?

Bachus joined Microsoft in June 1997, and a week later St. John got fired. But Bachus proceeded to try to get Microsoft to behave more like a console manufacturer with a dedication to games. It wasn't an easy task. In his new-employee orientation at Microsoft, he heard Chief Operating Officer Bob Herbold talk about marketing. When Bachus asked him if Microsoft would consider creating alternative brands that would allow Microsoft to market the more popular and violent games, Herbold said that the games business was so small that it hadn't warranted such discussion. From the very start of his job at Microsoft, Bachus heard developers say that Microsoft should do a console but they never believed the company would get its act together.

It didn't help when St. John got fired. Bachus soon after became a stepchild when his own manager moved to another division. He had six bosses in six months and he had no close ally. Meanwhile, Summers had been heavily recruited for months. Shortly after Bachus was hired, she joined Microsoft to manage one of the company's big online games, *Fighter Ace,* in which hundreds of players could duel each other in World War II aircraft simultaneously. The couple had been engaged for some time but kept putting off the wedding. They finally went off to Hawaii for nuptials. Bachus was ultimately assigned to work for Ted Hase, who became, Bachus said, the "best boss I ever had." Hase empowered Bachus to try to pursue his vision of making Microsoft empathize with game publishers. As the point marketing man for DirectX, Bachus had to keep current on all things game-related at Microsoft and build relationships with key businesspeople at game publishers.

When Blackley's proposal came to him, Bachus saw the same ideas that he had been touting for years. He sharpened the proposal because he knew about matters like royalty rates that game publishers paid to game hardware manufacturers, and he had a better idea of what kind of price the Xbox had to hit in order to take off. He also knew who to pitch.

Bachus got himself appointed to a group that was trying to figure out how to modify versions of Windows for the consumer market. David Cole, a vice president in charge of consumer Windows, led this group. Part of the three-year plan included PC appliances, which were stripped-down versions of computers that could be used for music playback or games. Among the slides in the group's standard presentation was one panicky bullet point: "Trojan Horse: Appliance cannibalizes PC purchases."

Bachus conducted numerous media interviews at the Game Developers Conference in 1999 where he was promoting the DirectX technology for the PC. Talking to a *Wall Street Journal* reporter, he seemed like he needed to shave a couple of times a day. He had tousled brown hair and penetrating blue eyes. His enormous height of 6'5" was disguised because during the whole interview he was leaning back in a chair and looking at his PowerPoint slides on a laptop computer. He seemed intent on going through all of his slides even though he was interrupted numerous times with questions.

Asked if the PC was in a weak position relative to the game consoles, he wouldn't let himself be pinned into a defensive position. He insisted that there was a great deal of crossover in the market. Many console owners also had PCs, and those who played PC games often didn't like console games. It was the duck strategy: Appear to be calm on the surface, but underneath, paddle like hell to get where you need to go.

SPREADING THE XBOX VIRUS

Bachus became Blackley's partner among the renegades not because he was a gamer, but because he loved the games industry. But it was Blackley's vision and his boisterous leadership style that made him the ringleader among the four renegades. As a natural performer with no fear, he could make presentations filled with words like "bad-ass" and not worry about what managers thought about him. He was certainly in a rush. All of his ideas pointed to launching some kind of product in 2000, not only to parry Sony's PlayStation 2, but to move ahead with speed to save PC gaming.

He and his cohorts all knew that the tradition at Microsoft was to rebel against bosses—at least to a limited degree—and to seize the opportunity to create a new business. Bachus had been at the Tokyo Game Show just after Sony announced its new box, and he had seen how excited fans were about it. Japanese game developers were wary about their dying arcade business, and they again asked Bachus to get Microsoft to do a game console. Watching the worldwide media attention that greeted Sony's PlayStation 2 announcement told the Xbox team they were on the right track.

"The Sony announcement really galvanized us," Blackley says. "We saw it was a valid business. We were thrilled the more we heard about the Sony plan."

The four renegades attended the Game Developers Conference in San Jose, California, in March 1999. Bachus sat in the audience among 3,500 other game developers as Sony unveiled the first demos of its PS 2. Phil Harrison, who, like Bachus, had once worked at Mindscape, led the Sony demo, showing how the prototype of the PS 2 could display spectacular fireworks and 3-D scenes with transparent clouds, and how all sorts of digital attachments, like camcorders or cameras, could be easily attached to the machine. Harrison got one of his biggest cheers when he said that the machine would use the free Linux operating system, because of its stability. Linux machines didn't crash nearly as often as computers using Microsoft software. As Harrison finished describing the "digital entertainment hub," the crowd erupted in a standing ovation. Louis Castle, a developer who was part of the Electronic Arts Westwood Studios unit and a longtime PC games loyalist, said he expected that his company would make games for the PS 2. In an interview that morning, Harrison defended Sony's decision not to use Microsoft software. "Sure, they are the standard in the PC market, but we set the standards in game technology," he said.

After the GDC, the Microsoft ringleaders returned to work with fresh visions of what the competition had in mind. The four men embraced the Japanese concept of *ringi*. Blackley had never been to Japan yet, but as he understood it, the word meant the process of achieving consensus without sacrificing the power of the original idea. Berkes focused on technical details such as a mock operating system while Blackley worked on demos. "We started booking meetings with all of the people we could to get them on board," Bachus said.

Ted Hase was good at picking which people to approach. With each meeting, he had the team rewrite the proposal so that it would be more easily understood and approved by the executive or manager being pitched.

"Microsoft is not an easy place to get things done," Hase said. "People don't understand why you're getting them involved in something that doesn't involve their current business. Sometimes it's a long way around the barn. But when you know you are going to get attacked by someone with another proposal, you have to make sure you have more allies than they do."

One of the first people the Four Musketeers recruited was Nat Brown, a software architect from Fairbanks, Alaska, who had a track record of working on big software projects at Microsoft. At 28 years old, Brown was a Microsoft lifer. He started as a summer intern in 1990 and returned full time in 1992 upon graduating with a computer science degree at Harvard University. (Had he dropped out of college, he would have made millions of dollars more in stock options; but he had already become rich as it was.) He worked on Microsoft's object linking and embedding technology, which made it easier to swap components between programs, as well as on Microsoft Publisher, the program that introduced the ubiquitous software wizards to offer easy tips on how to perform computing tasks.

He moved into systems software, worked on communications technology and browsing software, and worked his way up the program management ladder to planner. He got a lunch invitation from Ted Hase on April 5, 1999. They met at the Bento Box, a Japanese restaurant in Bellevue, a Seattle suburb. Brown knew some kind of conspiracy was afoot when the three other Musketeers showed up along with Hase. Brown had never met Blackley before, but he was familiar with him through e-mail.

Brown was part of David Cole's consumer Windows group and played a managerial role creating the strategic plan for Windows. He began working on the three-year plan in 1998, and this time he found the process was particularly slow because of all of the new threats to the PC. He was important to the Xbox team because he was part of the Windows establishment. He liked their proposal and that was important. He had worked at Microsoft since 1990, and he knew how to sell projects to Bill Gates. He regularly ate lunch with Eric Rudder, who was the technical assistant for Bill Gates. Those meetings gave Brown valuable insights into the mind of Microsoft's fearless leader. Brown signed up on the Xbox project because he saw a certain beauty in returning Windows to a simpler form. Windows had become complicated and bloated over the years, and Brown saw simplification as the only rescue. This debate had fractured Microsoft's executive ranks. One former member of Microsoft's executive committee, Brad Silverberg, had made the case for simplification and modernization of Windows to Bill Gates at around the same time that Brown signed up. When Silverberg lost the battle, he joined the exodus from Microsoft.[1] One of Brown's earliest contributions was to come up with the Xbox name, but the group was so cohesive that few remembered later who made that contribution.

About the same time that Brown joined, Blackley recruited one of his coworkers on the *Trespasser* project, Rob Wyatt, a 25-year-old graphics expert from Derbyshire, England. Wyatt was a longtime game programming veteran who had never wanted to work at Microsoft. But Blackley was so passionate about the Xbox that Wyatt couldn't pass it up. He went to work for Berkes and began helping with the operating system for the Xbox, launching the early work of evaluating different graphics chips for the Xbox.

One of the first outsiders to hear about the Xbox was David Kirk, chief scientist at Nvidia and a graphics geek. He visited Redmond just about every week to keep tabs on the newest versions of DirectX, which had become the standard for many computing technologies, including graphics. One day in early 1999, Otto Berkes asked Kirk to a meeting with the other Xbox cohorts. Berkes closed the door.

"We want to try this idea," he said. "Can you help us?"

The gray-bearded Kirk could detect angst about Sony, which was akin to the "barbarians at the gate" of the Microsoft empire. Kirk told them that the PlayStation 2 wouldn't live up to its specifications, dubbed "marketecture" in engineering slang, and that Nvidia's chips would surpass it by the time it hit the market. Nvidia had already begun work on its GeForce 3 chip, and he was confident that the GeForce 2, much further along in the design process, would easily beat the graphics on the PlayStation 2.

They asked him how much a console-like computer would cost. Kirk was pretty sure he could hit a target under $500. He suggested, for instance, that gamers wouldn't need much of a central processing unit, the Intel microprocessor that typically cost hundreds of dollars. Stick a state-of-the-art graphics chip in it, and gamers would notice the difference, Kirk said, with more than a little self-interest. Kirk knew that any one of several Nvidia chip projects under way could serve as the Xbox graphics chip, depending on when Microsoft actually planned to launch. Nvidia was preparing to launch what it would call the GeForce later that year. It was also working on the GeForce

2, the GeForce 3, and a highly integrated graphics chip set combination called the nForce. The team thought that the Xbox had to come out in the fall of 2000 to intercept the PS 2.

The proposal included alarmist bullet points like "The PS 2 is a huge competitor" and "We do not dominate an $8 billion industry. We are leaving significant money on the table." (Most other Microsoft veterans, wary of antitrust problems, had long since figured out they couldn't use words like *dominate*.) A risk, the proposal noted, was that there would be fewer Windows games as more developers moved to the console platforms.

Microsoft and Nvidia weren't the only ones concerned. Intel also felt threatened by the PlayStation 2. Jason Rubinstein had joined Intel in 1997 as its games evangelist. He got the company to invest in game software that could show off the power of Intel's latest microprocessors, and he helped steer Intel's marketing muscle behind many of the best games, so long as they relied upon Intel technology. Kevin Bachus and others on the Xbox team briefed Rubinstein, Andre Vrignaud, and a few other Intel representatives early in the development of the Xbox. Bachus believed that the Intel people would be dismissive at first. And they were.

"Microsoft was pretty pie in the sky," said an Intel source familiar with the meeting.

Some at Intel wanted to do a games console. Intel had created the home products group, a consumer-oriented division that took advantage of both PC and non-PC technologies. Claude Leglise, Rubinstein's boss in developer relations, was appointed to head the group. But Leglise didn't feel like there was money to be made in the games business. He was focusing on non-PC Internet appliances à la WebTV.

Intel vice president of desktop products Pat Gelsinger met with Berkes and Blackley's boss, David Cole, to flesh out the details of the project. But he warned that the costs of building the box were higher than the Xbox crew expected. Because of Intel's reluctance to provide chips at a low cost, the Xbox team expected to use AMD chips instead. Ned Finkle, an AMD executive, was more than happy to provide assistance with prototyping.

"We were looking for new markets for our chip architecture," Finkle said. "We were not incumbents like Intel and so we looked for new businesses. We were passionate about it."

Working with an outside company previously used by AMD, Blackley put together a BIOS—a basic input-output software program—that would enable the machine to turn on quickly. The box, unlike the PC, had to start, or boot, within seconds and be ready to run games immediately. The Xbox prototype, such as it was, could be up and running in nine seconds—versus two minutes for the average PC. Blackley used Eidos Interactive's *Tomb Raider*, a game featuring the buxom Lara Croft, as proof that the games could be easily loaded into the system.

"Consoles have to be magical," he argued. "They don't crash."

Ed Fries was an early and important convert. In the years he had been running the games group, Fries had always declined requests from other Microsoft divisions to make games for non-PC devices. He turned down, for instance, requests to make games for Sega's Dreamcast and felt justified in the decision when that console failed. Fries didn't want to distract his efforts from establishing Microsoft as a powerhouse in PC games. But Fries was impressed by the growth of game consoles and felt the Xbox plan would work because it focused solely on games, not on games as part of some larger software platform.

"They had a plan I believed in," Fries said.

Fries brought credibility to the project that would be important later on. He was the swing vote and proof that the Xbox pitch would appeal to game developers.

Nat Brown said, "We warned Eddie that his people might get stuck programming games for some weird custom hardware that the WebTV guys were talking about. So he started leaning our way because the Xbox was more like the PC."

But Fries worried what this would mean to his plan of growing the games business at a sensible rate. If the Xbox passed muster, he would have to double the size of the games division in just a year's time. "That wasn't a perfect fit, but there was no other way to go into the console business," he said. He began thinking about Microsoft-developed games that could run on the machine and began switching resources within his division to start work on Xbox games. He determined the best way to organize was to preserve his studios intact. These game designers worked with each other and were solid teams. There was no point in splitting them into two halves and designating some of them to be Xbox teams and some of them PC game teams. Rather, the studios would have a choice about working on either Xbox or PC games. They would determine on their own whether a particular game concept was best done as a console or PC game.

One of the victims and ultimate beneficiaries of the Xbox uncertainty was David Wu, Seamus Blackley's friend and fellow physics fan. Wu was the 25-year-old president of Pseudo Interactive, a game development studio in Toronto. He was gearing up to create *Full Auto,* a car combat game for the PC that was going to be published by Microsoft. But Wu's overseer at Microsoft left and in the ensuing turmoil, Fries canceled his game around May 1999. Ironically, one of the things he was told was that the action-based game was too "console-like." Wu was upset but he didn't break off relations with Microsoft. Tipped off by Blackley, Wu pitched Fries again with an Xbox title. It would be a game with cartoon-like characters driving around cars armed with bombs, rockets, machine guns, and giant hammers. The cars would fight in a demolition derby and they would be animated in a way that was physically accurate, although they would twist and turn, elongating like rubber bands when they turned corners. The graphics sounded original. Fries gave the idea the go-ahead.

"We wanted to get in early on the Xbox," Wu said. "We knew it was a risk. There was a 50 percent chance that it wouldn't happen. But it was a chance to be a player on a North American console. I knew we would have no chance to be early on the Japanese consoles because they focused on Japanese developers."

The Xbox took on a life of its own as it picked up more followers among the executives. Before every meeting, the Xbox boys were preparing at full speed. They'd have momentary panic attacks when copiers broke down or printers didn't work as they were assembling dozens of copies of white papers for high-level executives. When they arrived at their meetings, the rooms were often so full that they would have to ask vice presidents to surrender their seats so they could give the presentation.

Before one meeting, they were late so they asked Nat Brown to drive them from one part of the Microsoft campus to another. Brown obliged, but he had been so busy he forgot that day he was supposed to dump some garbage from his home at the garbage cans along the side of the road. He forgot to empty the garbage and left it in the backseat of his car instead. When Blackley stepped into the car, he complained of the reek. He tossed the garbage out the window as they sped to their appointment.

"Seamus pissed and moaned about that for the next two months," Brown said. "He called my car the Xbox garbage truck."

Such moments sealed the bond between the men. Along the way, Blackley kept getting encouragement from Microsoft veterans, who said the project reminded them of the old days at Microsoft, when people just took a good idea and ran with it without regard to convention or formal approval.

"We would go to all these Microsoft veterans and they would tell us that, after they heard us give our pitch, they kept thinking about it the whole weekend," Bachus said.

8

MEETING WARFARE

BY THE TIME BLACKLEY JOINED Microsoft in 1999, multiple threads were developing on the game front. The Xbox proposal had one big weakness, and rivals within Microsoft seized upon it. The Xbox was going to be the Ferrari of consoles. It had to be good to surpass the PS 2, but burdening it with a hard disk drive and borrowing so much from PC architecture meant higher costs.

Consoles were supposed to be cheap, as the team from WebTV insisted. Microsoft had acquired WebTV Networks in August 1997 for $425 million, and its leaders wanted to grow their platform from the Internet-on-TV to other things, like games. WebTV (founded in 1995 by former Apple engineers Steve Perlman, Bruce Leak, and Phil Goldman) was making a small box that turned a television into a pseudo-computer. It could run a Web browser, send e-mail, and allow people to chat with others while they watched their favorite TV shows. It was a simple device—manufactured by Sony and Philips Electronics—aimed at the people who found PCs too complex. Bill Gates trumpeted the WebTV acquisition as offering the benefits of combining the "Internet with emerging forms of digital broadcasting." Craig Mundie, the executive in charge of non-PC consumer technologies, was exploring whether WebTV and other set-top boxes could use the same graphics architecture as the increasingly TV-like graphics on the PC.

WebTV had been launched with much fanfare about how it might spell the end of the PC era. But the box used a slow modem and had quirks that made PC veterans scoff. After Microsoft bought the company, sales topped out and never grew much past a million units annually, compared to about 100 million a year for the PC. WebTV boxes sold for $99, but the manufacturing cost and the subsidy for original equipment manufacturers (the companies that actually made the things) added up to $215 on the classic model, resulting in a loss of $116 on each sale. Depending on the retailer's margin, the service fees began to generate a profit between nine and 25 months after purchase. But the churn rate of subscribers was running at about 20 percent a year. So even with more than a million users, WebTV was a big cash drain. About 40 percent of the subscribers felt the uses of WebTV were too limited. And 31 percent felt its Internet access was too slow. Everyone said in surveys that they might consider buying one for their parents, but never for their own use.

The WebTV engineers became interested in adding games, and, in 1998, WebTV bought a little graphics chip company called CagEnt Technologies, a 3DO spin-off whose team included designers of 3DO's second-generation console, the M2, which never came to market. On the team were game veterans like Tim Bucher, the lead hardware designer on 3DO's game consoles. 3DO had been the first company to try to create a console based on the CD-ROM, but its system was too pricey and fell victim to Sony's PlayStation. Bucher was now vice president of hardware engineering at WebTV. He was a soft-spoken man who wore glasses and watched a lot of TV. He knew how to design game consoles inside out, but lately he had become obsessed with how to enhance TV. After all, TV still consumed more hours a week of entertainment time than video games and it dwarfed all the other entertainment markets in overall revenues.

Bucher and his cohorts constituted the opposition party against the Xbox within Microsoft. In some ways, they were underdogs because their core business was a failure; on the other hand, they had many more resources than the Xbox crew. Steve Perlman was in the process of resigning from the company. He had had great hopes when Microsoft bought the company, but concluded that Microsoft saw WebTV in limited terms: as a way to thwart the enemies of the PC and as an avenue to sell more operating system software. To Perlman, WebTV had been an ambitious effort to create new categories of home entertainment gadgets around the Internet. But he admitted the revolution was falling short. He was planning to leave Microsoft and create a new start-up. WebTV was rudderless, and its hardware team was starting to unravel.

Nevertheless, others took on the task of pitching the WebTV game console. Chief among them was Dave Riola, the division's director of business development. He was a clean-cut man with classic Italian dark features, his hair combed back in waves on his high forehead. Riola had grown up in Schnecksville, Pennsylvania, north of Philadelphia. He bounced around various chip jobs, moving to Silicon Valley in 1990. He worked for Cypress Semiconductor as a marketing manager and for

3DO as director of business development. After leaving 3DO in 1997, Riola joined the graphics chip company that was later acquired by WebTV.

When Riola heard that Gates was interested in a response to the PS 2, he went into motion. He drew up a plan and submitted it to Jon Devaan, who was the senior vice president in charge of the WebTV unit on the corporate level at Microsoft. Riola strategized with Ted Kummert and Chris Phillips, who were in the Windows CE group and handled the Sega deal. Along with several others, they created a white paper—circulated after they heard about the Xbox plan—describing how Microsoft should launch a game console. Like the Xbox team, the WebTV side thought Sony was a threat.

"If Sony had kept their mouths shut, Microsoft would never have built a console in a million years," said one WebTV source. "Through their hubris, they moved us into action."

They figured that WebTV could easily converge with game consoles without adding much to its cost, since the box would likely share many common components with game consoles. Riola favored designing a game console that would be subsidized by royalties from games and sales of peripherals. It could use Windows CE and Intel-compatible microprocessors or some other operating system or other chips. By using less-expensive microprocessors and the same graphics chips used in other WebTV products, Microsoft could undercut its rivals and come up with a cheaper console (costing $200 at launch and falling quickly to $150 in the second year) that would be part and parcel of a larger entertainment system. It followed the typical model: Sell the hardware at cost or lose money on it; make money on the software.

One of the key lessons that Bucher learned from 3DO was that it was important to control your own destiny. 3DO's model was flawed in a fundamental way. The company designed technology for a game console and licensed it to the Panasonic division of Japan's Matsushita Electric Co. But Panasonic wanted to make a profit on the hardware, so it sold the box for $700 in comparison to much cheaper consoles from Nintendo and Sega, which could afford to sell their hardware cheap because they made up for the sales with software revenues. 3DO was helpless in getting the costs of the consoles down.

"Don't give up too much control of your business to other companies," Bucher said afterward.

This attitude was very similar to Ken Kutaragi's at Sony. With the launch of the PlayStation 2, Sony had decided to spend $1 billion on its own semiconductor fabrication plant to make its own graphics chip.

Later on, this argument held little sway. Bill Gates knew that Microsoft would be such a big customer for components that its suppliers would make sure they invested adequate resources in order to keep Microsoft's business. Blackley had little respect for the experience of the 3DO engineers.

"They learned that if your hardware is too expensive, you lose," Blackley said. "They were scarred by the 3DO experience like I was by *Trespasser*. They didn't learn that content is king. We said you have to empower the developers."

Jon Devaan, who became responsible for the WebTV unit after Craig Mundie engineered the acquisition, also favored the low-cost approach to the games business. This machine, he believed, would be able to address the rising category of "convergence games," where games became just one feature of a larger entertainment system. Since WebTV functioned as the larger entertainment system, Devaan and his group initially believed that they should be in charge of the design.

Out of self-preservation, the WebTV camp proposed that its console supplant the Xbox. Under instructions from Bill Gates, Craig Mundie called a meeting for March 31, 1999, to follow through on the executive retreat directive to explore an expansion of the games business. David Stutz, a researcher who was assigned to pull the meeting together, told Hase about the meeting over a dinner at the Game Developers Conference.

Hase wasn't initially invited, but he was added later. The Xbox team was just emerging from the underground, so in classic renegade fashion the team crashed the meeting.

Mundie, a veteran of the minicomputer industry, had been caught up in a similar kind of internal struggle at Data General in the late 1970s. In that battle, two different divisions of the company tried to develop a next-generation minicomputer. One project went forward, and one didn't make it. Mundie was on the losing team. Tracy Kidder, a journalist with a flair for detail, won a Pulitzer Prize for the book that chronicled the effort: *The Soul of a New Machine,* published by Little Brown in 1981. Mundie's experience with minicomputers had taught him an important lesson. He told journalists like the *Wall Street Journal*'s David Bank that the threat always comes from below.[1] Minicomputers had undercut mainframes, and PCs had undercut minicomputers. He backed the WebTV deal because it represented a similar threat to the PC as a lower-cost device. And, while he wasn't in charge of that operating unit any longer, Mundie had clout as a kind of ambassador for Gates.

The meeting was held in a conference room outside of Mundie's office. A couple dozen people attended, including the renegades from the Xbox group and their ally Ed Fries of the games division, along with people from hardware, research, and other groups. On the other side was an alliance of the Windows CE/Sega Dreamcast project and the WebTV contingent. The rivals included business executives Mundie and Jon Devaan as well as WebTV people Tim Bucher, Dave Riola, and Nick Baker. They were joined by Chris Phillips and Ted Kummert from the Windows CE team. Among the neutral parties in the room were Jim Kajiya and Alvy Ray Smith, a couple of graphics wizards from the research group. Some, like WebTV founder Steve Perlman, tuned in via speakerphone.

Mundie chaired the meeting, made the introductory remarks about "what Microsoft, as a company, should be doing in the game space." The Xbox team viewed him as less than neutral, Brown said, because "he had to justify why we spent so much money on WebTV."

Bachus took the audacious step of saying his group already had a plan to talk about, taking the WebTV camp by surprise. As they made their presentations, the two sides attacked each other and didn't hold back. They shouted at each other, and the polite ones grumbled at how unprofessional each side was. The Xbox team went first but they quickly ran into criticism of their use of the expensive hard disk drive. Dave Riola said that console game makers already knew how to program games without a hard disk, but Ed Fries jumped in and said that the hard drive would differentiate Xbox games. Craig Mundie sided with the WebTV group, noting it had been on a fruitless search to find cheap hard disks. At a subsequent meeting, Riola said the Xbox bill of materials didn't take into account small costs like screws.

"It was true," said Nat Brown. We didn't really have a good handle on the financials at all. They scored a big point against us in credibility."

Screws cost an estimated 75 cents in the Sony PlayStation 2.[2] But the point was that the Xbox team had no clue about real costs. Chris Phillips of the Windows CE team considered himself a veteran of the console wars through his experience with Sega. He was amused at how the Xbox presenters were pretending to be experts on consoles.

"Their list of parts costs was complete bullshit," Phillips said.

At the time, the WebTV plan called for a machine that used a low-cost Mips microprocessor and Windows CE, the same platform that WebTV was using. One executive suggested a hybrid of a Mips chip and an Intel-compatible chip so that the machine could run more than one operating system, but that was shot down for cost reasons. But the WebTV side said it was open to using a different platform as long as the console business model was used; this showed flexibility, but it also seemed indecisive. The WebTV side emphasized making a box with custom-designed chips because that was the way that Microsoft would be able to integrate multiple chips into one chip over time; they felt using off-the-shelf chips would never allow them to beat Sony on costs. Fries tried to appear impartial at first but he was leaning toward the Xbox team. That was vexing for him because he was close friends with Jon Devaan on the WebTV side. Devaan and Fries had worked together on the Microsoft Excel project in the mid-1980s and this was the first time they were on opposite sides of an argument within Microsoft.

The Xbox team's proposal had the data that showed how high-cost PC components today would become much cheaper over time. Everyone knew that PC volumes were so high that they created economies of scale. Aided by Moore's Law, the chips that would power the Xbox would become much cheaper over the five-year life of the product. And by borrowing from PC hardware and taking the code written for the PC based on DirectX tools, the Xbox would be able lower its overall component costs and get games to the market much more quickly because game developers knew the tools so well. By comparison, the WebTV approach would force developers to learn a whole new set of tools to write software for unfamiliar hardware. Riola said the WebTV Web-browsing functions would essentially be thrown in for free, but the Xbox team took this to mean that the WebTV box would have so many features that it would never be able to beat Sony at gaming.

"We did a lot of talking past each other," said one WebTV representative. "And anyone with actual game console experience was just ignored."

Even before this meeting, Nat Brown became fond of ridiculing the WebTV team. During the meeting, he let loose again. Both Mundie and Devaan asked him later why he had to be so antagonistic to the WebTV engineers during the public meetings with top executives.

"We said it's not our job to bring these guys up to speed," Brown said. "So right away we became enemies."

The Mundie meeting set off the competition between Xbox and WebTV. And while the winds favored the Xbox, no one had made a decision about which project to fund. A few days later, Mundie held a meeting to describe the "rules of engagement" for the meeting with Gates, which Hase termed the "come to Jesus meeting." Approval for the Xbox required a decision from the Overlord of Microsoft, Bill Gates.

Shortly after the Mundie meeting, the Xbox crew decided to send their proposal directly to Gates. Hase wanted to make sure the boss got the proposal without it being filtered by a hostile executive. The group prodded Bachus to e-mail the proposal to Gates on April 2, 1999. The next day, Gates sent a reply back, "This sounds great! Keep pushing ahead."

The team then passed this e-mail around widely to get more people on board because it implied that Gates liked the idea. Finally, a meeting with the top boss was set for May 5, 1999. It was like Judgement Day.

CHAPTER 9

THE BEAUTY CONTEST

THE GAME STRATEGY MEETING with Bill Gates occurred in the boardroom at Microsoft headquarters in Building 8, an office building that looks like a couple of small letter "t"s connected at the tips when viewed from the air. The room wasn't ostentatious. It had a big oak table that probably looked chic in the 1980s. There were big black leather chairs with soft cushions, enough to seat about 20 people. There were no exterior views, so the executives meeting in the room could gather without fear of eavesdropping. One wall of the room was made of glass; that was the side that bordered the hallway that led to Gates's office. Outside the entrance, stacks of papers were piled high. Several executive assistants to Bill Gates controlled access in the waiting room.

The atmosphere was nervous. The meeting was set up as a beauty contest. The Xbox presenters included the Four Musketeers, who were joined by Nat Brown, Ed Fries, Rick Thompson (vice president in charge of hardware), David Cole (vice president in charge of consumer Windows), Jay Torborg (the director of multimedia), and Rick Rashid (vice president of research). Nat Brown was the appointed speaker for the Xbox side.

The other side included WebTV's Dave Riola, Tim Bucher, Bruce Leak, and others; vice presidents Craig Mundie and Jon Devaan; and Ted Kummert, Chris Phillips, and Harel Kodesh of the Windows CE group. Neutrals included Eric Rudder (Bill Gates's technical assistant) as well as a variety of other executives. The timing of the meeting was good. The scheduled recess in the antitrust trial had stretched from five weeks to more than three months. Gates wasn't distracted. Noticeably absent was Steve Ballmer, Microsoft's president.

Craig Mundie began the meeting, saying that everyone believed there was a threat to the PC business in the home because of the PlayStation 2. The question at hand was whether Microsoft would come "down from the PC" to do battle with the PS 2 via the Xbox or come "up from the appliance world" via WebTV.

Nat Brown gave the Xbox presentation first, with Blackley and Bachus piping up to bolster him. Hase stayed silent so he could be the observer. He wanted to listen so he understood what every person's position was. His job was to read the body language to figure out who was engaged or detached from what was being said and then tell everyone about it in the postmortem. Brown began talking about slides showing the Xbox's "guiding principles," which included taking advantage of PC volume economics. He said the Xbox would capitalize on Windows assets for its operating system. It would try to harness the enthusiasm of game developers and rely on existing technology.

PC makers would launch the box in the fall of 2000 with a PC microprocessor, graphics from a company like Nvidia or 3Dfx, a network connection, a DVD player, 64 megabytes of dynamic random access memory, and, most controversial of all, a hard disk drive. The box would run PC games and Xbox games. The machine's graphics would process in practice about 50 million polygons per second, which was less than the PS 2's theoretical peak. But it would also be updated every two years, giving it a chance to leapfrog the PS 2 and take advantage of new graphics technology.

Brown said the goals were to make money, expand Microsoft's technology into the living room, and create the perception that Microsoft was leading the charge in the new era of consumer appliances. The initial cost estimate was for a machine with a bill of materials (engineering talk for cost) of $303. That machine would debut in the fall of 2000 and use a $20 microprocessor running at 350 megahertz from Advanced Micro Devices. The machine would also have a $55 hard disk drive with two gigabytes of storage, a $27 DVD drive to play movies, a $35 graphics chip, $25 worth of memory chips, and a collection of other standard parts like a motherboard and power supply. Over time, these prices would decline. The WebTV crew weighed in again with their objections. They said the hard disk drive was unnecessary and too expensive. Brown said hard disk drive prices were falling and that he had seen one priced as low as $35. But Chris Phillips remembers thinking, "Oh great, you found a cheap hard disk on eBay and now you think that's what they cost."

The PlayStation 2 didn't have a hard disk, though Sony was considering one as an add-on device. The WebTV team noted that Nintendo had planned to introduce a hard disk for the N64 as an add-on peripheral but found it would cost as much as the box itself. But Ed Fries piped up and said that the hard disk drive was key to online gaming and it represented the next evolution in console hardware.

"I believed the hard drive would fundamentally make on-line games possible, and make stand-alone single player games more interesting," Fries said. "It was just the next evolution of console hardware to me."

The endorsement from Fries caught Gates's attention. Like Fries's boss, Robbie Bach, he trusted the opinion of Fries, who had earned respect because he had made so much progress in growing the games business. The hard drive could store far more data than the 64-megabytes of DRAM chip memory in the rest of the box or the mere 40 megabytes in the Sony PS 2. As such, it could store much richer graphic details. The hard drive was also 100 times faster at fetching data than a DVD drive fetching data from a DVD disk. Hence, game developers would be able to create extremely detailed models and then transfer that data from the DVD disk to the hard drive as a cinematic clip was playing so that the player never noticed any delays. Such details could make game environments far more interactive and malleable than in current games.

Other chunks of the hard drive could be used to store saved games, so that users could pick up where they left off without having to plug a memory cartridge into the box. And the hard drive could store new levels for a game that could be downloaded from the Internet through the fast Ethernet connection in the back of the box.

Gates said he felt like the hard disk would help set the machine apart from the other consoles and create other business opportunities later on. Some debate focused on whether Microsoft would get more mileage by adding more chip memory, increasing it from 64 megabytes to 128 megabytes, rather than adding a hard drive. But Gates said he agreed with Fries. Bachus showed a demo of Bleem! software that could take a PlayStation game and run it on a PC to prove that the PC technology that would be used in an Xbox would be able to run console game code if so desired.

The WebTV team also said that there was no way that Microsoft would be able to create an Xbox operating system in time. But the Xbox team said they would adapt Neptune, a new version of the Windows 98 operating system, by focusing it on what was needed for gaming. The system would be less crash prone because the hardware would be stable and it would rely on known PC tools. The market target was the 29 million 16- to 26-year-old males who were the fanatical core of gaming.

The Xbox team by now expected their project to cost $500 million, but they really had no good numbers supporting the estimate. A "business model" spreadsheet in the presentation showed that the team expected to sell 1.8 million Xbox consoles in 2000, with steady improvement every year leading up to sales of 30.2 million consoles in 2005. Microsoft itself would lay out $226 million in expenses in the project's first year, not counting the costs its manufacturing partner would incur. Microsoft did not plan to charge royalties to developers, and this was considered a perk that would get developers to defect from Sony, which charged them $7 a game. Hence, Microsoft's cumulative loss for the first year was expected to be only $169 million. But by 2005, Microsoft's cumulative profit over five years was expected to hit $913 million. Microsoft's market share in the business could grow from 10 percent of annual sales in 2000 to 35 percent in 2005.

The early plan wasn't all that ambitious. It called for only 50 employees at first, largely because Microsoft would license and subcontract most of the work to others. The numbers weren't really an educated assessment of what it would take to succeed in the games business today. Rather, the numbers showed how naïve Microsoft was in its initial expectations as it marched off to battle—much like the troops in World War I. It expected to encounter little resistance, not prolonged trench warfare: Don't worry boys, we'll win this and be home by Christmas.

For much of the meeting, Gates listened quietly. He asked how easy it would be to convert games from the PC to the Xbox and visa versa. Blackley said it would be easy to switch between PC games and Xbox games because of the common DirectX architecture. Game developers already knew the DirectX tools that would be used for Xbox games, so there was no tiresome learning process for them. The team hadn't really decided exactly what it would put inside an Xbox operating system and what subset of PC applications an Xbox would be able to run. The Xbox team figured they had to say the box would be PC-compatible whether or not that was really the case in the end. Some of the team felt the box shouldn't run Windows, but they weren't prepared to tell Gates that yet.

"When we talked about PC-compatibility for the Xbox, that came from the fear of Bill," Blackley said.

Ted Kummert, head of the Windows CE contingent and Dave Riola of WebTV, spoke for the other side. But when they started talking, the meeting time was almost out.

"We need to build a product that competes head-to-head with Sony," Riola said. "We should embrace their business models."

The WebTV team described a subsidized console that would cost about $183 and quickly fall to $150 the year after launch. It would have no hard disk drive and would therefore match the other consoles on cost. Only such a console would do damage directly to Sony's business, they said. In contrast to the earlier proposal with non-PC components, this console now included a $20 Intel-compatible microprocessor and a $30 graphics chip from Nvidia. The highest-priced item on the list of materials was $40 for memory chips. But the rest of the bill of materials was complete, down to $2.14 for the cables and $4.85 for screws.

"I'm concerned that we're not trying to take money away from Sony and we're not trying to build a new business for the future," Riola said.

The WebTV box would also use Intel-compatible chips, but it would have a graphics chip that would be useful across a variety of devices, including WebTV, a game console, and other appliances. Consumers could pay extra to get additional advanced television features such as WebTV's Internet service, high-speed Internet access, or digital video recording. Microsoft would invest $300 million to design the console, spend another $500 million on marketing, and $200 million to build the machines. This effort could be a joint venture with Sega or Electronic Arts, but Microsoft might go it alone.

Riola said that Microsoft should take advantage of WebTV's world-class chip team to design the chips itself, rather than use technology from PC component makers. He said the console would be successful if Microsoft would throw things out of the PC architecture that weren't necessary in the console space. Kummert said the console could use the Dragon version of the Windows CE operating system that Sega was using. He said Microsoft should fund additional CE-based Sega games, and WebTV should provide Internet service for the Dreamcast in the United States.

"Windows CE is the only environment that provides predictability in the operating system," he said.

This software would be integrated with DirectX 8.0, the next version that Berkes would deliver after he finished DirectX 7.0. Berkes and Nat Brown looked at each other and raised their eyebrows. They were thinking the same thing.

Bill Gates also detected the problem. Windows CE had to be made compatible with the upcoming version of DirectX 8.0. He interrupted the presentation and asked who was working on this project. Berkes, who was in charge of developing the latest version of DirectX, said to Gates that he didn't know anything about it. He would need a lot more programming resources to make sure that this conversion would happen and if done it would be a slow process. "It wasn't a credible claim" that Windows CE would be synchronized with DirectX any-time soon, Berkes said. The Xbox team had considered using Windows CE, but they dropped it as soon as they discovered the file size for CE programs was limited to 32 megabytes; they would have had to partition a hard drive into thousands of parts just to make CE run. Hence, the WebTV people didn't have a good software story. They hadn't had the presence of mind or resources on short notice to put together a demo that showed Windows CE working with a new version of DirectX. Gates also hammered the failure of Windows CE in the Sega Dreamcast.

"Tell me who used Windows CE in a Dreamcast game," Gates demanded.

Kummert had to reply that very few game programmers had done so. He and Phillips offered a half-hearted response about why that was so. Gates knew the matter all too well already.

The Xbox team countered that the WebTV plan to create a custom graphics chip from scratch would take too long to de-sign given the short market window. Jay Torborg, Berkes's boss, thought that was the weakest part of the WebTV plan. Torborg had spearheaded a graphics chip project dubbed Talis-man years earlier that ended in failure because designs for the chips ran horribly off schedule. By the same token, the WebTV team didn't believe that the Xbox could produce a version of their operating system in time to finish a box for 2000.

Watching from the sidelines, Rick Thompson of the hard-ware group had taken a neutral stance in what he called the "peanut gallery." But he looked at the pedigrees of the players. Chris Phillips, Dave Riola and Ted Kummert had game market experience. Mundie and Devaan were high-ranking and seemed somewhat open-minded to Thompson in spite of how the Xbox team felt. WebTV's leader, Steve Perlman, was pretty much out the door. On the Xbox side, Blackley and his cohorts worked for technical stalwarts like David Cole of the consumer Windows group and his lieutenant Bill Veghte.

"These guys were known quantities," Thompson said his thoughts ran at the time. "Ted Kummert's group didn't have a deep keel. They didn't have a proven leader."

The strategy of Ted Hase was coming to fruition. He was beating the other guys by bringing more allies with heavyweight reputations to the fight.

Overall, Gates reacted more favorably to the Xbox team. "There is no doubt we need to do the PC-down approach. If we do anything, it will be more like the Xbox."

He liked the idea that the Xbox could run a broader class of software than the WebTV box, including educational software or productivity software. But Gates wondered how the business model would work, and he asked the teams to do more work figuring it out. Craig Mundie asked if there was a role for a machine that didn't have a hard disk.

"I'd love to attack [Sony] from both fronts, but can we really hope to execute on both plans?" Gates said.

He worried that software providers would be confused because there would be "no continuity of message" coming from Microsoft on games. Rick Rashid, an early convert among the executives and head of research, agreed that a two-pronged effort would be confusing, fragmenting the game developers into camps.

Blackley was surprised that Gates seemed so engaged in the proposal, and he was relieved that Gates was even paying attention, given all of his big responsibilities, not the least of which was the government's antitrust case aimed at breaking up Microsoft. Gates had other worries as well. He wondered aloud if America Online planned to dive into the games space. AOL had already talked about an AOL TV service that it planned to launch with cable TV companies like Time Warner, its future acquisition target.

At the time, Blackley got the impression that Gates thought of the Xbox as a pet project, and a WebTV representative agreed that Gates seemed biased.

"The Xbox team had the right idea" Gates said later. "Empower the artists with a platform that inspires them to do amazing work."

Blackley saw from Gates's questions that the company had to work through a lot of problems quickly if it was going to get a box out in 2000. Bachus was disappointed that he didn't see a flash of the legendary Gates temper. "I was looking forward to classic Bill," he said later.

But the Xbox crew had convincingly covered many points. "Our argument was to start where the company was strongest, with PC technology and PC software code," Bachus recalled. Microsoft faced an immediate threat with the PlayStation 2, and it needed to do something to stop Sony from taking all the hardcore gamers. If they failed to do that, then none of the other things would matter. And if WebTV's box spent its time doing a mix of functions, then it wouldn't do games well enough.

"Our goal needs to be to contain Sony," Gates said.

But Gates left a glimmer of hope for the WebTV team. He said he wanted a "common graphics architecture" between the PC, the Xbox, and WebTV. He said this would enable devices in the home to take advantage of high-bandwidth connections. This fateful suggestion turned into a new form of the old Microsoft strategy tax, slowing down the Xbox again.

"The strategy tax was very real," recalled Eric Engstrom, the former Microsoft "Beastie Boy" who had created DirectX and a few other Microsoft projects before leaving to start his own companies. "You never knew when the tax collector was going to come. You could be halfway done and then get hit with the tax bill."

CHAPTER 10

CIVIL WARS

GATES'S APPROVAL OF THE XBOX wasn't ironclad. Walking out of the meeting, Mundie told the WebTV crew, "We'll get you back in there. There is no way they can pull it off."

WebTV's team had been beaten, but it refused to die. Mundie said that Gates's decision was subject to interpretation. Gates had said that he wanted to explore whether the Xbox and WebTV could share a common graphics architecture. Since WebTV alone had chip designers, it had to play a part; the Xbox might even have to use WebTV's chips. The teams prepared for another round of meeting warfare.

The WebTV people argued that they should still be part of the project because they were the only ones who had ever built a machine that attached to a TV set.

"The WebTV people were relentless," says Blackley. "They kept coming back and proposing new things. They forced us to be more extreme about relying upon PC components and PC software tools."

But the WebTV group was so much in favor of *convergence,* the idea of consumer devices that packed in multiple functions—that it sacrificed some of the highest-performance features that hardcore gamers would demand. And they had no solution for making it simple for game developers to write software for their box.

Fundamentally, Blackley's team won because they had the credibility of knowing game developers, says Jon Devaan, who was at first one of Blackley's opponents on the WebTV side. Blackley enlisted the developers in the creation of the specifications for the Xbox, because he knew their support was crucial to the success of the Xbox. Throughout video game history, console makers like 3DO and Sega who didn't listen to the developers failed.

"The developers gave us air cover," Blackley said.

Blackley had been quietly consulting with his friends in the games industry for months. Tim Sweeney, a top programmer at Epic Games, knew about the Xbox because he was one of Blackley's confidants.

The two men had met years back when they were both in the middle of their giant games. Blackley had confided that he was forced to ship *Trespasser* when it wasn't done in part because he couldn't stand up to Spielberg. Meanwhile, Sweeney's project, a game called *Unreal,* ran beyond its original schedule as well. While Blackley's game was only a year or so overdue, Sweeney's was 18 months late. In the last few months, Sweeney changed his development plan so he could ship the game and still preserve the best parts. *Unreal* was one of the sensational hits of 1998, selling 1.3 million units. It was in the same shoot-everything-that-moves genre as *Doom*, but it extended the graphics artistry to a new level. The lesson of *Trespasser*, from Sweeney's view, wasn't that real-world physics failed. Rather, it was, "let your schedule slip and take the extra time you need to finish."

But Sweeney still had tremendous respect for Blackley, and they became good friends. And, as Blackley told him about what he was working on, Sweeney came to regard Blackley as the champion for the cause of developers and artists within the ordinarily nasty Microsoft empire. Lorne Lanning, president of Oddworld Inhabitants, a game developer in San Luis Obispo, California, shared that view.

"It was a huge relief to have a creatively-driven mind in charge of designing hardware for the industry," said Lanning. "Seamus was a huge breath of fresh air for developers, even though he was a royal wiseass."

Blackley tapped Sweeney to be an unofficial adviser to the Xbox team, along with other luminaries like John Carmack, the chief programmer at id Software. Much later, Blackley signed up 15 members to a "technical advisory board." They kept in touch on an e-mail group and offered detailed suggestions to Blackley, who in turn used the feedback as ammunition to satisfy the rest of the colleagues on the team as well as upper management.

The developers were strongly in favor of Nvidia, which they regarded as the "coolest" 3-D chip maker because of its consistent improvements in its chips every nine months and because its software was so stable.

"When we got our way on things, we were stunned," Sweeney said. "It's like, you guys are actually listening."

Ed Fries, head of the games division, was a critical ally during the beauty contest between the Xbox and WebTV. The WebTV competition drove the Xbox team to extremes, because it let them know that their project could be canceled at any moment.

"There was a polarization that happened, and they pushed us more toward Windows and tools that made it easy for developers," Blackley said.

On June 17, another showdown was scheduled in Gates's boardroom. This time, the teams gave their presentations on different days. Gates and Microsoft's No. 2 man, Steve Ballmer, were both present. Blackley and his team were in a state of panic because the AMD team had left the demo in a locked room. The AMD people weren't around and no one else had a key. The Xbox guys tried picking the lock but failed. Then they stacked a chair on a table and lifted the ceiling tiles outside the office in the hallway. Bachus climbed up into the ceiling hole, crawled over the office doorframe, and then dropped in behind the locked door. He got the demo out, but had to face Microsoft's security. Blackley showed his badge and told them they had a meeting with Bill Gates in 20 minutes. The security guard didn't believe him. So he called Gates's office and asked if the group had a meeting. The assistant confirmed the meeting and the security guard let the Xbox guys go.

The Xbox team again presented first. The WebTV team presented the next day, but they were allowed listen to the Xbox presentation before they gave their own, and in that sense they had leeway to change their presentation for the next day. Tension was still pretty high. Blackley took great umbrage at a sniping comment from one of the rivals, Chris Phillips, who said to Blackley's cohort, Colin McCartney, "So you're going to do a demo for Bill. Hope it works." It was just minutes before Gates arrived.

Once again, Nat Brown talked. He noted that there was a chance to create a common graphics architecture between the appliance-like PC, the high-end game console, and the high-end set-top box. Each shared features like hard drives—especially since digital recording was becoming a popular notion—as well as a microprocessor and 3-D graphics. He said that even if the microprocessor architectures weren't the same, the systems would all be able to use common software interfaces such as DirectX.

Blackley showed the BIOS prototype—which demonstrated that a game box could be rigged to start instantaneously—running on a jury-rigged system. It used a newfangled *legacy-free* system board, one that had stripped out old PC technology like an aging data pathway. The mock-up was so unreliable that it only worked about half the time. Blackley crossed his fingers, turned the system on. It didn't work and so Blackley confessed it worked only about 50 percent of the time. On the second try it worked flawlessly for Gates, who exclaimed he had pounded on programmers for years to get a version of Windows that would start instantaneously. Within nine seconds, Lara Croft was on the TV screen and talking seductively. It was flashy. And it proved that the PC was up to the challenge of displaying sophisticated animations on a TV. The group also showed the Bleem! demo again to display PlayStation games on a PC, and it showed an Xbox mock-up that had been designed by Microsoft industrial designer Jim Stewart.

Brown closed with a slide that urged Gates to approve the project.

"We can do it," he said. But he noted it was a big, upfront investment with no guarantee of a return. And time was very tight for a 2000 launch.

"We must push into the living room," Brown said.

He said that if Gates gave the order within two weeks, the Xbox team would quickly produce a prototype, get commitments from retailers, get computer makers signed up to build the machine and solicit publishers.

"If you say no, we go back to our day jobs," building the future versions of Windows, Brown said.

The Xbox team knew they had made an impression on Gates. In past meetings, Brown noticed that Gates would show up with a single sheet of paper and scrawl over a quarter of it. After this meeting, which lasted about 90 minutes, Brown saw that Gates had written all over the entire sheet of paper. Steve Ballmer, the No. 2 man, highlighted the importance of the discussion when he said that Microsoft should do one of these two projects or face a big retreat in the consumer software business. Gates said he didn't want Microsoft to be just a corporate software firm.

Bachus recalled he was amazed at the breadth of questions Gates asked, drawing upon his many meetings in the past with Sega's top executive, Isao Okawa, and online games companies like Mpath Interactive. Chris Phillips said it looked as though Ballmer and Gates had already decided before they heard any real arguments.

"I felt like I was having my coffin measured," he said. "I just wanted to make sure that Bill had his eyes open on this one. If we didn't succeed with it, we would really hurt the Microsoft brand in the home."

The next day at the WebTV meeting, the Xbox crew griped that the WebTV proposal now seemed remarkably similar to their own. When Chris Phillips made an assertion about game developers, Kevin Bachus jumped up and said he couldn't sit still anymore as the WebTV team passed bad information on to Gates. But while he still favored the Xbox, Gates didn't tell the WebTV crew to move on to something new. Bachus said the Xbox team was depressed that Gates didn't kill the WebTV plan outright because there was again no clear, definitive answer.

The internecine warfare within Microsoft took a toll on Blackley, but his team had the upper hand. Maddeningly, the WebTV crew still participated in the project until a showdown over graphics chips months later.

"It really was death by a thousand blows for WebTV," said Nat Brown.

Eventually, the WebTV opposition lost interest as it began to pull together a product that would replace WebTV. The engineers began working on it as early as July 1999. This product, dubbed Ultimate TV, integrated digital video recording capability into satellite TV, resulting in a box that TV lovers would froth over. WebTV had helped EchoStar introduce the DishPlayer 500, the first machine that could function as a digital VCR. But the launch was so quiet that nobody paid attention until a Silicon Valley company called Tivo announced a box with much more fanfare. Even though the sales of Tivo's first generation were slow to take off, it had a galvanizing effect on the WebTV team. Instead of the Xbox and PlayStation 2, they now had a new enemy. And their technology was much more suited for going after Tivo, which had left an opening for Microsoft because of its relatively weak product launch. Ultimate TV launched in the spring of 2001, with no video game technology in it. WebTV advocates like Jon Devaan said the Ultimate TV platform meant they needn't feel as bad about missing out on games. Devaan also said WebTV's outlook was good because it remained possible in the future, as the technology treadmill proceeded, to integrate Xbox functions into a WebTV box.

"The option was left open to build a hybrid device in the future," Devaan said.

Bucher, who later became vice president of consumer products in the WebTV unit, said the company made the right decision by separating the WebTV and Xbox products.

"When you integrate things that sacrifice the quality of experience, consumers won't adopt it," he said. "WebTV was about video and storage technology. Gaming was about graphics. Adding them together does not lead to better game experiences or better TV experiences. If you're playing a game, then the machine has to record a TV show, will it take resources from the game?"

Bucher also believed the Xbox team had an advantage because it worked from the inside out, whereas WebTV, which was acquired in 1997, had to work from the outside in. That is, WebTV's technology used non-Microsoft software such as its own proprietary operating system. That software wasn't easy to integrate with DirectX, which was the bedrock technology for games on computers.

"We had to shed older, non-standard technology as we transitioned into Microsoft," Bucher said.

"In an alternate universe, if it weren't for what we did, you'd be playing games on a WebTV machine today," Blackley later said.

Although the internal divisional conflict wound down, there was no armistice. And as a result, the civil war erupted once more, making Microsoft lose some critical time as it debated what to do between the Xbox and WebTV proposals.

Steve Perlman, who had watched from the sidelines as WebTV went down in defeat, said, "The consequences of that time of indecision are profound in this marketplace. That indecision could make or break the Xbox's performance in the market."

It remains to be seen whether or not that lost time will cost Microsoft dearly in the competition with Sony and Nintendo. Both those companies put years into planning their new products before Microsoft got into the action and they had a big head start.

"You wouldn't believe how much time we wasted," said Blackley, who always wanted to move at renegade speed.

11

GETTING TRACTION

THE XBOX BAND OF RENEGADES was growing more legitimate every day as the summer of 1999 pressed on. On July 12, they met with Robbie Bach, the senior vice president who ran the Home and Retail Products Division, which oversaw the games, hardware, and Office productivity software groups. Kevin Bachus had set up this meeting because he believed that the consumer Windows division didn't have the marketing skills to launch a consumer entertainment device. Bachus had been working with Home and Retail Products division marketers like Don Coyner and Jennifer Booth, who were both veterans of the video game industry. On July 16, they made a pitch to Rick Thompson, head of the hardware division. The Xbox crew had staged a classic business incubation. They didn't go outside for funding like traditional entrepreneurs. Instead, Blackley and his cohorts were *intrapreneurs,* doing the same thing as entrepreneurs except inside a big company. They cleared out the bureaucratic barriers and internal competition with other divisions and tried to make it into a real business. The group was familiar with a 1997 book by Harvard Business School professor Clay Christensen, *The Innovator's Dilemma,* which underscores how tough it is for companies with great franchises to embrace new ideas that threaten those franchises.

The Xbox could be a "disruptive technology," which in Christensen's terms meant it had the potential to unseat the hegemony of older product lines. But would the Xbox stop with disrupting Sony's business, or would it go after the PC as well?

After the first Gates meeting, the Xbox team met with Steve Ballmer alone one day at his office in Red West, a complex a mile or so from the main campus that housed the games and hardware groups and a variety of newfangled Internet-Microsoft businesses such as MSN. In a small conference room, Windows executive Bill Veghte asked Ballmer how much he knew about the Xbox. Ballmer bowled them over with a monologue. In his booming voice, he said, "The Xbox is the greatest fucking thing in the world! It's going to make billions! It's the greatest thing ever! It's going to do this, it's going to do that! I know! I know!"

He went on for a minute. Bachus said it was "the loudest sound I ever heard in my life. He was ribbing us, semi-sarcastically." The team took the loud harangue as a gentle joke making fun of their enthusiasm. But then Ballmer became serious. Patiently, like a college professor, he got down to work on the business model. His job was to take Gates's ideas and turn them into profitable businesses. He was paid to be skeptical of wild-eyed plans for new products.

"How are we going to make money?" he asked. "Let me tell you why it's not going to work."

He said he had been studying the WebTV model and couldn't make it work. He picked up a pen, walked over to the white board and asked them to give him numbers. "OK, what's in the box?" he said. They told him and he wrote the numbers down. "What about your allocation for returns? Your retailer margin? The retailers will never go for 6 percent. Restocking fees?" Ballmer didn't relent. "Give me a number. Just to write it down." At the time, the Xbox team still hoped they could get away without charging software developers a royalty. Sony and Nintendo charged a fee of $7 per game, in exchange for testing it and packaging it in a plastic jewel case. Without this fee, Microsoft could make a token fee on the sale of controllers as well as take profits on its own in-house games. Ballmer questioned the viability of the no-royalty model. He wondered if the hard drive was practical given its hefty cost, and he thought the retailer margin had to be set at a high 18 percent of the cost.

At the end of it, Ballmer said, "You're off by $100." Bachus said later, "He showed us we were pretty stupid."

Ballmer went on to offer a lot of encouragement to the Xbox team in his own fashion. For example, once when they were standing in line at a cafeteria, Ballmer sneaked up behind them and yelled in his salesman's voice, "It's the Xbox guys!" Blackley said, "I almost peed in my pants." He looked over at Bachus, whose face went white, like someone who had just been caught doing something bad.

Blackley added, "But at the same time, it was so motivating that he was showing to everyone else there exactly who we were." As Ballmer walked over, he asked more quietly, "Are you making any money yet?"

Now came the time to figure out who would really turn the proposal into a business. Periodically, the Four Musketeers and Nat Brown tried to figure out who would be the best person to run the business. Some thought that bringing in an experienced video game hardware leader was the only way to jump-start the Xbox. Sega's top executives like U.S. subsidiary president Bernard Stolar were natural candidates because of the close relationship between Sega and Microsoft over the years. Nat Brown, however, felt he had seen too many outside executives come into Microsoft and fail to adapt to the company's unique culture.

On July 21, 1999, a dozen executives and many more team members met for another meeting. Bill Gates and Steve Ballmer were there. Rick Thompson, the vice president in charge of the hardware business, walked in last because he had gone to the wrong building on campus. The group once again agreed to back the Xbox plan.

Toward the end of the meeting, Ballmer asked who should head the group. Nat Brown, who was on vacation and participating via speaker phone, suggested Thompson, whose face turned purple.

"My first reaction was that I was not big enough to do the job, that they needed somebody with more chutzpah," Thompson says.

He said just that to the group: "I'm not big enough for this job." That prompted a lot of obvious jokes but Ballmer took Thompson off the spot, saying, "You can't expect someone to make a career decision with dozens of people in the room."

Thompson was a 38-year-old vice president who had worked at Microsoft for 12 years. He was the son of a New Yorker who owned a tire shop. His mother died when he was 11 years old. He worked odd jobs in the tire shop and all of his way through high school to pay his way through a liberal arts college in Maine. A sales and product management veteran, he joined the hardware division—which included joysticks, steering wheels, and mice for personal computers—when it had only 14 people. Over the years, he grew the unit to 300 people. Sales went from $30 million to more than $600 million a year. The business wasn't core to Microsoft and if something had gone wrong, Microsoft would have shut it down quickly. But the hardware unit was innovative and profitable, so Thompson ran his own company within a company as he saw fit.

The Xbox boys already knew him well because they had lobbied him to get on board with the hardware for the Xbox. Ed Fries and Robbie Bach also liked him because he was the only executive who had run a hardware business where the key was finding a path to make razor-thin profit margins, as was necessary in the consumer market. Thompson had the reputation of a top-notch businessman who could figure out profit-and-loss models for a business that had hundreds of employees and produced hardware in high volumes. Thompson enjoyed the scrappy fights between the WebTV and Xbox teams, but he never really took sides. He was faithful to profit-and-loss plans.

"I was stiff-arming the Xbox team members," he said. "But I did go to the meetings."

Bachus couldn't understand why Thompson was such a reluctant general. "We kept saying he should lead this," Bachus said. "He kept saying 'I'm not the right guy.' We thought he was being modest." Thompson had talked the idea over with one of his good friends, Bob McBreen, who had been running the Actimates toy group for Microsoft Hardware. McBreen had been Thompson's college roommate, and the men coached Little League baseball together. Thompson said, "I'm about to get drafted for this thing." McBreen signed up to join that night.

The day after the July 21 meeting, Ballmer summoned Thompson and his boss, Robbie Bach, to his office. Ballmer was holding a baseball bat, as he often did to drive home points. He was holding the bat in one hand and slapping it against his other hand. But Thompson had endured that act before and didn't flinch. He presented a one-page memo on why he wasn't the man to do the job. Ballmer said that Thompson could keep his hardware job for the time being, but he had to take on the additional duty of planning the Xbox business. He thus became the first vice president of the business, still reporting to Bach, and the Xbox became legit.

"Up until that point, it was all a great technology," Thompson said. "But it needed a business side"

Gates agreed, noting that the team was heading down the right technical path, but it wasn't, he said, until Thompson joined the project that the business and technology visions came together. Thompson needed to study the games business and figure out if Microsoft could make money on it.

Thompson brought friends from the hardware division. Bob McBreen knew his role. He would drive the deals with strategic partners, mostly on the hardware side.

The decision to legitimize the project brought a high-level endorsement of the Xbox, a validation that it was an important enough business that Microsoft would transfer one of its highly respected managers to run the start-up division. And it was about time. Sony was planning to launch its PS 2 in March 2000 in Japan and in the fall of 2000 in the United States and Europe. (It later delayed the United States launch to October and the Europe launch to 2001). To get a box out in 2000, Microsoft had to go fast.

It had seemed like Microsoft had made this decision back in May. But, Fries explained, the company's culture was a methodical one. The company debated its ideas, sifting through evidence at periodic intervals, until it was clear that a project was a good one. Then it measured the project on a series of milestones to decide whether to keep funding it or to pull the plug.

"We would update Bill and Steve on things we had learned," he said. "Then we would get their feedback. This took time. We knew that when we told them something, we should be ready for them to drill into it and push back. So they gave us the go-ahead, but always for the time being."

Fries didn't mind the delays because the Xbox plan kept evolving for the better. Robbie Bach, who oversaw Thompson, regretted much later that he had not moved with the speed of a start-up early on.

As the Xbox became official, the onset of legitimacy also gave Blackley and his cohorts "a moment of supreme angst." All of a sudden, their baby wasn't theirs anymore.

Thompson had always been an adviser that the Xbox renegades had lobbied heavily to get involved.

"Everyone wanted Rick to be the head because of his disposition and his successful hardware business," Hase said. At the same time, they each wanted to play a big role in the project. Blackley harbored the unrealistic expectation that he should run the project himself, even though, as a first-year employee, he had no idea how to communicate up the chain to Bill Gates. In spite of his hopes, Blackley knew that none of the Xbox creators had any experience managing a business involving hundreds of millions of dollars, and upper management would have to find someone else.

At that point, the project reached a crisis. Otto Berkes, Nat Brown, and Ted Hase also didn't like the new decisions by people coming in to take over their project. Berkes and Hase decided to quit the Xbox and return to their own jobs, since they figured their work in getting it going was done.

"Once it shifted more to building a console rather than an improving on Windows play, it was less attractive to me," Hase says.

Hase told others he wasn't sure whether it would be a bad career decision. He put a premium on organizational loyalty, he had obligations on his old job, and he worried that too many people might defect to the Xbox camp and abandon Windows gaming. At an August 4, 1999, meeting with Thompson, Hase asked if his developer relations group could handle the evangelism for the Xbox. Thompson said he wanted the evangelists to be part of his own Xbox division. So Hase said that Bachus should move over to the Xbox, but he himself would stay behind. Hase said he had concerns about moving to a new division and having to prove himself all over again for a boss who didn't know him.

"In some ways, staying behind was a riskier decision because we knew the Xbox was going to get a lot of attention and resources," Hase said.

With Hase's departure, the Xbox lost one of its most fiercely competitive strategists.

Brown decided to take a leave of absence from Microsoft altogether. Thompson thought Brown was on vacation and would be back in a couple of weeks. He expected Brown to become the project manager and start assembling a software team upon his return. Brown, however, didn't feel like he was lined up for the exact job he wanted, and he had other reasons to leave.

Thompson comments, "It was the classic jerk thing to do. To get me involved and then to bug out. I never saw him again."

Brown had taken to calling his opponents within the company "pinheads." He had been at Microsoft for nearly 10 years, starting in 1991 as an intern and working his way up the chain of the Windows NT group. In the late 1990s, he switched to the consumer group because that was where he saw innovations in software. Within consumer Windows, he was the technical person who sold ideas to upper management. He tired of the never-ending arguments within Microsoft. And he and his wife wanted to take some time off and start a family.

Brown had gotten his way on most things, but not in one key respect. He wanted the Xbox project to be part of the consumer Windows division, headed by his boss David Cole. When Thompson and Robbie Bach, who ran the home and retail products group, signed on as the top executives, the project escaped from Brown's division. While he respected them, Brown felt that the "mouse guys" weren't going to ensure that the lessons of the Xbox were passed along to the core Windows team. He wanted Thompson to report to Windows. But Bach said it made sense to assign the Xbox to the division that was focused on products for the home. In addition, it would be the biggest project in the division and would therefore get the most management attention. By contrast, the Xbox would have been a stepchild project in the consumer Windows division, where the operating system was the priority.

Like other revolutionaries at Microsoft, Brown wanted to see a simplified version of Windows that could serve as the backbone of an Internet appliance. When he saw that Windows wasn't going to be transformed quickly, Brown decided it was time to hand the Xbox over to other people who would get it done.

The rest of the Xbox survivors were disappointed at the unraveling of their team. Berkes stayed on for a little longer than Brown. He needed to help with the technical work and he wanted to see if his original idea, which he called Xbox One, would prevail. Like Brown, he wanted the Xbox to be a version of PC, running Windows and PC games. But as the new managers came into the project, Berkes found he was on the losing side of the debate. Others insisted on turning the proposal into Xbox Two, which was a lot more like a console right off the bat. This machine wouldn't run Windows or be compatible with PC games. It would be an appliance, running a different operating system than the one Berkes was proposing.

"I had animated discussions about this," Berkes said. "They took the Xbox and narrowed its focus and constrained it."

Berkes also had a comfortable job making the new version of DirectX 8.0, which was also a necessary ingredient of the Xbox. He stuck with his day job.

As this happened, Microsoft lost what might have been an equal partner on the project—without even realizing it. When the box strayed from the original plan of running a version of Windows, Intel decided to back out of a plan among some of its own renegades to become a much bigger partner in the project. Jason Rubinstein at Intel had talked to his bosses about Microsoft's ideas for the Xbox. Pat Gelsinger, a vice president in charge of the desktop products group, was considering a plan to participate in the Xbox as a co-marketer and co-branding partner. He was having regular discussions with Microsoft's David Cole in the consumer Windows group. Intel had proposed not only to build the microprocessor, chipset, and motherboard for the device but to assemble it and put its name on the machine. Intel was starting a Web hosting business that was running up billions of dollars in start-up costs. Intel wanted to provide the online infrastructure that Microsoft would use to operate a worldwide online games network. The Xbox could be key to generating traffic on this network, and this network also might produce a new source of revenues beyond the traditional model of losing money on hardware and making up for it on software. Intel also liked the idea of doing more than just gaming on the box. In his speeches before Intel's developers, Gelsinger had talked about home PC appliances with the ability to share video files over the Internet, play digital music files, surf the Web, and do other things such as e-mail. Gelsinger and other Intel officials liked the fact that it was an open platform that didn't charge royalties and that it would run PC games. It was so attractive that Intel wanted to participate in a big way. Such a plan, built around Xbox One, could have brought the Wintel duopoly partners closer together than ever before.

Gelsinger got up at a meeting between the Microsoft and Intel brass and said that the Xbox team was wrong about its cost estimates. Backing up what Gates and Ballmer had already heard from the WebTV team, he said that the bill of materials cost on the Xbox was too low. Instead of $303, Gelsinger anticipated the costs would be more like $340 to $350. He had put his top chip architects to work studying the problem. Gelsinger predicted the Xbox plan would fail.

Ballmer became emotional. He was clearly upset with his own team, and he showed how much he differed from Gates in his opinion of the Xbox. He screamed, "Then why the hell are we doing this?"

The teams then argued about the cost estimates and talked about what they could change. Ultimately, Ballmer and Gates agreed that focusing the box on gaming was the first order of business. If they couldn't beat the PlayStation 2, then they had no business trying to do other things like providing e-mail or Web browsing. This was what some people in the project came to call Xbox Two.

Microsoft's executives weren't enthusiastic about Intel's plan to provide the network infrastructure for online gaming. Intel's executives believed that was where their profit opportunity lay—in collecting a kind of toll on online gaming. They were disturbed that Microsoft was willing to spend billions of dollars on the project and yet it still didn't have a clue about basic manufacturing costs. They didn't think the Xbox would stop Sony. They decided to back off.

"After that meeting, it unraveled," says an Intel person familiar with the matter. "We decided let's just be a chip supplier on this thing, not a partner. It was clear our opportunity would be smaller. We weren't even sure if we could make money as a chip supplier at the prices they were talking about. They appeared uncoordinated to us. We laughed at the idea they would blow a few billion dollars."

On Microsoft's side, some believed that Intel wouldn't be nimble enough as a partner. It might move too slowly for such a dynamic marketplace. Intel could still participate as the supplier of the motherboard, chipset, and microprocessor, but it wasn't going to be an equal partner.

Along with Intel, Berkes, Brown, and Hase dropped out of the limelight. The three men lost much of the credit for helping to create one of the biggest projects that they would ever participate in. They didn't second-guess their decisions, but they also weren't pleased when they didn't get much recognition for their efforts. The Microsoft PR department would later neglect requests for interviews with them. Hase was philosophical about it. Quoting former president George Bush, he said, "There is no limit to what can be accomplished as long as you're willing to let someone else have the credit."

While Brown took off, Berkes and Hase focused on their dream of improving the PC. And Berkes had to ship the next version of DirectX 8.0, which would form the core of the Xbox operating system as well as gaming technology on the PC. But this task would be far from the center of excitement.

"You can't fault the guys who took off," says Blackley. "We'd cry, feeling it was being hijacked."

The Xbox had started out as a project created by people who loved games, or at least knew the games industry well. They were not the most experienced in the games business, nor did they know much about console games. But they knew games. The WebTV and Windows CE people had console experience, but their advice was ignored because of their poor track records. As Xbox grew up, other people took over. These people believed they knew how to run the business better than the gamers. Some of them bragged that they were gamers, or that their kids were gamers. But not many of them as yet had the close, intimate connections with other game developers and years of friendships with such people. There was no single person who had the ideal combination of console game experience and business knowledge who could unify the different camps. This situation set up some conflicts for the future. The game experts would clash with the business experts again and again. And it would be the source of confusion for those on the outside who really wondered whether Microsoft grasped the games industry.

"You work in the industry for ten years and then these business guys come and think they can learn all of your knowledge in a month," Blackley said.

Of the original instigators, only Bachus, Wyatt, Fries, and Blackley stayed on board. Blackley, for one, had no job to return to. He was like an invader who had burned his ships and had to go on. He also didn't mind making compromises in order to get his grand vision into the market. Both Bachus and

Blackley would have to get used to the idea that their voices would carry less weight in the new regime.

"Part of it was *Trespasser*," Blackley recalled. "I was not going to fail again. I decided I could react to *Trespasser* by making it make me stronger or weaker."

Blackley and Bachus shared their grief that their baby was being taken away. Bachus recalled a debate they had over whether a group could build a great product with or without a strong visionary, like Steve Jobs, who had shepherded the Apple Macintosh to market in 1984.

"It was really hard for us to figure out what we really wanted to do," Bachus added. "I kept saying that it would be OK. The Boeing 777 had no single person who was its inventor, and Seamus would say that the 777 wasn't really as elegant as some of the early hand-built planes."

But they could see that the train was leaving the station and for better or worse they had better be on board. Otherwise, they worried that the project wouldn't be done right because they wouldn't be there as the constant voice of experience.

Blackley commiserated with Rob Wyatt, who also liked aerobatic flying. They would take off in a small plane from Boeing Field in Seattle and fly north to the San Juan Islands, an archipelago of 172 islands just off the coast of Washington, just to get above it all and talk things over.

Sometimes Blackley and Bachus would talk to each other on cell phones for a couple of hours at a time. Bachus stayed engaged in conversation with the more emotional Blackley until he could steer the conversation back to what really got Blackley excited. When Blackley remembered what was so exciting about the Xbox he was able to shelve his emotions and move on. Still, in dealing with the change, they sorely missed Nat Brown's experience.

"None of those guys had ever handed a project off before, but that is a classic thing to do at Microsoft," Brown said later.

"I think if I was around to tell them how to do it, it would have been easier to deal with."

Thompson had no sympathy for the Xbox founders. Much later, he said he had viewed them as "arrogant, obnoxious, and massively irresponsible." They were fame-seekers who were enamored with technology, but had no clue about the business side, Thompson felt. "My attitude was there is the door if you don't want to be part of it," Thompson recalled feeling.

Thompson admitted, however, that he himself had no real connections to game publishers and developers. And his assessment was unfair in one respect. The component vendors that the Xbox team had talked to had offered low-ball numbers to win favor from Microsoft. But when it came time to make bids for contracts, they pulled back and admitted they wanted higher prices. In doing so, they inadvertently shot down the credibility of Blackley, Bachus, and the other people who knew the games industry on the Xbox team. Their bill of materials was bogus. Of course, the Xbox guys should have known better than to trust the vendors. Thompson began to look elsewhere for gaming expertise.

Others watching from the sidelines felt that Thompson was too harsh on Blackley and Bachus. Jay Torborg, Otto Berkes's boss, had left Microsoft in July. But, as he heard about the transition difficulties, he believed that Thompson should have valued the duo for their gaming software expertise, even if they didn't know much about hardware.

"They didn't purport to be hardware experts, so it was unfair to penalize them for that," Torborg said.

Torborg felt it natural that business managers be brought in to run the business, but he was sad that there appeared to be so few roles for the original renegades.

For a time, Bachus felt like he had been put off in a corner with nothing to do. He viewed his time on the project as a sine wave, with plenty of ups and downs. And he was at a low point.

"I had an awesome amount of respect for Rick Thompson," Blackley says. "It was crushing when he didn't like me."

And Blackley couldn't help but feel disappointment when Thompson came to him one day in August and said, "This is your new boss."

THE NEW BOSS

The new man on board as project manager was James "J" Allard. He was a legendary figure within Microsoft because of the role he played in getting Microsoft to respond to the threat of the Internet. He was of medium build, with wire-rimmed glasses and a high forehead. He dyed his short buzzed hair blondish-white. Allard joined Microsoft in 1991 as a networking programmer even though he wasn't convinced that Microsoft had a clue about the Internet. His job was to build TCP/IP, the Internet communications protocol, into Microsoft's software products, and at the time it was only because then-Executive Vice President Steve Ballmer wanted to appease customers who were screaming for it.

"I was thinking big though, like how powerful it would be to marry the Internet and Windows," Allard recalls. "I entered into the job with the goal of getting my mom to do e-mail."

Allard was so wedded to e-mail that he adopted a shortened form of his logon, *jallard@microsoft.com,* as his nickname: J without a period.

Allard ran an unsanctioned project in early 1993 to build Microsoft's first Internet server, which could link Microsoft to other Web sites. But he was getting frustrated that Microsoft didn't understand the importance of the Internet, even after Marc Andreesen and other students at the University of Illinois released Mosaic, the first Web browser that made it easy to surf the Internet. On January 25, 1994, Allard penned a memo, "Windows: the Next Killer Application for the Internet." He ultimately inspired Gates to reorganize the entire company to focus on the Internet, a move that was later formalized on December 7, 1995, when Gates announced to the world that Microsoft would embrace and extend Web standards and be ready for the "Internet Tidal Wave." Microsoft would not only embrace the Net, it would build Internet capability into all of its products, even to the point of intertwining Web standards within the Windows operating system.

Indeed, all that followed—the intense browser war with Netscape Communications, the explosion of demand for browsers to cruise Web sites, the intense scrutiny by the federal government that ultimately brought an antitrust suit against Microsoft—could be laid at the feet of Allard. But none of the work was easy. Allard initially lost battles with Microsoft's MSN unit, which wanted to keep Microsoft's online network based on proprietary software. He ultimately prevailed, but the battles were debilitating. By the time he had shepherded many programs through the treadmill, he was tired.

"I was wildly proud of what I did," Allard said. "But I needed a change."

Allard had been assigned to lead a major Internet software effort called Project 42. But he had trouble getting along with his boss and he didn't want to make a required three-year commitment to the project, which was later renamed .Net, a collection of services provided over the Web. During the middle of 1999, Allard was on an extended leave of absence. He considered running an art gallery or bar on Seattle's trendy Capitol Hill, or a Web production company, or maybe something to do with digital video.[1] He was playing video games all the time, and he was thinking about how he wanted to become a part of the new world of digital entertainment. He had this vision that, because of the Web, computers were going to become the central console of the living room, a master control unit that would play movies, music, games, and just about anything else. He was nursing a broken ankle, but he was itchy to get to work on the idea, perhaps by starting up a new company on his own. He wanted it to be as big a deal as his previous gig and felt like he had to either "go big or go home." The phrase hearkened back to one of his original job interviews at Microsoft in 1991, when a networking manager asked Allard what he wanted his tombstone to read.

Nat Brown told Allard about the Xbox project. As he was deciding whether to stick around himself, Brown decided he needed to do the Xbox team one last favor. He wanted the software effort to be headed by a bulldog who had the ear of Gates and Ballmer. This bulldog would report to the business guys like Bach and Thompson, but he would also have to be a technical leader. Brown thought Allard, who had managed teams of 200 people, could do the job. In an e-mail note to Allard, Brown wrote:

> Wanted: energetic, maniac, manager-type, with biz, Web, and e-savvy to launch astoundingly fantastic new kick-ass product against entrenched competitor. Experienced gamers, high-speed racers, and drinkers only. Large discretionary budget. No strings attached. First name must be a consonant. Call Nat. . . .

But Allard said he didn't join immediately because he didn't think there was much point in doing a specialized version of Windows for entertainment. At first, Allard thought this effort was just another "eMachines for games," a reference to the easy-to-use, sub-$500 consumer computers that met with limited success over time.

Allard thought that the Windows Entertainment Platform might generate a million or two more sales of Windows. But Allard wanted to participate in a project that turned the games industry on its head. The original Xbox team had long ago dispensed with the Windows Entertainment Platform and had been calling the Xbox a game console for some time, but to Allard it wasn't necessarily going far enough in the console direction. The Xbox team believed their machine would augment the PC, not compete with it.

Allard met with Steve Ballmer again and asked if Microsoft wanted to "build another Microsoft in entertainment." He pressed Ballmer on whether he would investigate the Xbox idea as a potential multibillion-dollar business. Ballmer told him he should talk to Rick Thompson, adding, "We'll do a real investigation of this. Go make this real."

Hobbling on crutches, Allard went into Microsoft to meet with Thompson, and in a one-hour meeting he cemented his return to Microsoft. It all came rushing back to him. His first software code was writing a game. His first real job was selling games. He had missed gaming in all those intervening years writing code. All of the other consoles were just more of the same, and they weren't taking gaming to the next level.

"It was a chance to do something with a more profound impact on society," Allard recalls. "Games needed to be elevated to an art form. Until games were reviewed in the arts section of the *New York Times,* they weren't legitimate," Allard says, picking up a line from Blackley.

"The world's best storytellers aren't working on games, and until that's the case, we're not done. I wanted to be part of this revolution."

12

MAKING THE TEAM

ALLARD HAD TO SMOOTH THINGS OVER with his young rebels, and he didn't hit it off with Blackley at first. They argued about technical matters. Blackley eventually saw that Allard brought a lot of respect from the top and gave the Xbox more credibility among the top brass. Allard, for his part, was surprised at Blackley's naïveté. Blackley knew little about how to get things done at Microsoft. Allard had close personal ties with Gates and Ballmer; he'd worked on dozens of different products at Microsoft and knew what it took to convince the brass to get behind a product wholeheartedly. He had credibility based on his track record for spotting opportunities early and pulling together motivated teams.

He brought in his inseparable companion from the Internet wars, Cameron Ferroni. Ferroni, a 31-year-old programmer, had been at Microsoft for eight years and had worked alongside Allard for several of them. He was the guy who got things done while Allard stretched his vision. Working under Allard, Ferroni was responsible for system software for the Xbox and for planning the online strategy. Allard brought other friends aboard, including Jeff Henshaw, who headed the effort to create the software development kits.

Allard and Ferroni took the only space available near the hardware group, in an office in the middle of the team that created Microsoft Money personal finance software. Allard and Ferroni spent about $1,600 on a color TV, a Sega Dreamcast, and all the games they could get their hands on. For the first month, they played so much that the Money team thought they were nuts.

The Xbox team had to show the new bosses that they were smart enough to participate. Soon enough, they gravitated to their assigned roles. They found they had so much work to do they didn't need to argue about turf battles. Thompson recruited Todd Holmdahl, who was running Thompson's mouse business. A few numbers tell his story: Holmdahl was the son of an electrical engineer who called it quits and moved his family to Tonasket, a town of 1,000 in northern Washington. The nearest stoplight was 25 miles away, and the nearest McDonald's was 120 miles. He grew up hunting with a bow on a farm with 80 acres, but his father pushed him to go into technology. Holmdahl became a technical wizard in his own right. He attended Stanford University and got both bachelor's and master's degrees in electrical engineering. He went to work for a competitor of Microsoft's hardware division, and Thompson's people recruited him to join them. Eventually, Holmdahl ran the mouse unit, which at the time was making 20 million units a year via subcontractors such as Flextronics.

Thompson put Holmdahl in charge of designing and integrating the hardware for the Xbox. Holmdahl brought with him eight engineers, and he consulted Blackley's group for details on the hardware thinking. "I saw the Xbox as competing at the highest level," Holmdahl said.

While Thompson trusted his hardware teammates, Blackley and Bachus entered a new stage of proving themselves all over again. Rob Wyatt, the graphics specialist, was also dismayed.

"J [Allard] showed up and brought all these people with him," Wyatt said, recalling the arrival of the new Xbox project manager. "All of a sudden, all the top jobs were taken."

Blackley carved himself a congenial role in the project. He wanted to get people excited about the Xbox, a kind of evangelist in the tradition of Alex St. John. In visiting Japanese publishers, he needed a prestigious title just to get an audience. So he appointed himself director of advanced technology, and Allard signed off on the title. Blackley created a team of technical experts who would advise the hardware team and solicit opinions on technical matters from outside developers. Later, he would offer technical support for the developers and try to convince them that the Xbox was the artists' palette that they could use to realize their visions for great games. He truly believed this pitch, which made him the natural choice to carry the message.

"From my view, Seamus was the only guy who could have run this team," said Wyatt, who joined Blackley as a graphics specialist in the Advanced Technology Group.

In addition to selling the Xbox in the first place, the Advanced Technology Group had the responsibility of coming up with new ways to exploit Xbox hardware and sharing them with game developers within Microsoft and among third-party teams. Sony had groups that did such things, but not necessarily to the same degree that Blackley envisioned. He began building an enthusiastic team—putting together a couple of dozen people with a broad array of talents.

To help him understand the Xbox hardware better and how it would run software, Blackley hired experts like the respected programmer Michael Abrash, who'd worked on the hit game *Quake* at id Software and had a long list of technical credits, as well as graphics expert Rob Wyatt and Microsoft program manager Linda Jeffries. Blackley considered his recruits the bad asses of the gaming industry, and he eventually expanded the group to more than 50 people. They figured out how to push the Xbox to its limits. Blackley got them to work on demos to spread Xbox fever.

Early on, the group had no assigned budget but began spending money on prototypes and travel. Drew Angeloff, a code tester in Microsoft's Visual Studio development tool group, joined and helped create demos and Xbox prototypes. Angeloff, a 26-year-old with a shaved head and a foul mouth, hit it off with Blackley right away because they both loved to curse in their everyday talk and they both had take-charge-and-get-it-done personalities.

"Seamus was very direct," Angeloff said. "He would say, 'Dude, you really fucked it up' when he thought I did something wrong."

Blackley and Angeloff worked tirelessly on their prototypes in the offices that housed the hardware group. They commandeered part of a lab that was next door to the product group that made computer-driven dolls. For much of the day, they had to listen to Power Rangers dolls drone, "Light, Speed, Power!" The lab workers had to live with the smell of Indian food, which Blackley and Angeloff ordered frequently. The early team members got little sleep, especially if they copied Blackley's own random behavior. In spite of quirks like "I thought of something" calls at 3 A.M., Blackley's instincts and ideas were strong enough for Angeloff to believe in him.

"It felt like a start-up," Angeloff said. "Seamus was the best boss I ever had and probably the best boss I'll ever have."

Blackley established such relationships with many of the people he met on the Xbox project. He tried to do a better job managing the team than he did on *Trespasser,* but he was still impulsive. He had to remember to tell the team that he had made promises to other managers, but he moved so fast that he sometimes forgot. That drove colleagues like Wyatt into frenzied tantrums—some so prolonged that the neighbors in the Money section of the Microsoft online business lodged formal complaints.

"Traveling with Seamus was a nightmare," Wyatt said. "He would spring surprise trips to Japan or Los Angeles on me and we'd have to change tickets or get a rental car and then find a hotel at the last minute."

Fortunately Blackley picked up an able assistant, Avril Daly. She had been working in the mail room until the company outsourced the work. Then she became a contractor doing the same job, but she was bored. She moved over to work for a manager in the hardware group. Then she passed by a room one day where she saw Angeloff carving foam in the form of a big X. He asked her if she could help and she said yes. Another man came storming into the lab, cursing that the prototype wasn't working. That was her first introduction to Blackley. She could tell he had a sense of humor and figured she could work with him. As she learned about the Xbox mission, she became hooked and joined the team. At first she split her time between Blackley and another manager, but she eventually stayed with him full time. She didn't mind him or the long hours, which kept her busy seven days a week for weeks at a time.

"I told them I would do it for free," she said. "I pretty much became Seamus's personal digital assistant. I would call him on his cell to tell him where to go next."

Constantly reminded by other employees of Blackley's value, Rick Thompson decided that Blackley was earning his keep. "Seamus in hindsight figured out what he could and couldn't do and took great satisfaction from the evangelist role he had created for himself," Thompson says.

Meanwhile, Bachus was appointed director of third-party publishing, the direct contact between the Xbox team and the outside game publishers. This important job included making initial decisions on whether proposed games were appropriate for the Xbox and setting up deals for those that passed muster. He had become what Allard described as an "information powerhouse" on games and their publishers.

After Blackley wowed the talent with technology, Bachus had to close a deal with the business side. His work as a DirectX product marketing manager had led him to establish personal relationships with scores of publishers, connections that made all the difference on whether the publishers would trust Microsoft in such a crapshoot. He began recruiting a team of account managers—eventually numbering more than 20— whose job it was to keep close tabs on certain game publishers. At his first team meeting, Bachus tried to motivate his team by giving them cans of a high-caffeine drink called "Whoop Ass"—which the whole team adopted as the official drink of the Xbox. Visitors to the Xbox team were always treated to a free case of Whoop Ass.

Among Bachus's most important tasks was screening the initial proposals for games from third-party publishers. Upon receiving the proposal, Bachus's account managers presented it to a panel of marketing and technical people, including Blackley and Allard. Internally, this group was nicknamed the "Star Chamber"—named after a 1980s movie, which itself was named after a medieval court whose judges were viewed as a secretive and vindictive society that abused its powers. Not everyone on this Xbox Concept Review Team had game development experience, but it was a cross section of the Xbox team and it strove to be fair, in contrast to the rumors of biased approval committees at other console makers. Whenever Blackley ran into Phil Harrison, who approved many of Sony's games, Blackley would find a way to say, "I'm not impressed with that"—because that was supposedly what Harrison said to developers proposing games.

The Star Chamber could avoid being capricious, but it couldn't please everyone. It had the important job of making sure that the pipeline for making games was full and that there was enough variety to the platform and timing of releases to keep the attention of all types of gamers. The approvals were tough for Blackley because many of the developers coming through were his personal friends.

"It's brutal," he said. "You look at people's babies and investigate them in an honest light."

It was hard to judge a game just from a sheet of paper. But Blackley made sure that the process offered some clues; he asked, for instance, that every proposal include a description of everything that happens in 60 seconds of the game. Overall, it was refreshing for Blackley to see how much creativity existed across the entire video game industry.

Bachus's involvement in the Xbox was all consuming, and so it was fitting that he was married to Chanel Summers, who worked for Ted Hase as the evangelist for DirectX's audio technology. She went to so many audio conferences that her rival at Sony nicknamed her Microsoft's Rock Chick.

She eventually got so psyched about the Xbox that she decided to take a job working for Blackley as the audio technologist on the Xbox developer support team, helping design the audio chip. She had a hard time leaving Hase because he had given her free rein to make ideas happen. But she saw the audio project as a challenge she couldn't turn down because she felt the audio technology in games had been ignored for too long, even though movie directors like Steven Spielberg said that getting audio right was half the illusion. Summers wanted to get game developers to adopt new effects like environmental audio, reverberation, echoes, and anything else that engrossed the gamer. Here was an opportunity to take audio on consoles a leap forward. So she talked to Blackley and signed up. She would help push to make sure that Xbox games had the best possible audio, with effects like the ability to hear footsteps sneaking up behind a player in a hunting game. This was too good to pass up.

"It isn't every day that someone starts a new console," she said. "We were making history."

She also felt that the other people on Blackley's team were kindred spirits. "I liked it because it was a group of creative people, free thinkers," she said.

Summers herself was an iconoclast. She wore rings through holes pierced in her nose and chin. She saw the body as a tapestry or a photo album, and body piercing was a form of expression. She showed enthusiasm for her new job by putting a tattoo of the Xbox on her lower back. On top of the Xbox was a butterfly, in honor of the demo where she first got the box to play audio.

"It was a trophy," she said—and she posed part-naked to show off the tattoo for photographers at *Next Generation* magazine.

"Everybody needs a hobby, and that's hers," said Bachus, philosophically. She had an artist's sensibility for expression, and so she fit right in with those who believed games were an avant garde art form.

Bachus and Summers—the Xbox couple—could talk to each other about their obsession with their jobs without driving each other crazy, but Bachus said they occasionally had to forget about work just to balance their relationship. Summers said they had learned over the years to keep a strictly professional relationship at work. They had to bend over backwards to show everyone else that they didn't favor each other because they were married. Despite their shared passion for gaming, they were an odd couple, with Bachus being so quiet and Summers so extroverted.

"We balance each other out," Summers said.

As project manager, Allard had the job of putting the Xbox together on a technical level and keeping upper management informed. While Thompson ran the business, Allard had to deliver the technology. If they needed resources, he passed the message up to Thompson. The job was perfect for him because he was so well established at Microsoft that no one would question his ability to balance technical matters and business matters alike.

"J could manage upward into Microsoft," Blackley said. "And he came to trust that I could make some of the right technical decisions."

Allard decided that Blackley was indeed a brilliant contributor to the team—the ideal missionary for the machine among game developers . . . as well as a crucial technical mind on hardware design. He said, "I take bets. I bet on Seamus every day. I give Seamus a lot of leash. Someone else might not do that, but I have an entrepreneurial nature, and Bill had given me a lot of leash."

After so many delays in making decisions, the group now started operating like a start-up. Allard had to recruit an entire team—the Xbox group was still small when he joined. Thompson transferred trusted employees from the hardware group, but he had to stop the raid or risk hurting that business. He had few leads on recruiting the software team, however. Since Brown had bugged out, Thompson was grateful that Allard was on board. Without him, recruiting would have taken much longer. Allard wanted to get off the ground.

"Let's get going," he kept telling Thompson. "Enough fooling around with the business model."

Robbie Bach, who was Thompson's boss, transferred some of his fellow stars from the Microsoft Office team, including marketing director John O'Rourke, a longtime Microsoft veteran with a straitlaced look but a fondness for playing guitars. He was the youngest of eight children and had 35 nieces and nephews, enough for his own focus group of young video gamers. In turn, O'Rourke became the boss of other marketing people like Don Coyner, a former Nintendo marketer, and

Jennifer Booth, who once worked at Sony. They had been involved in the project early on, giving advice to Rick Thompson and Kevin Bachus. The whole group came from a variety of backgrounds, but they were united as Xbox commandos.

"These guys would never meet accidentally by walking into the same bar," Allard said.

CHAPTER 13

THE XBOX TAKES SHAPE

TIME HAD COME TO DECIDE what operating system and components would be in the Xbox. The clock was ticking down for a product launch in 2000.

The graphics chip makers such as ATI Technologies, Nvidia, and 3Dfx Interactive visited Microsoft to pitch the Xbox team on graphics chips. The only candidates for the microprocessor were Advanced Micro Devices and Intel. Early on, Intel's enthusiasm was limited because it wasn't particularly interested in selling low-cost microprocessors. Over time, all these companies offered engineers as consultants in a kind of virtual design team.

Allard took charge of defining what would be in the Xbox, and he assigned Ferroni to develop the operating system for the box. Allard's team had started out with the notion that they would have to modify Windows to fit into the Xbox. They found that the console would not be able to run Windows and still be fast enough for games with split-second timing. Otto Berkes had always wanted the Xbox to be an entertainment PC capable of running different kinds of PC software beyond games. He favored putting more Windows technology into the Xbox. He had heated debates with Allard and his team about the operating system. But Berkes lost the debate, in part because Blackley's game developer friends chimed in and said they wanted a lightweight operating system that did little but make their games run as fast as possible. Allard overruled Berkes and backed Jon Thomason.

Thomason, a veteran of prior operating-system efforts such as Windows 95, picked Windows NT (later known as Windows 2000) as the starting point, because this corporate version of Windows was the newest operating system, it had a full set of features, and it was more stable and secure than Windows 98, the consumer operating system. Because of its modular design, it was easy to take things out without making the entire machine go haywire. Thomason figured that most of the operating system could reside on the DVD disk with the game, rather than on the hard disk. The idea was a good one because it gave flexibility to developers. They could put a wide variety of code modules into their own custom operating system, using only what they needed and thereby reducing memory usage. (For example, if the game wasn't online, they could leave the networking code out of the operating system.) And because the operating system shipped on the DVD, they could be certain as they developed their game that their code worked with its own particular version of the operating system.

Allard's team then made a list of the things required to execute DirectX, the software that let games make use of different pieces of hardware like the sound or graphics components. They altered the operating system in one key respect, changing it so it would boot, or start, from flash ROM (read-only memory) instead of a hard disk, so that the speed of start-up could be much faster. It would also operate in a more stable manner than a PC. Because the operating system was on the DVD, games would not rely on the dynamically linkable libraries (DLLs—shared files spread all over a hard disk in a PC) that were a frequent source of software crashes. PCs suffered from a problem known as DLL Hell, where one application would quietly change a DLL in ways that crashed other applications relying on the same DLL. The solution: Get rid of the DLLs altogether and have applications draw on operating system files stored on their own DVDs. Such a system also had the advantage of avoiding conflicts between programs contending for the same system resources such as memory, and it freed up space on the hard drive to store saved games, new levels downloaded from the Internet, or repositories of art.

All told, the Xbox operating system wound up at less than 500,000 kilobytes—small enough to fit on a floppy disk. The resulting system was streamlined to do one thing really well: play games.

"We started taking things out of Windows NT, or rather putting things into DirectX, to put the software together," Allard said. "It was more or less a DirectX operating system."

In the next meeting with Gates, Allard, Ferroni, and Thomason broke the news that the machine wouldn't be able to run the full Windows operating system, the flagship of the empire. Hase says he admired Allard for "having the stones" to "rip Windows to shreds, one of the sacred cows at Microsoft." Gates knew that the machine wasn't going to run all of Windows. But, like Berkes and Brown, he held out hope that the machine could be fashioned so that, one day, someone could flip a switch and Microsoft's Office software could be dropped into an Xbox and run. The WebTV crew, which was working on a machine using a version of the Windows CE operating system, was still arguing that the Xbox might one day be integrated into a more powerful WebTV box. So Gates wondered if it might be possible to make the combination box sooner. Allard shook his head.

"What do you mean?" Gates yelled, as he stared across his desk at Allard.

"We're not going to run Windows," Allard said.

Allard recalled later, "I think that was the closest Bill ever got to strangling me. But he ultimately came around."

Gates had never insisted on a particular design for the Xbox. He left that to the team to decide. He had only articulated which approach he was more comfortable with. Starting from Windows was less of a risk. Rick Thompson, Allard's boss, said that Gates knew that the box had to be designed for gamers or it would lose out to its rivals.

"It wasn't so much that it wouldn't run Windows," Thompson said. "It was more that it would never be a productivity platform, or an e-commerce or e-mail platform. That made Bill apoplectic. He understood why the box had to be for gamers, but he just didn't want to leave the other functionality behind."

In a sense, Gates had been hoodwinked. He chose the Xbox because its roots came from Microsoft's strengths in the PC and because it enhanced the core Windows product. He bought into the Xbox because it leveraged Windows and offered a platform for further strategic moves in the living room. If people wanted to surf the Web or send e-mail on their TV sets in the future, the Xbox would be ready to do it. This was the kind of box that Hase and Berkes had wanted to create, the heart of their original Xbox pitch. But now Allard was turning that plan upside down.

The decision to delete Windows had a cascading effect. Now the team had to decide whether PC games should run on the Xbox and vice versa. Already, it was clear from the business model discussions that Microsoft would have to charge third parties a $7 royalty per game. But there were no royalties on

PC games, so it would be asking for trouble to let them run on the Xbox—developers would use them to skirt the Xbox royalty. An open question remained whether Xbox games would run on both the PC and the Xbox. The team decided that the technical differences between the Xbox and Windows meant that Xbox content was now going to diverge from PC content.

"The fundamental debate was whether we would run console content or PC content," Allard said. "Since the goal was to sell tens of millions of consoles, the choice became clear."

Cameron Ferroni, J Allard, and Rick Thompson talked through the issue with a list that they called the "Ten Lies of the Xbox." They decided that people who said there was no distinction between PC games and console games just weren't paying close attention. "We called bullshit on that," Allard said. That meant the Xbox had to target one or the other or it might fail to make either side happy.

From the outset, Ed Fries realized that making PC games was far different from making console games. PC gaming was typically a solitary experience, where players sat with their nose about two feet from the monitor. They were alone, contemplating strategy, or playing over the Internet with people they had never met before. Console games, on the other hand, were social games. They were played in the living room with friends watching or joining in. The most popular kinds of console games were racing games or fighting games, in contrast to shooting and strategy games on the PC. They duplicated the arcade experience, where players talked trash to each other as they scored points in fast and furious battles.

Another myth of the early days was that Microsoft could allow anybody to make Xbox games. Fries and the new leaders believed that Microsoft would have to play gatekeeper. By controlling the approval of Xbox titles, Microsoft could keep out the trash that flooded the PC platform. It could also stop developers from doing quick and dirty *ports,* that is, transferring PC titles to the console format with little or no modification to the games. Such titles, Fries saw, could lower the level of quality and diminish the consumer experience on the Xbox. Hence he was an early advocate of charging royalties to developers, like Sony and Nintendo did, to keep out the amateurs as well as off-set the hardware losses.

The original Xbox team—particularly Blackley and Bachus—had wanted to do a console as well, but they started out with Project Midway because they felt they needed not only to start a new console business but to use what they learned in the process to improve Windows. Now with Allard leading the charge, Blackley and Bachus could say what they really wanted to do. Allard's proposal to use a stripped-down operating system was starting to look a lot more like a traditional console. Gates had already rejected such a plan from the WebTV group. Frus-trated WebTV advocates felt vindicated as the Xbox planners woke up, but Gates didn't contradict Allard at this stage because so many game developers were in favor of Allard's solution.

"I guess you could say we did a bait and switch," said Nat Brown, who was still watching from the sidelines. "It was less intentional, and more circumstantial. If we had said we weren't going to run Windows, we wouldn't have gotten very far. We got approval, and then we took Windows out. But it wasn't truly intentional."

The Xbox team also argued that the box should not have an ordinary phone-line modem; rather, it would have only high-speed networking capability, with an Ethernet adapter that could connect to the Internet at speeds of 10 megabits a second. They decided to leave out the 56 kilobit-per-second modem that connected users via ordinary phone lines. Upon hearing that the box would have no modem, Gates said at first, "You must not have thought about that very carefully."

The decision was tough because developers thought Allard was insane to bet that broadband would reach broad deploy-ment during the life of the Xbox. But the team argued that gamers would jump to get fast connections. And making the

Xbox broadband-only would make life much simpler for game developers, who wouldn't have to worry whether to design games for phone lines or for high-speed Internet connections such as cable modems or digital subscriber lines. If the modem was in the box, developers would develop for it as the least common denominator that would ensure they would have a large audience. DSL connections or cable modems (which could plug into an Ethernet adapter) could run very fast, but such technologies were only beginning to roll out. Sega, out of the gate earlier with its Dreamcast, put a 56K modem on its machine. Sony eventually announced it had made its system expandable to include a 56K modem and a network adapter.

"Putting a 56K modem on the Xbox would be akin to putting cloth seats in a Ferrari," said Allard (who owned a bright-red Ferrari). "We wanted to bring games to the next level. If you could download new levels to a game, you could bring an episodic experience almost like TV."

If the online network launched with a blockbuster game, it might inspire more gamers to adopt broadband. In addition, knocking off the modem saved $5.18 per box. That added up to $221 million in savings over sales of 43 million units. At the end, Gates agreed that taking out the modem was correct. Todd Holmdahl was all for it. He was already looking at the top ten components that would account for 80 percent of the costs. It wasn't looking good, and the big hard drive was making him wince.

These technical decisions took place over months and involved dozens of people. So much work was involved that Ferroni couldn't see an end to it.

"There were a half-dozen times when I thought this is stupid and we should just bail," he recalled.

Now the time had come to figure out what the Xbox would look like on the outside, and for that the team needed an artist. Jim Stewart, Microsoft's top industrial design manager, asked Horace Luke, a 29-year-old industrial designer who had been in the business for nearly a decade, to start work on a prototype for the Xbox. Luke, a high-strung man with short black hair and designer glasses, worked obsessively. As a contractor for Microsoft, he had designed mice and joysticks in the hardware group. Before that he had worked at Nike designing brands for a wide variety of sports lines, from the X Games to the Tiger Woods line. He had designed jeans, trade show booths, and store displays. He grew up in Hong Kong and moved to the Seattle area when he was 13. He attended high school in Seattle and went to the University of Washington, where he almost got a degree in sculpture. At the last minute, he switched to commercial art and industrial design. He put himself through college creating sterling silver jewelry.

He was already doodling around with Xbox designs before Stewart formally assigned him to the project as creative director. During October 1999, Luke got around to making his first sketches of the Xbox. The only marker he had at the time was green. So his four sketches all used green in some way. He didn't know it then, but one of them would become the Xbox design.

Green had a lot of meaning to people in the field of design. Luke had done many focus groups over the years and people always associated green with technology.

"Green is the signature color of technology ever since the beginning of time," he said. "Look at the green screens of the early monochrome Apple computers. It's wizard-like and magical. Think of witches stirring a pot of something secret, or the blood of aliens in the movies." Even better, Sony, Nintendo, and Sega had all avoided green for some reason.

Luke had to do a great deal of research with outside consultants, focus groups, other designers at Microsoft, and upper management. He had to check his whimsical inspirations with the engineering requirements laid down by hardware chief Todd Holmdahl as well as the priorities of John O'Rourke, who was handling marketing.

In Luke's view, he wasn't just creating a box design. He had to pull the team together in its mission. By designing a prototype, he would give people something they could show the rest of the world. It meant the Xbox was real. Microsoft was serious about it. He had to convey that it was a done deal, even though it was nowhere near that at the moment.

"I design the esprit of the business," he said.

Luke soon had a wall full of sketches of the Xbox. He hooked up with the usability and user experience teams, which did research in the field to judge consumer tastes. Microsoft fortunately had vast resources for testing its ideas among consumers worldwide before it launched anything. Luke's team came up with a few key points. The Xbox had to have a sense of power, advanced technology, innovation, and immediacy. So Luke sent the teams out to find relevant images that already communicated these points in the homes of real people, as well as to assess real-world use of game boxes. Luke visited dozens of homes of people who didn't mind being surveyed in exchange for some trifles or money. In many homes, he saw that the game consoles they already owned were kept on the floor because the controller cables were too short. He made sure that the Xbox controller cables would be nine feet long instead of the usual six feet. And with cords that long, Microsoft would need to build a safety mechanism into the cord so that if someone tripped on it, it wouldn't tear a hole in the box. He also noticed a lot of Coke cans sitting on top of the boxes, so that meant there could be no air vents on the top of the machine that would allow spillage into the delicate electronics.

Not that everything he saw was directly useful, of course. For example, in one home he asked, "What does power mean to you?" The man went to another room and came back with a gun. "This is power," he said. Luke found an excuse to quickly end the visit.

Armed with that database, Luke then went to all the magazines he could find and cut out pictures of sexy consumer gadgets, from new cars to phones. He plastered the images across one wall of his workshop. That gave him what he called a "comfort zone" of images. Then he shut a team of five designers in a room, opened a bottle of wine, and ordered pizza. They worked into the night.

They stayed within engineering's constraints, which were being figured out on the fly by Holmdahl's group and vendors like Flextronics, a contract manufacturer that was a leading candidate to assemble the box. The Xbox was loaded full of electronics. Systems like the hard drive and the DVD player couldn't be bunched too close together or else they could overheat—or damage each other if the box fell on the ground. That required more space—but the box couldn't be bigger than a standard video cassette recorder and still fit in many crowded home entertainment systems. The favored sketch was Luke's rendition of the box as a rectangle with a big X emblazoned on its cover. At first, he wanted the X to be a separate color, but the mechanical engineers said that would cost an extra $1 on every box. Luke wanted the box to be symmetrical so he put the DVD tray in the center, but it had to be moved to one side for better internal airflow. Rick Vingerelli in the hardware group and Jim Sacherman at contract manufacturer Flextronics had figured out from visits to Taiwan that front-loading DVD players cost $10 more than side-loading models. In addition, the players that used no trays—where users simply inserted a disk into a slot—were also $10 more than regular tray-based players.

Blackley liked Luke's efforts to put pizzazz in the product. He felt that Microsoft's products were never designed with the same style and flair as Apple's or Sony's. He wanted some style in the Xbox, cost be damned.

"It drove me mad," Blackley said. "It reminds me of the first time you go skiing. Your object is survival. A really good skier will go down the hill with style. But for us, they just wanted to make sure that we got the box down to a reasonable cost. It hurt the design. I think we needed to learn that cool was just as important as cost."

But only Holmdahl and his crew knew what it would take to integrate more than a thousand components into an Xbox and secure suppliers for every piece. Early on, he created a production schedule that ticked off the number of days until manufacturing had to start. The engineers figured out that 45 of the components were critical because of their cost or because they came from single sources of supply.

Once the hardware team got a good idea of the dimensions the box needed to house the electronics, then Luke's team began to carve foam images in three dimensions. Luke spent hours mixing new kinds of paint, coming up with weird variations of colors until it made him ill. Luke desperately wanted a silver box but it proved too costly. In most of his designs, Luke included in the center of the box a glowing green orb, a jewel that exuded what he called "nuclear energy." He wanted the orb to glow when the machine turned on, as if the machine were "thinking," much like the advertisements for the Sega Dreamcast, which suggested the box was so smart that it could think and that it knew what you were thinking as you played it.

"The green jewel was part of the emotional mark of the box," Luke said. "It's a journey. It's an escape. You don't know where you go when you get sucked into that thing."

Luke's team worked with beehive intensity. He got the operating system team to farm work out to companies like Rezn8, which helped design the user interface screens that the players would see when they turned the machine on. He worked with Kirk James of Cinco Design Office in Portland, Oregon, to develop the logo for the machine. James, another former Nike designer and a consultant who helped companies create brand identities, caught the Xbox fever from Luke and worked on what he called a "brand mythology."

The logo had to reflect the meaning of the brand, which would be accompanied by a back story. It sounded like mumbo-jumbo, but the bigger the company and the bigger the project, the more effort a company had to put behind its identity. James wrote a simple story about the X logo, which stood for the experience of playing an Xbox game. The story involved a team of explorers in the Antarctic who stumble upon glowing green pods in the ice. They uncover one and find the acid-green X, which transports them to another world, like a wormhole in a science-fiction movie. A kid turning on the Xbox would be accessing a source of energy on the other side of the universe. The pods containing the X were originally titanium cubes with the X on them. But after Nintendo announced it would call its product the GameCube, Microsoft had to steer clear of cubes.

"This X is peeling open and revealing the access to this energy," James said.

To some inside Microsoft, such notions sounded ridiculous. But Luke and James believed in their branding message; they saw it was as important as choosing which special effects to put in a movie. They wanted people to fall in love with the Xbox, not just the games. James recruited Blur Studio in Los Angeles to bring the logo to life as a 3-D animation. Tim Miller, the head of Blur, agreed that his team would help, even though he couldn't stand all the marketing and design hype.

"Branding bullshit talk makes me sick," he said. "Once Horace gets started talking, it's horrible. I like him and his passion, but he's just relentless on the crap that it all means and how it tests in the focus group."

On the other hand, Don Coyner, one of the marketing directors for the Xbox, found Luke's passion refreshing. "You always want someone who worries about the incredible subtleties of things like how big a logo should be or what message it sends."

Once Blur and Cinco came up with the acid-green X logo, they had to refine it. Cinco presented four versions in the end, but it had worked on 40 or 50 different variations of those designs over the course of five months.

Each of the ideas had to be tested by consumers along the way. Luke felt that 18 months was a short window to develop the box. He had to finish all of his work in half that interval. That was still enough time because he could bring to bear all of Microsoft's resources in industrial design, market research, and practical things like an in-house shop for making models of prototypes. The design that came back with the highest approval rating was one of Luke's original black boxes with the X on top of it. Luke was thinking of the Xbox as a BMW, not a Range Rover, as he perceived the PS 2 to be in its design.

Next, Luke had to design the controller. He sketched some quick designs that he gave to Blackley the night before Blackley took off on a trip to Tokyo. Then, for the real controller, he began working with designers in the hardware group, which already made console-like controllers for the PC. Soon, Luke's wall was full of scrawls of controllers. He used a carving knife to create foam controllers that fit into his hands comfortably. Once again, one of his own designs—this one sketched on the back of a tax form—was the winner. But research led the company astray on the controllers, J Allard said. Because the company focused on listening to 16- to 26-year-old gamers, it designed a controller for people with big hands. This later caused complaints in the United States, and in Japan the feedback was even worse. Follow-up research showed that a vocal minority of Japanese consumers hated the design so much that Microsoft decided to introduce new controllers. Alan Han, another designer, set about creating a smaller controller for the Japanese.

Once Luke was done with the real box and controller, he had to create the show box. That was around Thanksgiving in 1999. Kevin Bachus wanted to make sure this box didn't look anything like a PC, but he also didn't want it to be mistaken for the final form of the console. This would be the prototype shown to early allies and the box that Bill Gates would take on stage with him when he announced the Xbox to the world. In the meantime, the real box would remain a secret until much closer to the launch. Luke could go all-out on this box. Luke's boss, Jim Stewart, suggested that they make a gigantic X. Luke liked the idea and designed a machine that sported silver chrome, had a big green jewel at the center, and was shaped in the form of a three-dimensional X.

"It was a machine that just brought out the essence," he said.

Working day and night, Blackley designed the contents of the silver X-shaped boxes. He made sure that the machines would have plenty of gills for cooling and could withstand rough handling. Drew Angeloff had the tough job of making them work. Soldering gun in hand, he had to jam most of the contents of a personal computer into a space half the size. He welded the aluminum together, but Luke didn't like the ugly welding marks on the metal. So Angeloff had machinists carve the silver X shapes out of solid billets of aluminum. With frequent trips to electronics stores, he spent $18,000 on each of the custom boxes.

"Dude, these silver X's will look awesome," Luke said. "We need a fucking green laser. Go buy it. It's going to be awesome!"

Luke was so passionate about his work that he clicked well with Blackley. He saw Blackley as all soul, not body.

"Soul is this thing that is spiritual," he said. "We both aggressively communicate our passions." Of course, Blackley liked Luke's spirit too, but occasionally he wished Luke had more technical brains. Angeloff and Blackley wasted half a day once trying to get a prototype to work; they discovered that Luke had bought the wrong kind of switch at Radio Shack because he liked the look of it.

At the same time, Blackley's relationship with his on-and-off-again girlfriend was on the rocks. Unlike Bachus, who was happily married to someone on the team, Blackley found the Xbox killed his social life. The situation, Blackley said, was "no different than any dot-com girlfriend." For a while there, his only outside support was Paco, the pit bull he had nursed back to health after someone tossed him out of a moving car.

CHAPTER 14

WORD LEAKS OUT

WHEN MICROSOFT BEGAN SOLICITING feedback from the rest of the games industry and regular consumers, that raised the risk of discovery. The team had many debates about when and how they should tell developers about the plan. Some feared that developers would quickly leak it to the press or rivals.

For the Xbox team, the Internet age comes with a curse. A horde of Internet game news Web sites devote themselves to the mission of covering games in ways that would make tabloid editors blush. The teenagers who founded many of these sites to get free games sometimes have no regard for journalistic ethics. They print rumors just to drive traffic to their sites, and they don't bother with corrections when proved wrong. Legitimate journalists track many of the Web sites and check out their rumors, just in case real news breaks there. Back in 1998, some of these rabid fans-turned-gumshoes faked credentials to get into the E3 trade show, but in 1999 the exhibitors had to agree to allow many of them into the show as long as they could prove they published stories. A lot of the Web sites posted more photos of the scantily clad women at the show booths than of the games they were reviewing. But many CEOs of graphics chip makers and game publishers said that they had arranged interviews with these kids because they were so influential with game buyers.

The legitimate trade press regularly beat the neophytes. Tom Russo, then a senior editor at gaming enthusiast magazine *Next Generation,* was just as plugged in as anybody. He was a 30-year-old diehard fan of gaming who had covered the industry for eight years. Hailing from Hanson, Massachusetts, he had a heavy New England accent. He bounced around at news jobs that didn't pay well until he saw an opening for a job writing about video games for promotional materials. He did that for 18 months and then got a job at *GamePro,* an established game review magazine. He joined *Next Generation* in 1996 and watched with delight as the industry steadily grew.

Russo had a fat Rolodex file of sources. Among them was Seamus Blackley, whom Russo had met while Blackley was promoting *Trespasser* at DreamWorks. In an article in 1997, Russo described Blackley as playful like a "deviant school boy" whose idea of fun was probably inventing new ways to blow up toilet seats. Russo and his boss Chris Charla ran down the tip on the Xbox and published a story that ran in the magazine and on the Web site at the same time, just before Labor Day in 1999.

"I was calling Seamus two times a day, but he was telling me he had nothing to do with it," Russo said. "But I kept hearing from other people that he was involved in it."

The story was thin, but *Next Generation* wasn't just one of the rumormongers. It had a good reputation for its dedication to covering the games business. Russo's story described the machine as having an Nvidia graphics chip and a 600-megahertz AMD microprocessor.

"After that story ran, all hell broke loose," said Bachus.

Everyone was expecting an announcement in the fall of 1999 or early 2000. But the plans were only beginning to take shape within Microsoft. And the product had a lot of hurdles to meet before final approval. Some people began to sense that Microsoft was paralyzed by indecision. Would it take the plunge or pull the plug?

PITCHING THE INDUSTRY

From July through September 1999, most of the Xbox crew was canvassing the game development and publishing community. Bachus and Blackley traveled to the ECTS trade show in London, where the top publishers and developers gathered to show off games for the European market. Ted Hase, who had not yet quit the Xbox team, had directed one of his evangelists to set up meetings with all the European game developers. But Bachus didn't find this out until just before the trip. On the flight to London, he began furiously revising the slides for a presentation to outsiders. He was on the air phone back home for much of the time to figure out if Microsoft was prepared to tell publishers that Microsoft would not charge a royalty. The answer: yes. That decision would later haunt the team.

Bachus flipped through a games magazine and was surprised to see that someone was claiming they were considering making an Xbox game. So Bachus met with Jez San, the game developer at Argonaut in the United Kingdom. San was making a game called *Malice* that was going to demand the utmost from a next-generation game console. It was originally planned for the Play-Station, but that plan faltered since the aging console would become obsolete by the time the game would appear. Since San found the PlayStation 2 architecture inadequate, he was searching for a new console. Yet he was skeptical that the Xbox crew knew what it was talking about since it was shooting for a cheaper console than the PlayStation 2 and yet had no plans to charge a royalty for each game.

"Later on, they got the math right and figured out that the royalty was necessary," San recalled.

San and his team went to work on a version of *Malice* for the Xbox. Blackley coached them, giving them lots of advice on how to pull the game together. He also had thrills serving shots of vodka-Redbull in various London bars. Those who drank it reported feeling sick but wide awake. The potent mixture sent waves of alcohol and caffeine racing to take control of the victim's body. Blackley could take the reeling effect better, San said, because of his "substantial body mass."

Some publishers, such as Bruno Bonnell of Infogrames, were excited about creating Xbox games. Bonnell liked the fact that the machine had a hard disk drive and broadband capability to set it apart from the other consoles. But he wanted to make sure that the hard disk drive was going to be reliable enough for a machine that sat on the floor and took some abuse from kids.

"We were an early supporter," Bonnell said. "We stressed that online was only interesting if it was broadband. Otherwise, the modem was useless."

But overall, the briefings were pretty much a fiasco, Bachus said.

"I couldn't tell if they were really serious," said the chief executive officer of one of the game publishers that met with Microsoft at ECTS.

"That's the same question we got from everybody," said Bachus. "The level of skepticism was very high."

The no-royalty plan was at the top of the list of complaints. Microsoft felt that would attract more developers to its platform, as was the case with the PC. But the best developers felt that free access was the reason for the glut of trash on the PC. A couple of thousand PC titles appeared every year, yet million-unit hits on the PC were rarer than on the consoles. The console makers used royalties not only to enrich themselves and recover the cost of the hardware but also as a form of quality control. Rather than stick with a bad plan, Microsoft decided to take the advice and implement royalties.

"We were very enthusiastic about the technology they were coming up with in the fall," said Tom Dusenberry, who at the time was the president of Hasbro Interactive, the electronic games unit of toymaker Hasbro Inc. "As they gained feedback from developers, they adjusted what their targets were in hardware."

During the fall of 1999, a thousand consumers came through Microsoft's headquarters to participate in focus groups. All told, Microsoft representatives interviewed more than 5,000 people worldwide. Blackley was stunned at the amount of research Microsoft was willing to do, and how quietly it did so. Consumers said in no uncertain terms that Microsoft's brand had a lot of meaning when it came to business software, but not much when it came to games.

Bachus saw that consumers didn't believe in packing a lot of functions into one box that sat on top of the TV set like WebTV. It reinforced the beliefs that the Xbox team had from the start.

"Convergence is bullshit," said Blackley when he heard about the research. He and Bachus felt more right than ever that the Xbox should be just about "games games games." This was more ammo against rivals like WebTV, though that debate was largely over.

The newly formed marketing department started talking to retailers. Some of Microsoft's marketing experts had been drafted over the years from Nintendo, which had its U.S. headquarters in Redmond. They knew how to play the retail game, and what they heard from retailers was frustration. Why, for instance, were separately sold controllers always in such short supply at launch? Game console makers always included just one controller with the machine, but almost everybody bought an extra controller so friends could play. Kevin Bachus read a book by former Coca-Cola marketer Sergio Zyman. It was all about how to overcome established brands, so he invited Zyman in to give a lecture to the team, which would very soon need to figure out how to overcome Sony's PlayStation 2 brand. Zyman advised the group to run the marketing event much like a presidential campaign. They liked his tips so much they kept him on retainer for six months. Jim Whims, a former Sony marketer who helped launch the original PlayStation, told the group not to worry about the absence of a mascot character. Sony's main hit, *Crash Bandicoot,* showed up in the second year and surprised everyone.

Rick Thompson visited PC makers along with his sidekick Bob McBreen, who turned into Thompson's deal maker, and with others on the team. They came back with confirmation of what the Xbox team expected. No PC makers wanted to make the box, because they saw no way to make money on it. The whirlwind tour took Thompson, Blackley, Bachus, and a few others to Austin on September 1, 1999.

Michael Dell, CEO one of the most successful makers of personal computers, told them that the business model for the Xbox had no place for a company like his. "When Sony cuts prices on their PlayStations, their stock price goes up. Every time I cut prices, my stock price goes down," Dell said. "If you don't understand why that happens, you don't understand the console business. I understand why this is strategic to Microsoft. I don't understand why this is strategic to Dell."

Thompson had to take no for an answer. He also went to Japan to visit Panasonic, NEC, Sharp, Casio, Toshiba, and Mitsubishi. Their reaction, Thompson recalled, was, "Why are you doing this? You gotta be nuts." Daeje Chin, CEO of Samsung Electronics' digital media business, recalled, "Microsoft wanted to squeeze us on price. We saw no way for us to make money. And why should we build their product? We are interested in building products with the Samsung name." Samsung would later bid to supply parts.

Traditional console makers lost money on the hardware and made up for it in game sales. Since PC makers didn't sell software, they were out of luck trying to make console hardware. Thompson realized that he had a much bigger project to sell to his bosses back in Redmond: Microsoft had to build these consoles on its own.

Upon returning, Thompson delivered the news to Todd Holmdahl, whose job it was to design the Xbox electronics. Holmdahl assembled a team of engineers that scoured the globe for parts.

Although the manufacturing job was big, Microsoft had an edge. It already relied on large contract manufacturers to make the hardware for its mouse and joystick products. Holmdahl was familiar with companies like Singapore-based Flextronics, which had become a multibillion-dollar company making everything from printers for Hewlett-Packard to cellular phones for Ericsson. Analysts estimated that contract manufacturers accounted for about 13 percent of the $800 billion electronics industry's annual sales. Consumers never gave a thought to the fact that their machines were manufactured by subcontractors in big factories in Asia, Europe, or Latin America by low-paid workers.[1] Holmdahl and his lieutenant Rick Vingerelli collected bids from Flextronics, Solectron, SCI Systems, and others. It was clear that the Xbox contract would be so valuable to these companies that many were willing to build new factories just to handle the Xbox assembly alone.

Even with the promise of contract manufacturing, Thompson was disturbed. Vendors began filing bids for work, and it was clear that the original Xbox team had grossly underestimated how much it would cost to make an Xbox—the estimates were running well over $400, not near $300. Many

Xbox team members saw Nvidia as the clear choice for graphics because the developers favored it, but they were upset that Nvidia quoted a price so much higher than other graphics vendors offered. The schedule for the box would depend on the graphics chip, which was the most customized component in the entire system. The graphics chip was expected to start out at a high price and then fall each year over the next five years. But for some reason Nvidia wasn't playing the game; the bid didn't go down steeply enough over time.

"Jen-Hsun was a sharp businessman," said Bob McBreen, Thompson's deal maker. "I think he thought he couldn't lose."

Huang's executives had been meeting with Microsoft's buyers over the course of the summer. Chris Malachowsky, co-founder of Nvidia and head of engineering, shared the sentiments of all at the company when he said, "graphics was the soul of the new machine."

Huang, remembering later and trying to sound diplomatic, said, "There was displeasure that Microsoft saw us as a resistor supplier," that is, as someone who makes commodity components such as resistors for pennies.

Microsoft's buyers were fairly clear about what they wanted. They were fascinated by the new technology in Nvidia's GeForce 3 chip, which was scheduled to launch for the PC in spring of 2001. The chip was one of the most ambitious ever attempted in the chip industry, with 57 million transistors, compared to about 42 million for Intel's latest Pentium 4 microprocessor. It had a technology called "programmable pixel shaders," which allowed game programmers to create their own unique special effects using software tools. If they wanted an explosion with a bluish-green fire, they could program it just the way they wanted rather than rely upon some prefabricated special effects. With only 23 million transistors, the GeForce 2 had lower performance; it didn't have the pixel shaders, and it was shipping in the summer of 2000. The GeForce 3 wasn't finished yet, while the GeForce 2 was getting close. Huang had no clue how much it would initially cost to manufacture a GeForce 3. The *manufacturing yields*—the percentage of good chips out of the total batch—on brand-new chips were often low. As a result, chip makers had to produce a lot of scrap just to get some good working chips.

"The Microsoft people said we'll take a GeForce 3 but for the price of a GeForce 2," said Dan Vivoli, vice president of sales and marketing at Nvidia.

That was out of the question. Huang knew that the initial manufacturing costs on the GeForce 3 were likely to be $100 a chip. Yet he was being asked to supply them initially at $40 to $50. That made the negotiations particularly irksome.

"I wanted to do the deal," Huang said. "But not if it was going to kill the company."

Huang was already nervous because he had begun to assign engineers to figure out how to combine different projects into a single chip for Microsoft. As a result, he had to scale back or cancel some of the company's efforts in making laptop chips and core logic chipsets. If Microsoft flaked out and canceled the Xbox altogether, or if it went with another vendor's chip, Huang was going to be left holding the bag.

Thompson felt he had been sold a bill of goods, and it took Blackley and Bachus a lot of effort to keep Nvidia in the game. Blackley had been traveling so much that he failed to keep up to date on his expense reports. On a trip to Toronto, his American Express card didn't work, and so Bachus had to use his card to pay Blackley's way. The only rental car available was an old Volkswagen Beetle. So the dynamic duo rented the car and drove it to graphics chip maker ATI. There, they got a pitch from ATI about the R200, the code name for what the company would later call Radeon. It was running behind Nvidia's schedule, and it was also underpowered.

Thompson, meanwhile, began to favor a counterproposal that came from the WebTV team. They had proposed licensing a graphics architecture from a Silicon Valley start-up called

GigaPixel. WebTV would take the technology and design the graphics chip as well as the rest of the console. Tim Bucher, the hardware vice president at the WebTV group, was friends with Rick Thompson. By staying in touch with Thompson, Bucher caught up on the Xbox and lent his advice even though the Xbox crew thought he was out of the picture. Bucher reminded Thompson of the importance of controlling his fate.

"In Rick's eyes, this reduced the risk of the Xbox because more of the technology was going to be built in-house," Bachus said.

Thompson also consulted with and tried to recruit top business executives. He talked to Bernard Stolar, the former president of Sega's U.S. unit (dismissed in August 1999 for not getting along with his Japanese bosses), about strategies to follow. He consulted with Paul Eibeler, a former executive at Acclaim Entertainment, about marketing plans. But neither man signed on to participate in the project. Thompson had concluded that an executive who didn't know the ropes at Microsoft would never stand a chance.

A few Microsoft people, led by Margaret Johnson, a longtime veteran in the operating system group, thought about making the Xboy, a handheld game player that would challenge Nintendo, which had 97 percent of the market for handheld games. Nintendo's upcoming GameBoy Advance was a step up in picture quality, but it still featured relatively primitive 2-D graphics. Microsoft, using 3-D graphics, might have a chance to enter the high end of the market with a more advanced device.

The discussion went up and down the executive chain, but ultimately the team decided such a project would be a distraction from the Xbox. If the initial Xbox were successful, then Microsoft could think about the Xboy project for 2002 or later. Eventually, it was tabled.

Robbie Bach said, "I'm focused on one thing and one thing only. If I take my eye off the Xbox mission for two seconds, I'll lose. I can think about [portable games] when I have time to think about those things."

If Microsoft were to launch an Xboy, it would first have to arbitrate an internal debate about whether a handheld game player might cannibalize the market for PocketPC handheld players that used the Windows CE operating system. That was all Microsoft needed: another turf war. Had it engaged in it, chances were good the company would have moved too slowly to field even one product, let alone two.

CHAPTER 15

GAMES AND DEMOS

ED FRIES KNEW THE BURDEN of creating blockbuster games would fall on his shoulders. If Microsoft's own game group couldn't show what could be done on its own console, then who else would do it?

But Fries had to balance staffing Xbox games with the need to continue the established franchises on the PC. As the Xbox gathered steam, he had 400 people at 10 internal studios at Microsoft and relations with nearly 20 outside studios. By 2000, Microsoft planned to be releasing 20 games a year. This focused so much energy on PC games that Fries couldn't pull the plug without wrecking his own profit-and-loss figures. At the same time, Fries needed exclusive, must-have titles for the Xbox. Third-party game publishers like Electronic Arts would certainly flock to the Xbox, but those companies were going to play it smart and spread their bets across all the consoles so they could maximize the return on a game. It fell to Fries to generate exclusive Xbox games through Microsoft's own network of in-house developers and exclusive-contract external developers. He began an investment and acquisition binge that eventually increased his staff by hundreds.

At the same time, Fries didn't simply divide his team into PC developers and Xbox developers. The creative talent wanted the freedom to work within their own studios—beside familiar colleagues—and have the freedom to choose whether their particular game ideas could be best done as PC games or Xbox games. So Fries kept his studios intact, forming multiple teams within the studios. And those teams could choose to do Xbox or PC games. This allowed Fries to minimize the disruption to his creative teams and avoid staff turnover.

Fries had to study his rivals and figure out how to challenge them. For Nintendo, mascot characters were key. Cute, cuddly, memorable characters like Mario were crucial to winning over the young or young at heart. In one meeting, Gates asked, "Do we need those cute mascots? Do we have any?" Fries had heard that question from Gates for years. But he preferred to make investments in talented developers rather than big-budget licenses. He looked at the expected launch schedule for the fall of 2001 and he calculated how much he would have to step up his development program. For a time, Microsoft considered buying Midway Games, one of many publishers that was struggling with the transition between game consoles. Midway wanted the deal to happen, but Fries still didn't think there was much value in acquiring a publisher, even one like Midway that brought with it numerous franchises. The talks continued for a time and then fizzled out.

Even though Microsoft decided to block developers from dumping titles on the Xbox, the company knew it would be useful to be extremely friendly to developers in ways that the other console makers weren't. The tools used for creating the Xbox games were the same as the PC game tools. Small developers looking to break into the games market could rally behind the Xbox with less risk and less cost and very little backing.

In the fall of 1999, none of the game developers were ready to commit themselves to the Xbox until Microsoft came back with more precise specifications. As mentioned, the transition to next-generation consoles was taking a toll on developers and publishers, who were leery of new risks. Anticipating this head wind, Bachus told Blackley that he should jump-start some demonstrations so that, when the two of them took off on a developer road show, he could begin to show just what the Xbox could do.

He turned to a small game development company in Eugene, Oregon, called Pipeworks Software. Blackley had known Dan Duncalf and Dan White, the company's founders, ever since 1995, when he'd interviewed with them at a flight sim company called Dynamix before joining DreamWorks. White and Duncalf had since been laid off from Dynamix and joined up with about seven of their friends to create Pipeworks. They were looking for work, and Pat Cook, a product manager and well-known maker of football games at Microsoft, reintroduced the men to Blackley in October 1999.

Blackley wanted them to participate in his secret project: a killer demo. He gave them the specifications for a 450-megahertz microprocessor and a GeForce graphics chip from Nvidia, which was only available in prototype form at the time.

"Go do some cool stuff with it," Blackley said.

The Pipeworks team was anxious to do the work, and not just because it meant Microsoft would be paying them. They came up with a few ideas and began working on them furiously. One, which they called Desk Toys, showed a 3-D scene of a room with a huge amount of detail. The scene had a picture of Bill Gates on the wall and a computer sitting atop a desk. In final form, the demo could focus in on any object in the room and show extreme details. If someone clicked on the keyboard, it displayed individual keys that lit up. On the monitor, the image showed a reflection of the actual Xbox prototype; the Pipeworks designers were among the first outside Microsoft to get a look at that prototype since they needed to see it to complete the demo. Blackley visited a couple of times and gave his recommendations, sprinkling his comments with vulgar jokes involving pigs. He checked in on the progress, but he entrusted oversight to Drew Angeloff.

The Pipeworks work was important because it proved Blackley's original point. The tools the developers used were the same as the ones they used for PC games. Because the developers knew the tools, they had no surprises. They could develop the demos quickly, and they knew exactly how to debug their work.

Once they were done, the Pipeworks crew went on to do several more demos. Blackley had funded Pipeworks on his own authority, as part of his newly formed Advanced Technology Group. But after the demos were done, Duncalf started working with Microsoft's game division to develop an actual game.

After lining up Pipeworks, Blackley made one more call—to Tim Miller's Blur Studio, the special effects and animation house that was working with Horace Luke on the logo animation. Bachus wanted at least one computer-generated film that showed the potential of Xbox hardware running at a much higher speed than was available on demonstration hardware. Blackley said he needed some "eye candy" for a demo to show off a new game platform. Blackley visited the studio and, upon seeing all of the crew engaged in a game of multiplayer *Quake*, hired them after a 10-minute conversation. He asked Miller to put together a computer-animated video in three weeks to show off the animation capabilities of the Xbox. Blackley gave them the specifications for what the Xbox could do and asked them to stay within that technology envelope, even though they were capable of doing much more in animation quality. Blackley knew that if Blur exaggerated the capabilities of the Xbox, game developers would know.

Miller was a fan of *Mindbridge,* a science-fiction novel by Joe Haldeman in which the characters explored planets in 16-foot-tall robot suits. He'd already optioned the rights to the story and created 3-D animations based on the robot characters. He showed it to Blackley, who loved the idea. In the short animation, Miller proposed having a woman character get into the robot and have it perform some martial arts maneuvers. Blackley okayed the idea, but asked Miller to have the woman get out of the suit to do the maneuvers and have the robot copy her. That meant a lot of reworking of the animations, but Miller agreed. His team worked furiously to get it done.

"He said OK and we didn't talk again until we showed him the demo," Miller said. When Blackley saw it, he called Miller and said, "This is fucking great!"

Blackley had expanded his role on the Xbox team: He was now the Demo Guy. It was, Bill Gates would later say, the perfect job for Blackley.

Jonathan "Seamus" Blackley shows off one of the Xbox prototypes at Sony's game division headquarters in the Aoyama district of Tokyo. He was one of four renegades who proposed the Xbox, and he was the only one who stayed on the team through the launch of the console.

Kevin Bachus was the chief coconspirator with Blackley on the Xbox. The two became fast friends during the project, but Bachus resigned in May 2001.

Ted Hase, a former Army sergeant, was the politically savvy strategist and cocreator of the Xbox. He helped secure support from key executives, but he returned to his old Microsoft role in the fall of 1999.

Otto Berkes was a cocreator of the Xbox, which he originally envisioned as a Windows Entertainment Platform.
A graphics expert, he left the Xbox project in the fall of
1999 and later became a program manager of Windows
Innovation.

Ed Fries is vice president of games at Microsoft. He was an early
believer in the Xbox and architect of the strategy to deliver in-house
games for the Xbox. Here he gives a captivating speech about the
challenge of making games into art at the Gamestock conference.

Rick Thompson was vice president of Microsoft's hardware division before he became general manager of the Xbox group in July 1999. He created the business plan and tried to acquire game publishers such as Nintendo, Sega, and Square. He resigned in April 2000 to join a dot-com start-up.

J Allard was a revolutionary twice. First, he got Bill Gates to wake up to the Internet opportunity, then he joined the Xbox team to lead the charge as project manager.

Drew Angeloff was Seamus Blackley's sidekick in the Advanced Technology Group. He got the prototypes in shape and made sure the demos worked.

Todd Holmdahl directed the hardware design of the Xbox. He orchestrated the manufacturing logistics that enabled Microsoft to launch in the fall of 2001.

Horace Luke was the industrial designer behind the Xbox and the reason why it had an acid-green color. He polished the prototypes until his fingernails turned black.

Chanel Summers became the audio evangelist for the Xbox in Seamus Blackley's Advanced Technology Group. She had the Xbox logo tattooed on her lower back.

A production version of the Xbox. It was stylish in black and acid-green, but not as wild or outlandishly expensive as the original chrome prototypes.

Master Chief, the lead character of Bungie's *Halo* game for the Xbox, packs heavy weaponry as he saves humankind from alien races.

Seamus Blackley being interviewed by Japanese journalists at the Xbox Unleashed event in the fall of 2001.

Flextronics's factory in Guadalajara produced an Xbox every 20 to 40 seconds as it raced to make enough consoles for the launch.

Ed Fries (left) and Robbie Bach, chief Xbox officer, beam at the U.S. launch as the Xbox goes on sale November 16, 2001.

Microsoft spent part of its $500 million Xbox marketing budget by lighting up Times Square in green light for the Xbox launch.

John O'Rourke, director of Xbox sales and marketing, stands in front of the Toys 'R Us flagship store in Times Square on the night of the launch.

Bill Gates greets the crowd of hundreds lined up to buy the Xbox on opening night.

Seamus Blackley proposes marriage to Van Burnham just after the launch of the Xbox at the Toys 'R Us store in New York's Times Square. Blackley recruited Bill Gates to give him the ring at the appointed moment.

CHAPTER 16

HAIL MARY

MICROSOFT HADN'T BEEN SITTING STILL. Rick Thompson met with Bill Gates and Steve Ballmer again on September 29. Thompson told them about the resistance from Michael Dell and others. He now believed that Microsoft had to make the box itself—and commit to spending billions of dollars over the next five years.

Debate continued on whether to include the hard disk drive. Rick Thompson opposed it because it stretched the budget too far. Moreover, it was a component that was made in the millions for the PC, so it had already been cost reduced. In the third, fourth, and fifth years of production,

Thompson believed it wouldn't be possible to squeeze more cost out of the hard drive. But the proponents won the day, saying that the hard drive was a key difference between the Xbox and the PlayStation 2.

Thompson had argued that building the box wouldn't be as big a burden for Microsoft as it would have been in years past because of the rise of contract manufacturers. And without PC makers in an intermediary role, Microsoft could keep total control of the Xbox, from the games to the hardware. In doing so, it would have a lock on the project in the same way that its Japanese rivals had.

By now, Thompson also knew that Microsoft would have to collect royalties from third-party game developers who made games for the Xbox. He was still looking at the traditional $7, but it might include rebates for higher volume games. Thompson asked for $1 billion to spend on the initial machines for the launch, and another $200 million to spend on marketing to ensure that consumers bought the machines. Kevin Bachus needed another $50 million as a war chest to spend on acquiring exclusive titles. The goal was that Microsoft garner about 30 percent of the revenues for titles sold for the Xbox. In addition to the game creators in Ed Fries's group, Thompson believed he needed about 110 employees to ship the Xbox. Microsoft would ship 20 of its own games for the Xbox in the first year and grow that to 40 games a year over time.

Bill Gates and Steve Ballmer signed off because they understood that the Xbox was the best chance to stake a claim in the living room. Gates said that in the strategic picture, Microsoft needed twin pillars with the PC in the den and the Xbox in the living room. He and Ballmer said they knew that the message from the start had to be that this would be the "ultimate game box for the ultimate gamer to play the ultimate games." The only other ways to break into the living room involved acquiring the pipes that brought programming into the TV, like cable

TV businesses or satellite TV—an even more unrealistic and expensive proposition.

"The only door that was open for Microsoft was the console," Thompson said. "If we could have a direct relationship with 50 million consumers, that could be worth the costs in the long run." It wasn't altogether clear exactly where the Xbox fit into the living room in comparison to set-top boxes and other devices, but that was obviously its best bet. The executive team asked Thompson to give up his day job running the hardware division. He had to commit to the Xbox project full time and fill out the team, and the next day he asked his Xbox volunteers to do the same.

"It's time to either commit or get out," Thompson said. "This is going to be one of the most audacious projects Microsoft has ever undertaken."

Although Thompson felt he could now race ahead, many plans still had to take shape before Gates and Ballmer would truly commit. One of the questions at hand was whether to stay on Sony's schedule, which meant a launch in Japan in early 2000 and a launch in the United States in the fall of that year.

Bill Gates gave the keynote speech at Comdex on the first night of the big computer trade show in Las Vegas, a geek fest that drew about 200,000 people. But those who attended were disappointed since he didn't mention the Xbox. Microsoft employees had to sit through a keynote speech the next day in which Sony's Nobuyuki Idei declared that the PlayStation 2 would be the comet that hit Earth and wiped out the dinosaurs.

Idei said that the PS 2 was more than the PC, and that it would define the future of entertainment. In a press conference, Idei said he had heard rumors about Microsoft's plans to create a game console. But he noted that Microsoft had little experience in the console business. For all the work the Xbox team was doing, they still had to operate in secret—so they had to sit back and listen to the guff from Sony.

Microsoft wasn't alone in contemplating a game console at this point; another company was visiting game publishers in Thompson's shadow. Intel officials were thinking about proposing their own game box. They had bailed out of Microsoft's effort, but now they had a far-fetched scheme of their own.

"We were threatened by the PlayStation 2," said one Intel official. "We didn't want to lose equity in the home. We started working on our own alternative strategies."

Intel's desktop products group under Pat Gelsinger was exploring the possibility of creating a game console that could run Linux. That would have amounted to a declaration of war against Sony, which was one of Intel's big microprocessor customers. Intel's officials saw the chance to become a vertical powerhouse. They could build the game box themselves, buy Sega to do the games for it, and contract with a network provider for the online connectivity. Armed with these ideas, the desktop products group made the rounds at the Japanese video game publishers. Rather than any love for Microsoft, they immediately detected a preference for Intel's idea of embracing open-standard Linux software.

"We asked everyone we met with what they thought of Microsoft," said an Intel official. "Every company we met with said they would be happier if Intel made this game platform. The proposal went to the highest levels at Intel."

At one point, the team met with Electronic Arts. The companies considered the possibility of jointly making a game console, co-branded with Electronic Arts and Intel and geared toward the sports market.

The proposal was a bold one, and Intel's leaders decided they couldn't take the risk. Intel had around $10 billion in cash, but it needed that money to plow capital back into its chip factories. It didn't have the kind of money to burn that Microsoft did. Intel was already investing billions of dollars in communications chips and Web hosting businesses. So it backed off on the console.

"This never went anywhere," said John Riccitiello, president and chief operating officer of Electronic Arts. "Intel raised the idea. They showed us the financials. They approached us, we listened. One discussion and it died."

Intel wasn't exactly going behind Microsoft's back. Pat Gelsinger had pitched this box in various forms to Rick Thompson, but Microsoft wanted to do more than just provide an operating system. Gelsinger's own renegades weren't nearly as organized, passionate, or persuasive as Microsoft's. Intel didn't have an internal games division already, so it would have had to build it from scratch.

By December, there were 60 people working on various parts of the Xbox. On December 21, 1999, the Xbox team met one more time with the top brass. The whole leadership chain for the console was present. Thompson had to talk about how the project would make money.

Thompson always liked to deliver his bottom line first. He opened his slide presentation with the title *Hail Mary.* That was his conclusion about the business model. He told them that the Xbox couldn't be justified on a profit-and-loss basis. He used supporting slides that spelled out the costs and how many games Microsoft would have to sell. He had visited the top game publishers and noted their advice.

"If you do this, you will lose $900 million over eight years," Thompson said.

Bill Gates asked Thompson, "Can't you do better than that?" Thompson had been conservative because he didn't want Steve Ballmer pounding on him for failing to make his numbers, but he didn't budge. He still expected the company to spend $1 billion making the initial supply of boxes. But now he needed 315 employees in addition to Ed Fries's group. Acquiring additional content would be another $1 billion, not just the $50 million that Kevin Bachus originally anticipated. Marketing would be more than the previous estimate of $200 million.

The problems in the budget were plentiful. The cost of the goods, not including items like retailer margin, fell from $291 in the first year to $171 in the sixth year. So Thompson estimated that the price of the Xbox would never fall lower than $179. However, if Microsoft were forced to match Sony's prices, the Xbox project would lose $3.3 billion over its lifetime. The model assumed that Sony would be aggressive about cutting its prices. There were some huge unknowns that could swing the finances up or down. If Microsoft made more on the games than expected, then the benefit to the bottom line would be $621 million. But if memory chip prices were to double, then the hit would be $785 million in further losses. Thompson offered a couple of ways to save money, like removing the DVD function by putting it in a separately sold remote control, and by cutting out the modem.

Online gaming remained a wild card, particularly since Microsoft hadn't figured out how to charge for its own MSN Gaming Zone, which had 18 million PC users, most of them playing free games instead of paying the $10 a month subscription for the restricted offerings. Robbie Bach, who was Thompson's boss, observed, "It's a business with very big dials that are set very sensitive. If you change one thing here, you get a big change on the bottom line."

Thompson knew from his own estimates that Sony had been able to bring the cost of the original PlayStation down from $450 at the outset to $80 five years later. He believed it would do the same with the PS 2. According to Portelligent, a consulting firm that took apart a PlayStation 2, the Sony machine cost $441.09 to manufacture, even without a hard disk drive. The machine contained 48 chips that cost a total of $187.61. The DVD drive itself cost $65, and the main chip, the Emotion Engine, cost $59.20. Sony would reduce the chip count by shrinking chips and combining multiple chips into one, just as Microsoft would. The problem with the Xbox was that it was using parts like the Intel chip and the hard disk drive that had already been mass produced and thus cost reduced.

The loss figures scared Thompson. Microsoft wouldn't break even unless it could sell 9 games for every Xbox, including 3 produced in-house. Sony had achieved that goal over the life of the PlayStation, but Nintendo had only sold 6.7 games for every Nintendo 64 system and 3.9 for every GameBoy. Sega needed to sell 4 games for every Dreamcast to break even, but it was only selling between 2.5 and 3 titles.

Others like Ed Fries saw an acceptable risk. "If you look at Microsoft's history, most of Microsoft's great products were not profit driven at the beginning," Fries said. "With the Xbox, I could see how we were going to get from point A to point B." Allard also noted that, if the Xbox managed to get a spectacular ratio of 12 or 14 games for every box, then it would make a profit of billions.

"We said we can make this a good business, but we said to Bill and Steve, you have to be prepared to lose this much money," Allard said.

Robbie Bach was also on board. He said, "This business is a three-dimensional jigsaw puzzle on a good day."

Thompson said there were still reasons to go ahead. The Xbox would hook the crucial constituency of enthusiast gamers, who were key influencers of a much larger community of consumers and thus opened that key gateway into the living room.

Microsoft couldn't match the Japan launch schedule, but perhaps it could launch worldwide in the fall of 2000, less than a year away. Gates and Ballmer asked the group what it could accomplish with a fall 2000 launch.

The answer was that Microsoft would be able to field a machine that was roughly on par with Sony's PS 2. It would have an off-the-shelf graphics chip based on the NV10 (GeForce) or NV15 (GeForce 2) chips from Nvidia or an equivalent chip from ATI. It would have a microprocessor from Advanced

Micro Devices that ran at a speed no greater than 600 mega-hertz. And it would have a hard disk drive with a few gigabytes of storage.

Gates didn't like that strategy, even if it meant beating Sony to the starting line. If Microsoft were to enter the market, he felt it should have a superior product. He opted to skip the fall 2000 launch.

"We aren't aiming to build a parity product," Gates said. "If there was a benchmark for consoles, you guys would prob-ably win with this product. But not by enough that anyone would be able to tell the difference. I want to be able to see a difference between Xbox and every other console."

He asked the team about its other option. The team said it could do a machine that debuted in the fall of 2001. That ma-chine would have triple the graphics capability of the PS 2, using an NV20 (GeForce 3) graphics chip from Nvidia or equivalent ATI chip and a 733-megahertz microprocessor. Moreover, that graphics chip could be custom designed to fit the requirements of the Xbox instead of being retooled from the PC. The hard disk drive could hold eight gigabytes of data. Better yet, all of these components could be designed from the ground up if the launch date was postponed.

But there was a trade-off. The risk was that Sony might ce-ment itself in the market. How much could Sony sell by the time the Xbox hit the streets? The group estimated it might take Sony a year and a half to hit 10 million units of the PS 2 worldwide. Would Microsoft ever be able to catch up if Sony had such a big head start? If Microsoft set its specifications high enough, gamers would love the machine. Microsoft would sell more boxes, per-haps even enough to make up for the lost time. Losing time didn't scare Thompson. He had been in business long enough to know that you don't launch a business half-cocked. He had to find the right business model before rushing into execution.

"I was not prepared to commit myself to a plan that I couldn't deliver," he said.

Thompson had taken a lot of grief for this attitude from other people on the Xbox team. He was investigating alternatives to a plan that he considered too brash and bold to begin executing. Blackley—who was certain that gamers were unlikely to settle for anything but Nvidia—thought Thompson took far too long to decide on the graphics chip.

Asked if he was concerned that Sony might sell 20 million boxes before he sold his first one, Thompson said, "That didn't bother me at all."

Thompson left open the possibility of making money on the Xbox sooner if the company would consider a major acquisition. Microsoft had talked to everyone in the industry and had considered acquiring Nintendo, Sega, Electronic Arts, and Square. Shoring up Sega would take an estimated $2 billion investment. Such a move would guarantee that Microsoft would sell many more first-party titles for every Xbox, giving it a much better chance of hitting its break-even target of nine games for every piece of hardware sold. Thompson had great admiration for Electronic Arts, and Robbie Bach had a good relationship with its CEO, Larry Probst. EA's market capitalization was around $5 billion to $7 billion, well within Microsoft's reach. It had an excellent history, but most of its revenues were coming from the PlayStation. If Microsoft bought EA, it would have to stop its heartbeat, switch it off the PlayStation, and then get its heart going again, Thompson said. That wasn't attractive, and EA never discussed selling.

So far, nothing was panning out. Steve Ballmer made a visit to Square in Japan in the fall of 1999. Bob McBreen participated in the meetings and said Microsoft made it clear "we were willing to overpay for them." Square executives wanted to sell only 40 percent of the company to Microsoft at a price that exceeded the $2.5 billion market capitalization of the entire company. "It was a laughable price," Thompson said. Ironically, Square's movie *Final Fantasy: The Spirits Within* bombed in the summer of 2001, and Sony had to bail the publisher out.

It bought 19 percent of the company for $124 million, a fire-sale price compared to the original demand it made to Microsoft. Square's CEO, Hisashi Suzuki, resigned as the company reported a big loss.

Thompson also believed that costs could be cut if Microsoft adopted Tim Bucher's plan to have WebTV create a graphics chip based on technology from GigaPixel. That way, Microsoft could cut Nvidia out of the picture and lower console prices in the future. Moreover, GigaPixel's chip used a different architecture; the company promised that it could more efficiently design a chip so that it would be a quarter of the size of Nvidia's. If it turned out to be possible, such a design would cut the final costs of the graphics chip a great deal.

Since Microsoft was generating $1.5 billion in cash a month from its Windows and PC applications monopolies, it could afford to make big gambles. That cash was useful, but it alone wouldn't be enough to drive the other players out of the market. Sega had been bled dry as it had to borrow more and more money to finance its hardware sales. But no one now would have the same problem. Sony had $5 billion and Nintendo had $7 billion in cash. And Microsoft was approaching $30 billion. During the week of the late-December meeting, Microsoft's market capitalization hit a record of $620 billion as its stock shot to almost $120 a share.

There were big worries. Microsoft needed more time to get the hardware together. The plan for the games on the Xbox wasn't set yet. The schedule at the time called for final Xbox hardware in January 2001, in time for a launch in September 2001. But that January date was only a year away and no vendors, including the all-important graphics chip vendors, had been hired yet. Even all-star companies like Nvidia typically took 18 months to design a chip from the ground up. Moreover, Fries argued that the games that would make or break the console wouldn't be ready for the earlier launch date. By waiting, he said, the games would be much better. Ballmer weighed in and asked if the team really knew what they were asking him to do in giving approval.

"You could lose the company a lot of money!" he thundered.

Then came the moment of decision. Gates said the team should make plans for a 2001 launch. Ballmer, of course, was more theatrical. He was like the George Patton of Microsoft, the general leading the army. At the end of the meeting, he said, "You're asking me for a decision on this with a Big 'D,' not a little 'd,'" meaning it was a long-term bet. Ballmer turned to Thompson and said yes.

Thompson felt a sense of restlessness and exhilaration, but no feeling of celebration. Only that feeling of a workload that never ended.

"It was opening the gates for us to work harder than we ever had in our lives," Thompson said.

CHAPTER 17

LAST-MINUTE DETAILS

WITH THE XBOX PUSHED TO 2001, Microsoft was in no rush to make its announcement. Bill Gates was the keynote speaker at the Consumer Electronics Show in January 2000, but the Xbox public relations team canceled its plans to unveil the Xbox there, in part because it wasn't a venue for the games industry anymore. So now the announcement was set for the Game Developers Conference in San Jose, California, in March 2000. The extra time gave Rick Thompson another chance to investigate other options for the business.

Thompson's office was only a few hundred yards from the headquarters of Nintendo of America in Redmond. He and Don Coyner, a former Nintendo marketer now working on the Xbox, decided to call upon Minoru Arakawa, president of the unit. Thompson asked if Nintendo wanted to work with Microsoft on the Xbox or if Nintendo would care to be acquired. Arakawa seemed stunned.

"I was surprised," Arakawa said later. "We didn't need money. I thought it was a joke."

Arakawa told Thompson he needed to take the proposal to the corporate office in Japan. The two companies signed nondisclosure agreements and shared their plans with each other. Thompson visited Nintendo's headquarters in Kyoto. He wanted Microsoft to buy Nintendo, which had a market capitalization of $25 billion. It was a price that Microsoft could afford to pay if it really wanted to. With Nintendo, the P&L on the Xbox would become positive very quickly. Nintendo usually made 50 percent or more of the games on its own consoles, so it reaped profits of $700 million a year or more. By contrast, Ed Fries's plan called for Microsoft to make as little as 17 percent of the games on its console.

Some Nintendo executives seemed interested and the meetings went on through the winter. The parties met six or seven times. Microsoft wanted Nintendo to drop its GameCube console and get behind the Xbox. But Hiroshi Yamauchi, the aging CEO of Nintendo, didn't like the idea. By January 2000, the talks were over.

"We said good luck and see you later," Thompson said.

Peter Main, executive vice president of Nintendo of America, sat through some of the meetings but saw the sides were far apart.

"Our ability to remain independent was unquestioned due to our financial status," he said. "And it became clear that our objectives and their objectives were not the same. We think Sony and Microsoft have similar strategies. But we think the $20 billion games industry is a market unto itself. The notion that the digital world is going to converge and combine markets—we have no need to share our assets across media in that respect. We believe a single-minded focus on game content has stood us in good stead."

Another plan involved buying Sega, the maker of the Dreamcast console. As far back as 1998, Microsoft had initiated talks to acquire Sega. The companies already had a working relationship since Microsoft provided software for the Dreamcast, but relations had soured in part because game developers didn't use that software. Sega was in third place with its console and was still losing a lot of money.

Worldwide, Sega had barely sold 5 million units as of early 2000, giving it a base far smaller than Sony's estimated 73 million units. Moreover, the older Sony machine and the Nintendo 64 continued to outsell the Dreamcast. Sega had launched dozens of games in the United States, but only one of the titles, a football game, sold over a million units. Sega didn't have the financial wherewithal to stay in the race, and that prompted third-party publishers like Electronic Arts to support the other consoles instead.

By buying Sega or otherwise investing about $2 billion in the company, Microsoft could acquire not only the Dreamcast technology but a lot of talent that it didn't have, like Sega's nine game development studios—which had consistently created hits like *Sonic The Hedgehog,* key sports titles, and *Virtua Fighter.* Sega also had a hardware design group that crafted new consoles.

Shoichiro Irimajiri, who was then CEO of Sega Enterprises in Japan, said his company was surprised to learn first from other game developers that Microsoft was planning to enter the console business. He was angry that he hadn't heard it from Microsoft first. His complaints led to meetings to discuss whether Microsoft and Sega could work together on the next-generation console. At first, he wasn't interested in selling out to Microsoft because the Dreamcast appeared to be doing well in the United States. The Microsoft side was equally lukewarm to the idea.

"Every time we looked at them, we thought all we wanted was the software," said Chris Phillips, who managed the Sega relationship until he left Microsoft in early 2000. "They weren't willing to sell just their software business. They wanted Microsoft to do a box that could combine the Xbox and the Dreamcast 2."

Yet like a bad rerun, Sega kept coming back and getting audiences with Bill Gates. One of Sega's top messengers was Kay Nishi, a former Microsoft employee and the CEO of ASCII in Japan. Nishi had a very close friendship with Bill Gates. Whenever he came to town, he could get meetings on short notice with Gates. He used that influence to get Gates together with Sega's top executives, Isao Okawa and Shoichiro Irimajiri.

In some ways, Sega was appealing. Some Microsoft executives had their doubts about the feasibility of coming up with a truly killer application that would drive people to buy the console over other systems. Ed Fries, who had confidence in his own game group of 700 developers, opposed the Sega deal because he believed Microsoft could create its own hit games.

Irimajiri said Sega wanted Microsoft to make the Xbox compatible with the upcoming Dreamcast 2. Okawa also wanted the Xbox to run games made for the original Dreamcast. Some key developers, such as Yuji Naka, the creator of *Sonic The Hedgehog,* insisted that he would create games for the Dreamcast or not at all.

"At that point, we weren't willing to give up the hardware," Irimajiri said.

Microsoft wasn't interested in saddling the Xbox with such an albatross. Ed Fries noted that the relationship between Sega and Microsoft on the Dreamcast wasn't successful, and in some ways there was no point in extending a failing relationship.

Nevertheless, Irimajiri met several times with Gates in Tokyo and in Redmond. Microsoft's Chris Phillips recalled attending a meeting on November 11, 1999. Irimajiri didn't think Gates knew much about the games industry. But Gates said that he was confident because of Microsoft's past history on execution and because it had so much cash. Gates said he was willing to bet $3 billion, and Irimajiri said he just might have to lose that much. Gates said that the Xbox would use a 450-megahertz microprocessor. Irimajiri said that wasn't good enough. He said that game consoles were like sports cars, not passenger cars.

"Okawa was like a high roller in Vegas," Phillips said. "He wanted to roll the dice one more time. He wanted to do something with the Internet and entertainment and leave a lasting impact on Japan before he died. So they asked each other how they could work together and it fizzled."

The visits stopped in early 2000. Talks had broken down.

"Sega had been one way for Microsoft to put its toes in the waters of games," said Sega of America's Peter Moore. "They learned a lot from us. There were talks about more formal relationships."

But Okawa wasn't a patient man when it came to his plans for Sega. He was in his 70s and had chronic health problems. His vision was to take games to a higher level, but he always wanted to move fast.

"I sensed that the negotiations came down to issues of control of the business," Moore said. "You had two strong leaders set in their ways."

So while Microsoft kicked the tires on Sega and just about every other large publisher, it didn't buy.

At one meeting, Ed Fries said, "Bill looked at me and said we aren't going to do a big acquisition early on. That was enough for me to follow my strategy"—which involved developing Microsoft's internal game studios. Fries's boss, Robbie Bach, fully supported the plan to grow the business organically through internal expansion and the acquisition of small development teams.

Bachus and Blackley were growing impatient. They felt acquiring publishers or console makers made no sense at all because of integration difficulties that could slow the project down. They figured it was only a matter of time before Microsoft would conclude it had to go it alone, and the less time that process took, the better. Bachus was worried that Microsoft had not yet made commitments to publishers and it was running out of time to get launch titles under way.

At the end of January, Blackley and Bachus went on a whirlwind tour, visiting about 40 game publishers in three weeks in Tokyo, Seattle, Los Angeles, San Francisco, New York, and London. They presented their plans for the Xbox. At the outset, they told people that they wouldn't have all the answers on how they would take the market from Sony and Nintendo, but they said they were pretty sure at the end of it that the developer or publisher would see that the system was powerful and that developers would be excited about the prospect of making games for it.

Bachus had heard from the publishers how tough it was to work with Sony, and he had experienced it himself. Blackley got them excited by showing off his prototypes and demos. Bachus would try to get them to make a commitment on game development. The two roving ambassadors solidified their friendship during their 8 A.M. to 8 P.M. rounds, even though there was little time to relax. They had a unique chemistry, and they enjoyed being on the road because it seemed like they were appreciated much more by the development community than they were at Microsoft.

"We were superheroes on the road," Blackley said.

Upon hearing that Microsoft would do a console, most developers said, "What took you guys so long?" While not many people appreciated it at the time, these trips were crucial for the early credibility of the Xbox, according to Mike Abrash, a programmer and graphics expert who worked for Blackley.

"If Seamus had not gone out and gotten those demos early, then Xbox might not have had the momentum to be taken seriously," Abrash said. "There was a critical period there when someone had to make the outside world and people inside Microsoft feel like this was a project that was going to keep going. He did that."

HIRED GUNS

Picking a contract manufacturer to assemble the parts into the Xbox wasn't too difficult. After scouring the vendors, Todd Holmdahl's team came up with a short list consisting of Flextronics, SCI, and Solectron. Flextronics wanted the business badly, and it beat its rivals on cost.

"In our business, there isn't as much magic," said Jim Sacherman, vice president of business development at the Flextronics offices in San Jose, California. "We build similar boxes and our yields and metrics are a lot easier to estimate in advance compared to the people making chips."

Sacherman had a unique viewpoint. When the Xbox first appeared on the horizon, he was president of a mechanical engineering company called Palo Alto Products, which did design work for contract manufacturers. Two of his company's clients were bidding for the Xbox business and thinking in terms of using it as a supplier. Meanwhile, he was negotiating to sell his company to Flextronics. It got dicey when he bumped into some executives from a rival contract manufacturer while he was meeting with Flextronics and Microsoft officials at a restaurant in Guadalajara.

"It was awkward because it was obvious what we were meeting about," Sacherman said.

Microsoft needed good mechanical designers to supplement the procurement specialists who wrote the specifications for parts. Not only did the team have to figure out the parts, they had to make sure that the factory tooling wasn't too complicated and that the parts could be made easily. The task at hand was like making a PC to fit in a box smaller than a VCR.

Starting in November 1999, Sacherman and other Flextronics executives began negotiations with Holmdahl, who already knew them through the mouse business. At first, they pitched a manufacturing plant in China to build the product. But Holmdahl and his group had decided that manufacturing the product in the areas where it would be sold could give it cost advantages. Sony, for instance, had a tough time replenishing supplies in the United States because it had to use shipping lines or air freight. But by building the box in Guadalajara, Flextronics proposed to cut those costs by trucking the boxes north. Flextronics could also open a site in Hungary.

On January 19, 2000, Flextronics made its final bid for the Xbox contract at a meeting in Guadalajara. Todd Holmdahl gave a verbal OK the following week. It would be months before Microsoft and Flextronics signed a formal contract, but the companies stuck together. In February they began discussing the launch schedule.

Launching in the fall of 2001 was no problem. On most jobs Flextronics has to begin making a product within three months of being hired, so Microsoft's 18-month schedule made life easy. Microsoft had to wait until it had hardware superior to its rivals' offerings, and it also had to wait until the games were ready. That gave Flextronics plenty of time to design and build new tools as well as new factories. The company determined that it would build the initial allotment of up to 5 million boxes in its two factories, which would each have a capacity of 100,000 boxes a week. The company would hire 2,000 employees in Mexico and another 1,500 in Hungary. It would pay each employee $3 to $4 an hour, a little higher than in Asia but cheap when the lower shipping costs were factored in, and it would design and manufacture more than 50 different types of custom assembly tools for the plants. It seemed like there was plenty of time.

THE GRAPHICS SHOOTOUT

Jockeying among graphics vendors wasn't unusual. Graphics chip makers knew that getting locked into a console meant five years of steady sales in the millions of units, and they did anything to win contracts.

Since July 1999, Rick Thompson and Todd Holmdahl and his technical experts had been formally searching for the right graphics chip. One of Holmdahl's messengers, Manolito Adan, asked all the companies to sign nondisclosure agreements and then presented them with a spreadsheet that had a list of features that the Xbox graphics chip had to have. As he visited more vendors and took suggestions, the list of features kept growing, says Nvidia's chief scientist, David Kirk. Nvidia was the front-runner, but the company's CEO, Jen-Hsun Huang, says his company lost the contract six or seven times. Nvidia always had the problem of bidding too high compared to other graphics chip makers, who were willing to take much bigger risks to get the Microsoft business.

Todd Holmdahl was telling the buyers not to focus primarily on cost. Rather, he wanted them to make sure that they could get a continuous supply of goods from whomever they were buying from. The worst thing that could happen was that a company would turn out to be too small to finish its component on time or make it in sufficient quantity. Even so, Nvidia didn't always come out on top in this equation, and its price was almost always at the high end of the bids. The hardware buyers recruited Mike Abrash, who had the skills to evaluate the claims of graphics companies, to help sift the bids.

The competition was reset to the starting point when Gates and Ballmer postponed the launch from 2000 to 2001. That opened the door for a new round of bidding, and for the WebTV group to make another pitch to participate in the Xbox project.

Now that there was more time, Thompson and Jon DeVaan recommended that the WebTV team design the graphics chip for the box as well as its hardware, largely because its team had done such boxes before and they had engineers like Tim Bucher who could design chips. Bucher's team had hooked up with GigaPixel, which could license a powerful graphics chip technology to WebTV.

This made the Xbox team groan. Rob Wyatt, the graphics specialist working with Blackley, felt that Nvidia was a must. The company had the best technology and it had a track record for delivering on time. It offered a combination of raw graphics performance and features that increased the realism of the illusion, providing better shadowing, lighting, and surfaces. But Wyatt and Abrash had to examine the technical claims behind each proposal. The runners-up, 3Dfx Interactive and ATI Technologies, both made big promises but had poor execution records.

"There was one clear winner," Wyatt said. "Everyone on the technical side was getting impatient. We knew we had to work with Nvidia. We said the game developers will rip you to shreds if you don't use them."

Abrash was more objective than Wyatt. He said that the GigaPixel solution could be interesting if it could meet its promises. Still, he said that the best technical and practical choice was Nvidia.

"From a technical side, GigaPixel would have been interesting to see," Abrash said. "But when you're rolling the dice for a couple of billion dollars, I don't know."

But Todd Holmdahl, the head of the hardware integration task, said that Nvidia made an unacceptably high bid. Nvidia said it could only supply its top chip for $90 if it were delivered in 2000, while ATI was in the mid-$30 range. As a result, the WebTV solution starting looking better to Rick Thompson, and the advice from his games experts looked dubious.

The Xbox technical team would have to work with the WebTV hardware team to finish the design for the box. No longer was WebTV arguing that the Xbox should be part of

WebTV. Tim Bucher and his crew knew the Xbox had to be deployed as a stand-alone game box, at least in this generation. But the teams went to war once again over the choice of the components for the box, and the graphics chip vendors were caught in the middle.

Nvidia figured something was wrong when Microsoft went into radio silence around November 1999. All information stopped flowing from them. "We knew they were talking to someone else," Kirk recalls.

WebTV was going to support the Xbox, but it wanted to create the graphics for the Xbox at WebTV's headquarters, which by now had moved to Mountain View, California. Tim Bucher's chip designers figured they could take technology licensed from GigaPixel and build a very powerful graphics system for the console. Plus, he thought it would serve as part of WebTV's own boxes in the future.

Bucher's plan complemented some of WebTV's other ambitions. WebTV had earlier proposed what it called a common graphics architecture between the PC and interactive TV. Both machines could use the same graphics technology since 3-D graphics had become as photorealistic as television images. Thompson described the WebTV idea as an "all-or-nothing bet." The Xbox people had no alternative since they had no chip design team, and Nvidia's bid was too high.

In the end, the battle for control of the Xbox became a horse race between Nvidia and GigaPixel. Like Huang at Nvidia, GigaPixel's leader, George Haber, was one of the colorful characters of the Xbox story. He was a fierce survivor and competitor. He was born in Transylvania, in a city near Romania's border with Hungary, and he grew up speaking Hungarian, Romanian, and French. His mother, a survivor of the Auschwitz concentration camp, always told him that material goods didn't matter, since you can lose them overnight. "The only thing that matters is what you know and who you are," Haber recalled her saying. "She said no one can ever take that away from you." His father, an electrician during the war, was deported to a forced-labor camp first by the Germans and then by the Russians. Haber's father used to tell him, "the only reason I am alive is that I was strong and could work harder than anybody else." Growing up in communist Romania, Haber was a rebellious, long-haired musician, and because he loved music he became adept at electrical work because he needed to make his own amplifiers. Haber couldn't stand the lies of the communist society, where everyone pretended to be loyal as if they were in a big surrealistic theater. "You couldn't believe anything or anybody and when this goes on in all walks of life it's awful," he said.

In the late 1970s, at age 21, he got a chance to immigrate to Israel. As part of a trade deal, President Jimmy Carter had negotiated a deal that let a limited number of Jews leave Romania. "If it weren't for that, I would have run over the border for sure," Haber said.

In Israel, Haber got a job as a disc jockey. He studied electronics and earned more money as a electronics repairman. He enrolled in Israel's prestigious Technion Institute in Haifa and worked and studied so much he slept only a few hours a night. But he found time to get married and brought his parents over from Romania. He began to specialize in designing custom chips, and, in 1988, he immigrated with his family to the United States. Here, he joined Sun Microsystems, becoming its 100th employee. In 1993 he founded CompCore Multimedia, which made software for displaying video images and DVD movies on computers. In 1996, he sold the company to chip maker Zoran Corp. for $60 million, a deal that netted him about $15 million. He built a home for his parents and another for his own family.

Oddly enough, Haber became good friends with Nvidia's Jen-Hsun Huang as they worked together to enable Nvidia's chips to play DVD software smoothly.

"We were good pals and had some good times together," Haber said.

But Haber had start-up fever. He said the experience was "better than sex, and it lasts much longer." So in August 1997, he founded GigaPixel, which would create graphics chips that could work much faster because of a unique processing architecture. Haber raised $5 million from US Venture Partners, a venture capital firm, and Creative Labs, famous for its computer sound and video hardware. It was pretty late in the graphics chip wars to start such a company. But it happened that his graphics technology was just about ready by the time Microsoft was lining up its Xbox partners.

GigaPixel claimed it had an edge over Nvidia. When Haber and his crew visited Redmond, they argued that their "chunking" technology was streamlined to be faster. Instead of drawing every object on the screen and then deleting from the display image the part that couldn't be seen, GigaPixel's chip first calculated what parts of the objects could be visible. Then the graphics processor would conserve its energy by drawing only the visible objects rather than the entire scene. Haber's first prototype came back from the factory in October, and Microsoft's team was impressed with the results.

In January 2000, Haber signed his contract with Microsoft. The software giant agreed to invest $10 million in GigaPixel, grant it some royalties, and pay $15 million to help develop the final chip for the actual Xbox. If GigaPixel eventually went public, Microsoft's return on its investment would be so big that it would effectively get its graphics chips for free, in contrast to paying a lot of money to Nvidia. Haber was ecstatic. With such a large customer, Haber figured he would be able to take GigaPixel all the way to an initial public offering on the stock market. With a blessing from Rick Thompson, Bob McBreen had stayed in touch with Nvidia. McBreen told Nvidia that GigaPixel had won. The only way that Huang could get back in the game was if Nvidia made a bid to buy GigaPixel.

Haber had done damage to his top competitor, Nvidia. And Huang knew it. According to Haber, Huang called him up that day and said, "Don't sign the deal, I'll buy you instead." Haber said that Huang used crude language to suggest that he would be beholden to Microsoft for the rest of his life. Haber replied, "We'll sign the deal, and then you can buy us after that."

Huang says he indeed called to stop the deal. But he had good reasons. He says that if GigaPixel signed the deal, it would have been terrible for Nvidia to follow through with an acquisition of GigaPixel. That's because GigaPixel was merely licensing its intellectual property to Microsoft, which would codesign the final chip. The royalties on such a deal would be a few dollars per chip.

"It started out with a low price, and it went lower and lower over the years," Huang said.

Rather than just get a licensing fee, Huang wanted to design and make the chip for Microsoft—and sell the final product for a much bigger sum, somewhere in the $20 to $50 range that Nvidia usually got for its chips. (The launch date had pushed back far enough so that the $90 to $100 bid was no longer applicable.)

"It would have been a bad deal for us," Huang said.

Haber knew that Nvidia's size and track record were big advantages over GigaPixel. He started talks with companies from Intel to 3Dfx to see if they would acquire GigaPixel or otherwise ally with it. He was surprised to learn that few potential partners considered the Xbox a once-in-a-lifetime opportunity.

Haber now moved his 33 employees into the WebTV building in Palo Alto, where the teams worked on putting together the final design for the graphics chip. Another 55 or so WebTV engineers and support staff joined the project. They toiled away on the design until they were rudely interrupted.

THE ST. VALENTINE'S DAY MASSACRE

Ed Fries had to dodge questions about the Xbox at the company's annual game fest, dubbed "Gamestock," in early February 2000. He walked out on stage before an unusually large crowd of press and developers and asked, "Who wants to hear about the Xbox?" Most of the hands in the room went up. But Fries said, "That guy over there didn't raise his hand so I guess I won't talk about it today."

Meanwhile, Blackley was learning that, at Microsoft, decisions were never really final. The Xbox team was getting its ducks lined up, details were falling into place, and schedules were being locked down.

But the team had to go through one more review. It happened to be on Valentine's Day, February 14, 2000. Bill Gates and Steve Ballmer called together a final meeting to go through all the plans once again. It was clear that Microsoft had to spend $5 billion or $6 billion over five years on the Xbox, and that was only the ante for the game. No amount of money would guarantee that Microsoft would win.

Thompson said, "We looked around at each other around the table and asked if we really wanted to lose billions of dollars over eight years."

Ed Fries had to present his plan for gearing up for first-party content. He said he planned to spend money beefing up his developer staffs but wasn't going to acquire big publishers. He had a plan ready to execute that would divide the management staff—with Fries managing Xbox games and Stuart Moulder managing PC games—while keeping the studios intact. Allard was as impatient as anyone and kept telling Rick Thompson "we have to stop fucking around." At the meeting, Allard wanted to make sure that, as Xbox moved forward, the rest of the company would now stay out of its way. Gates went over dozens of decisions that the team had made, and asked for the explanations for every one again. They focused on details like what level of the operating system the game developers would be able to access. Cameron Ferroni and his software team had agreed with game developers on allowing them complete access to the lowest levels of the operating system, known as the kernel. In Windows, developers couldn't get to such a level; it was a matter of control. Microsoft had to make sure in a PC that many different things could happen at the same time. If a user was using chat software, a program would sit in the deepest level of the operating system and scan for messages. If one arrived, it would interrupt the machine and pop up a note on the screen. But games were different. Developers didn't want anything else running in the background to slow the game.

As the team pored over these details, the meeting stretched into several hours. Thompson had reported back to Gates on the progress of various efforts, from the graphics chip choice to the details of the business model. Robbie Bach says it was Ballmer who said, "If we do this, we don't ever revisit this decision. We support these guys."

At the end of it, everyone was exhausted. "We all stepped out of the meeting at the same time to call our wives and tell them we wouldn't be home for dinner," says Allard.

The meeting came to be called the St. Valentine's Day Massacre, but it was just an exhausting meeting. And, of course, a romantic evening with spouses was pretty much slaughtered by the long meeting. WebTV suffered another grievous wound but did not take its death blow just yet. For Ed Fries, the conclusion to plough ahead came as a relief. He could finally dedicate large resources to making Xbox games and make big changes in his network of studios. Every one of his lieutenants had to figure out how to double up. As the meeting ended, various groups from systems software to online got the approval to staff up to dozens of people.

Much later, in the summer of 2001, Bill Gates said in an interview, "It was a really serious business decision. It's a big step. Five years from now you can figure out if we were right. I feel pretty good about it. We've got a breakthrough technology. We're learning new things. It's one of the more risky things we've ever done. So far, everything has gone unbelievably well."

CHAPTER 18

DOWN TO THE WIRE

AFTER THE VALENTINE'S DAY MEETING, Microsoft's commitment was finally fixed. To the relief of the Xbox team, Bill Gates agreed to personally announce the Xbox in a speech before the Game Developers Conference in San Jose, California, in March. With Gates making the announcement, Microsoft would prove it was serious.

Setting off solo was a tremendous commitment for Microsoft, so the Xbox team arranged one last-ditch meeting with Sony. The Japanese section of the team sat down with Ken Kutaragi, Sony's top games executive. They told Kutaragi that Microsoft planned to enter the games business, but they also asked, "Is there any way we can work together, as partners?" They asked if Sony would consider using Microsoft's software in the PlayStation 2, or working with Microsoft in developing software for online games on the console. But Kutaragi declined, saying he felt Sony had what it needed to make its business successful. It was more or less a courtesy call before competition started, like two boxers shaking hands before they come out punching. Diplomacy was over. Now it was time to go to war.

Gates was scheduled to speak in the morning on March 10, 2000, just about a year after the first Xbox proposal and just days after Sony had launched its PS 2 in Japan. The clock was ticking down to the unveiling. The tension on the project was hitting the maximum.

Just a week before the announcement, some of the most important product specs were not yet nailed down. Now it was George Haber's turn to learn that Microsoft's decisions were never final. Haber secretly regretted talking to Huang in January, suspecting that the supercharged Huang would go all out in an attempt to win back the Xbox account. In his desperate counteroffers, Huang decided to up the ante. He could dedicate hundreds of people to the effort of finishing the graphics chip, helping Microsoft design the box, and updating the DirectX software for the console.

"For Jen-Hsun, it became a holy war," Haber said. "I should have kept my mouth shut."

Word began to leak out as well, and some game developers were not pleased. A Web site reported that GigaPixel had the upper hand, and word had circulated through Blackley's group of technical advisers. Tim Sweeney at Epic Games argued that the Nvidia chips would outperform GigaPixel's. Blackley and his graphics specialists, Mike Abrash and Rob Wyatt, had long been tilting toward Nvidia. Blackley had once taken Sweeney from office to office within the Xbox executive group and had him explain why the Nvidia technology was better for developers and faster than benchmarks showed. Now Sweeney and others chimed in again.

"We had a huge backlash from the gaming community," said Bob McBreen.

There were moments when Blackley almost despaired and wondered if he should quit. He confided in Sweeney, who goaded Blackley to continue. Sometimes Sweeney went too far. Sweeney drew a crimson response from Blackley when Sweeney sent an e-mail that said, "Is this another situation when you are going to say, 'Yes sir, Mr. Spielberg?'" Blackley didn't talk to him for a week.

There was another problem with GigaPixel: The company hadn't made a chip before, so not only did it have no track record but the game developers had nothing to use as a reference to design their games. They would have to learn something new, and that had its risks. Haber realized this and made arrangements to deliver an earlier version of the GigaPixel chip, which would be housed in a graphics card. These prototypes would be given to game developers, who could use them to learn how to program games for GigaPixel. But Rob Wyatt and Mike Abrash thought that scheme was far-fetched; the earlier GigaPixel chip didn't begin to have all the features planned for the Xbox chip. It would be useless to developers who really wanted to know how their game would run on the final hardware. By contrast, Nvidia rarely changed the driver software built into each generation of its chips. The software was stable and once developers learned how to write code for it, they could easily adapt to subsequent generations. Wyatt and Abrash believed it would be far easier to finish games on time using the Nvidia graphics chip.

Now David Kirk and the other Nvidia executives had a new proposal to enhance the GeForce 3 product for the PC. The Xbox chip would combine the "north bridge" functions— which routed data within the system—in Nvidia's integrated chipset, the nForce, with the GeForce 3. So it would marry two chips together, resulting in lower combined costs and higher performance. Microsoft would get the programmable pixel shaders and higher performance that could give it two to three times better performance than the PlayStation 2 offered. It would also be half a generation ahead of the PC because of the integration of the north bridge and the graphics chip. Nvidia was also putting together a sound chip with other "south bridge" functions into another chip called the "media communications processor" that it could sell to Microsoft as part of a package deal. Sweeney, Blackley, and others ticked off the advantages of going with Nvidia. Blackley quietly reassured his friends, "Don't worry, it's going to be Nvidia in the end."

The WebTV group liked GigaPixel because they foresaw the day when GigaPixel's graphics technology could be incorporated into the WebTV box itself. As they jointly designed the hardware with GigaPixel, this was in their minds. GigaPixel also had Nvidia beat on one kind of benchmark, raw pixel processing performance, and it came with a low price. But in the upper ranks of management, Bach favored the idea of going with a proven company, and so he liked Nvidia, even if it wasn't going to hit a revolutionary performance level.

Huang's secret channel into Microsoft remained open. Bob McBreen told Huang that he had to step up or forget about the deal. "I put a deal sheet together with terms and told Jen-Hsun to put it on his stationery and tell us that he was willing to go along with it."

There was no more room for dickering. On the graphics chip alone, Microsoft would pay Nvidia a maximum of $48 for the first 5 million chips. That cost was relatively low compared to an estimated $59 cost for the Sony Emotion Engine. In addition, Microsoft allowed Nvidia a gross profit of $11 a chip. That meant Nvidia would have to charge less than $48 per chip if it could make the chips for less than $37. For the next 5 million to 10 million chips the maximum price was $44.25 a chip with a gross profit maximum of $9.25 a chip. The scale slid accordingly over time as Nvidia cut its manufacturing costs. For 30 million or more chips, Nvidia would charge $30 a chip or a maximum gross profit of $5.25 a chip. Microsoft would also reserve the right to manufacture the chip elsewhere and pay a royalty to Nvidia. This deal was acceptable to Huang. The maximum amount of revenue that Nvidia could make on the sales of 30 million chips would be $1.32 billion. The pendulum was swinging back to Nvidia.

Huang in the meantime was working furiously. He complied with McBreen's request and sent a deal sheet back to McBreen on Nvidia's letterhead. McBreen cut Nvidia's financial risk by agreeing to give Nvidia $200 million in cash up front as an advance on chip payments. Nvidia, which only had $61 million at the time, needed the money from Microsoft to expand its engineering efforts because it would have to finish the chip in less than a year, about six months less than it usually took. McBreen floated it upstairs to Thompson, Bach, and Gates. (Ballmer wasn't involved in the decision because his father was dying of cancer.) On Saturday, March 4, Bach called Thompson's cell phone while McBreen and Thompson were coaching a Little League baseball game. He gave the deal the thumbs up. The next morning, on a Sunday, McBreen and Thompson flew down to the San Jose airport and drove to Nvidia's headquarters in Santa Clara. They met in the boardroom behind white-frosted glass walls. Huang and his lawyers hammered out the agreement.

There were some interruptions. Chris Malachowsky's mother was visiting that weekend and he took her in to meet Jen-Hsun. During a break, Huang popped his head out to say hello and shake her hand.

Huang, for his part, knew that the Microsoft deal would bring a cachet to Nvidia. He could relax a little on the financial terms in return for gaining a foothold in a fast-growing part of the graphics chip business. The Xbox also represented a coup in that it would allow Nvidia to get its "programmable pixel shading" adopted by game developers far faster than it would have done via the personal computer. Once the artists got hooked on it, it would be even harder for other chip makers to dislodge Nvidia. After the day-long meeting, Nvidia was back in.

"Microsoft got a great price," Huang said. "At the time we signed up, the price was lower than what it was going to cost us to make it."

"What turned it around? Everyone got a cooler head. As time got closer, and the decisions were getting more concrete, I think they realized that they would never finish if they went with GigaPixel."

There wasn't much of a celebration at Nvidia. After the deal was signed, everyone left to go to a nearby seafood restaurant, Birk's. Together they toasted each other. Thompson and McBreen were visibly relieved. Huang went home that night and wanted to sleep. But he wrote an e-mail message to the entire staff at Nvidia saying that they had won the Xbox deal. It was not yet public information and Nvidia did not plan to release it until the day Microsoft announced the Xbox. But the next day, one of Nvidia's engineers, Manu Shrivastava, allegedly read the e-mail and began buying options on the company's stock. The trades netted him a profit of $446,742. Months later he was charged with insider trading by federal regulators and fired. The resulting investigation led to fines against 11 more Nvidia employees and some criminal charges.

On March 6, 2000, things came to a head at GigaPixel. Haber began calling the press, saying he would have an announcement to make that Friday and wanted to arrange interviews under embargos. Then he had to reverse himself. Haber got a call that morning from Rick Thompson. "He said it wasn't good news, and could I come over to visit him at WebTV," Haber recalled. The meeting the next morning was attended by Thompson, WebTV overseer John DeVaan, Tim Bucher, and Haber's vice president of engineering, Phil Carmack. Thompson spoke up.

"We signed a deal with Nvidia last night," he said. "We've been happy with the work you've done, but we will do it with them."

Microsoft, Thompson said, would still follow through with its contractual commitment to invest in GigaPixel and pay for development costs incurred.

Haber was stunned. He gathered his employees together and broke the news. Some of the WebTV employees present, as well as Haber himself, shed tears. Indeed, as Nat Brown had said, this was the final, thousandth blow to WebTV's ambitions. But they weren't as downtrodden as Haber. WebTV had a promising new project going in Ultimate TV, a satellite set-top box for DirecTV that had digital recording capability. It was aimed at Microsoft's newest rival, Tivo. The deal with Nvidia was the final nail in the coffin for WebTV's involvement in the Xbox. Most of the participants in the battle said that the arguments between the WebTV and Xbox crews made the Xbox better.

"We started from two ends of the spectrum, and we met in the middle," said Ed Fries. "I don't see either side as a winner or loser."

In his staff meeting, Haber said he took responsibility for the loss. He said the company would still prevail in the long run. To his surprise, in the following days, no one tendered a resignation.

As it turned out, Haber said later, "The real war was inside Microsoft. It was not between us and Nvidia."

SNATCHING DEFEAT FROM VICTORY

There would be one more upset before the GDC. Advanced Micro Devices, the No. 2 maker of PC microprocessors, had believed it had a deal for months to have its 600-megahertz Athlon microprocessors used in the Xbox. The Athlon debuted with faster performance than Intel's Pentium III chips, and PC gamers often chose to put it in their high-end computers. But sometime late the night of March 9, Bob McBreen faxed the final terms to Rick Thompson in Japan and Microsoft chose Intel.

The No. 1 chip maker in the world had steadfastly refused to sell chips to Microsoft for much less than the $62 limit that had always been the bottom of its price list. Any lower than that and Intel figured it wasn't worth the factory capacity to make the chips. If a chip ever fell below the $62 value, then Intel took it off its price list altogether. It came up with faster and faster chips, and those chips kept bumping the older chips out of the product catalog. It was like the Red Queen in *Through the Looking Glass,* running just to stay in the same place. AMD was the No. 2-ranked microprocessor company with market share that ranged from 10 percent to 20 percent, compared with Intel's share of 80 percent to 90 percent. Several times in the 1990s AMD suffered big losses as Intel raced ahead of it. Earlier in 1999, as AMD and Microsoft began their talks, AMD officials were determined to break into a new market and were much more willing to supply the parts for the Microsoft Xbox at close to manufacturing cost. Throughout 1999, AMD had been in such bad shape that any new business was welcome.

But now AMD wanted to renegotiate. In December 1999, AMD was winding up a blow-out quarter. Sales hit a record $969 million and net income was $65 million. Microprocessor sales grew 67 percent over the prior quarter. The company's Athlon was shipping in high volumes and had saved the company from disaster. The management was no longer desperate to fill factory capacity. So in December 1999 and again in January 2000, AMD officials contacted Rick Thompson and said they were rethinking the price. They also wanted Microsoft to make an equity investment of $200 million to $400 million in AMD so that it would be able to build more factory capacity. That opened the door for Intel to come back in. Ned Finkle, an AMD executive, knew that was risky but he felt AMD had no choice. The company didn't have a half-dozen manufacturing plants sitting around making older parts for customers the way Intel did.

"We pretty much had one leading-edge factory going up and one factory making current products," Finkle said. "Our situation was more complex than Intel's. We had an opportunity cost. For every chip we made for the Xbox, we could have been making a higher-priced part for the PC."

AMD had found itself in Intel's original position. Paul Otellini, Intel's third-highest executive, took charge of the negotiations. When they first heard about the Xbox, Intel officials hadn't altogether believed that Microsoft would really launch the Xbox so they hadn't taken the negotiations seriously. Now they knew otherwise, and Otellini was determined to get the deal. The conversations had focused at first on a 600-megahertz part. But it soon became apparent that Intel could now provide a 733-megahertz Pentium III for the Xbox. This faster chip compensated for one of Intel's shortcomings: AMD offered a faster bus, a datapath from the microprocessor to the rest of the system that served as a kind of freeway. AMD's bus operated at 200 megahertz, while Intel's operated at 133 megahertz. For Intel, the faster chip made up for the slower bus. The increase in cost to move up to the faster chip was less than the cost would have been to increase the bus speed on the slower chip. Microsoft had pushed off its date for the launch and so Intel could work on cost reductions over a longer period of time. Intel also decided it could go lower by using its depreciated factories (which were no longer useful for the newest products) to make the chips for Microsoft.

"The AMD people had the deal," said Rick Thompson. "Then they blinked. Intel came back and had the attitude like they weren't going to lose this deal."

The negotiations on Microsoft's side fell to Bob McBreen once again. McBreen told Intel that its price had to come down and the company would have to meet the terms of a data sheet he was going to fax to them. He was under pressure from Bill

Gates and Robbie Bach to cut a deal with Intel. On a Thursday afternoon, the final OKs were given. McBreen called Thompson, who by now was in Japan to talk to journalists about the launch of the Xbox.

Now Intel had come down on price. It was willing to supply 733-megahertz Pentium III chips for $35 a chip in 2001. The prices declined each year to $30, $25, $22, $20, and $19 by 2006. That wasn't as low as AMD's best offer, which started at $30 and declined to $17.50 by 2006. But AMD was not only asking for the $400 million investment, it also wanted a $300 million guarantee on chip purchases.

Paul Otellini at Intel later said that the deal was a good one and important to Intel because of the potential volume. Intel could also cash in by designing the motherboard for the system as well. Intel also said the prices were modified.

Late in the afternoon on Thursday, March 9, Intel began contacting the press. Not only would Intel supply the chip, it would provide debugging tools and design the main system board of the Xbox. The AMD representatives, whose early work made the Xbox possible, were completely surprised when Bill Gates confirmed the Intel deal the next day.

"I was sitting next to the AMD people, and their jaws just fell open in shock," said Tim Sweeney, the game developer at Epic Games.

The choice of Intel may look inevitable after the fact, but it was far from a done deal before the last minute. Intel had had a two-decade partnership with Microsoft as the main supplier of microprocessors for the PC. But one of Intel's executives, Steven McGeady, had also testified against Microsoft in its antitrust case. He was kind of a lone wolf, but it was never clear whether Intel was silently gleeful about the damage he did to Microsoft by testifying that Microsoft had bullied Intel into dropping multimedia software that conflicted with Microsoft's aims. The only loyalty between the companies seemed to be the result of convenience. Andrew Grove, chairman of Intel, had once described the two as fellow travelers rather than partners. Now it seemed that the stars had aligned once again so that their paths went the same way.

To bring Nvidia and Intel into the fold, Microsoft had engaged in some serious brinkmanship. Most of it wasn't planned. If Microsoft had planned to use Nvidia from the start, it would never have invested money in GigaPixel. This last chapter of negotiations showed how fluid the plans for the Xbox were, and how some of the most important decisions came down to the very last minute, creating anxiety for everyone working on the Xbox.

Haber called Huang with congratulations, catching him as he and two engineers were driving back from the conference. In a friendly tone, Haber joked that Huang was now beholden to Microsoft for the rest of his life.

CHAPTER 19

THE COMING-OUT PARTY

BILL GATES WAS GIDDY during the rehearsals the night before the Xbox unveiling at the Game Developers Conference in San Jose, as he and 30 other Microsoft people prepared for his keynote speech under strict security. Sitting in the back of the auditorium, Alan Yu, the program director for the GDC, was soaking it in.

"Gates would walk from one place to another and people were following him around like a school of fish," Yu said.

Gates watched one of the promotional Xbox video sequences, based on Midway Games's *Ready 2 Rumble* boxing franchise. Afro Thunder, an animated black fighter with a huge 1970s-style afro haircut, was primping and talking jive about how the Xbox animation made him so much more appealing. Afro Thunder was using so much street slang that Bill Gates and his PR people asked, "Is this politically correct?" Blackley piped up and said it was OK. Bachus had already argued that the character was familiar to gamers. Some of the handlers thought they should yank it from the speech. One said that the headlines would read, "Bill Gates mocks black people." The Xbox team agreed to take one line out, and Gates decided to keep the demo.

Bachus got someone to introduce Jen-Hsun Huang and David Kirk to Bill Gates during the rehearsals. Kirk and Gates talked technology for a while. Kirk forgot himself and mentioned that Nvidia used racks of Linux machines in chip design. That didn't go over so well with Gates, even though Bachus (who was helping write the slides) had briefed Gates earlier about how game developers weren't big Microsoft fans, noting that the GDC audience cheered a year earlier at the mention of Linux. Bachus said to expect a harsh crowd. For most of the day before the speech, the Xbox team holed up in the top-floor suites at the Fairmont Hotel near the convention center. From that perch, they did press and analyst interviews.

Blackley had been making a name as a charismatic speaker, and no one was worried about how he would do—except Blackley himself. He spent many long hours in the days leading up to the GDC making sure that his demos would work right. He had two Xbox prototypes on-site just in case one of them failed at the last minute (another was in Japan, and a fourth in London).

Drew Angeloff, one of Blackley's developer support staffers, had to babysit the prototypes. Upon arriving in San Jose, he found that neither of the boxes was working. In a state of panic, and with Blackley breathing down his neck, Angeloff asked to be left alone with the boxes so he could get them operational. The prototypes had the first NV 15 graphics chips in the world, fresh from Nvidia's contract manufacturer in Taiwan. At last, he got them running—only to watch them start to overheat. Angeloff realized that if Gates rambled on a bit during his keynote, the boxes would fry before the end of the speech. He had to carefully time when to turn on the boxes. Meanwhile, Horace Luke was exhausted. He hadn't been happy with the effect that welding had on his chrome boxes. So he bought some metal polish and spent a whole day applying it to the prototypes.

"I polished until the aluminum turned my hands black," he said.

The Civic Auditorium in San Jose was crowded on March 10, 2000. A long line snaked around the building as game developers and the press waited for Gates. He got up on stage in his signature sweater and glasses and began talking to the audience of 3,500 in the same room where, a year earlier, Phil Harrison held everyone spellbound with his demo of the PS 2. The speech was simulcast to even more people in the convention center across the street.

"It's very exciting to be here today and have the opportunity to announce a whole new platform, that all of you are going to take in directions that we can't even imagine," Gates started.

He went on to describe Microsoft's vision for entertainment technology, which spanned the breadth from the high-end PC to cellular phones and systems for cars.

"We believe the definition of a game is going to become a lot broader," Gates said. "The whole notion of what games are going to be is going to expand quite a bit."

Gates had to make sure that the audience knew Microsoft wasn't abandoning PC games. He had good things to say about Windows games but asked the audience to consider what it would take to move gaming to an audience four or five times larger than it was currently. The answer, he hinted coyly, was a "secret, a very deep secret." The audience laughed since the Xbox had been rumored for months. He teased the audience more by having an employee come out and demonstrate the latest in PC games. Finally, he got to the Xbox, recounting the tale of how some Microsoft insiders came up with the idea to do a console. So then he pulled a black shroud off a table and there was Horace Luke's shiny Xbox.

He described its specifications, with the Intel microprocessor and the Nvidia graphics chip. The machine ran DirectX with some parts of the Windows 2000 operating system. It had 64 megabytes of DRAM memory chips, compared to only 40 in the Sony box. The graphics would run at a theoretical maximum of more than 150 million polygons per second, compared to 66 million polygons per second with the PS 2. Everything was better in head-to-head comparisons, and it was appropriate since the Xbox would be out so much later.

To demonstrate the power of the machine, Gates had a prototype with an Nvidia chip that was running at only 10 percent of the performance of the real machine. And Seamus Blackley walked out on stage to run the demo.

"I was worried sick," Blackley said. "I was half-concerned people would boo, and that came from my own sense of self-importance, as if anyone would really think about *Trespasser* right then. I was under so much stress, it was remarkable I didn't explode."

But none of that showed in the performance the fast-talking Blackley gave. As he came out he gave Gates a leather jacket with a big green X on it, and Blackley wore one himself. Blackley grabbed a controller and showed off the demos from Pipeworks—the Desk Toys demo that showed a ton of detail like the picture of Gates and the first set of employees at Microsoft. Blackley pressed a freeze button on the controller and the action stopped in mid-air. For a second, Drew Angeloff nearly died, not realizing what Blackley had done. He looked at Rob Wyatt, and both had that "Oh shit" look on their faces. "I felt close to death," Angeloff said. Had the Xbox crashed? Fortunately, Blackley unfroze the action and proceeded, prompting sighs of relief backstage. He showed a scene with a beautiful Japanese garden with a koi pond that reflected the images of butterflies floating above it. Blackley pointed out the ripples on the surface of the water in the pond.

"The other cool thing, aside from all the lighting I'm showing you, and this is kind of neat because you can see that these are real environments updating in real time, and they have reflections underneath these and it's crazy," he said, speaking from one engineer to many.

As he introduced the next demo, he said, "In my high school physics class I was scarred with the image of chain reaction as demonstrated by the old ping-pong ball and mousetrap demo. So I felt it was only appropriate that I would scar all of you today with that same image."

He set off a mousetrap with a ping-pong ball atop it, igniting a chain reaction in a room filled with mousetraps and ping pong balls. Blackley got a roar of applause. He showed them butterflies dancing above a koi pond with perfect reflections in the shimmering water, and a room with a desk that was detailed down to the tiniest items like a working computer keyboard. Then he showed them the Blur Studio demo of the woman and the giant robot moving in perfect synchronization as they executed martial arts moves. This animation wowed the audience and showed what kind of games would really be possible on the Xbox. The woman had dark skin and Asian eyes and short hair. She had an X tattooed on her rippling abdomen, and it seemed like Microsoft had a mascot character at last. (But she seems to have made people uncomfortable. At any rate, in later appearances, her skin tones were noticeably lighter and she looked less aggressive.) Now that the box was ready, Gates said, it was time to start openly recruiting developers.

"We've put quite a budget behind this one, and we're going to break through in a very big way," Gates said in closing.

The demo reel of Afro Thunder played. Blackley introduced the video, partly as a way of shielding Gates from any criticism that the video might create. Most people chuckled, but one person in the audience shouted, "Sambo!"

Offstage, Blackley finally felt like he had completed a marathon. The project was announced and, for Gates and everyone else, there was no going back.

"I felt we were safe at home base," said Blackley, who had had very little sleep. Alan Yu congratulated Blackley, and said later, "It was like he was very proud to show off his baby."

Rick Thompson pulled off the Xbox unveiling in Japan without a hitch. Overseas, in London, other Xbox team members were about to unveil the Xbox to Europeans. John O'Rourke, director of marketing for the Xbox, was feeling good about the upcoming demo when he got a call from J Allard.

"Dude," Allard said. "I blew up the Xbox."

Allard explained that he had turned the switch on the Xbox without first flipping a control that adapted the box to European electrical current. The power supply was fried, and it was just the night before a meeting with the press and games community. They called Drew Angeloff back in the United States, and he told them how to fix it.

So the two men started a frantic search. Allard found a replacement power supply, but he had to solder it into the machine. The two men convinced the staff at the Metropolitan Hotel to allow them into the basement repair shop, where they found a soldering gun. They proceeded to solder 36 wires to the new power supply.

"It was quite an experience, and J and I bonded," O'Rourke recalled.

The next day, the London demo went off without a hitch. After that, big green stickers were put on all of the developer kits that went out in the coming months. The stickers told the developers to switch up for 220 volts and down for 110 volts.

"We called it the J sticker," Blackley said. "I have a picture of one that someone took off their machine and stuck on a urinal."

Back at the GDC, it was party time. The Xbox team gathered for dinner at Scott's seafood restaurant atop a building in San Jose. It was Ed Fries's birthday. They ordered champagne and were generally rowdy. Nearby, some game developers from Ensemble Studios started a chant: "Xbox—Xbox—Xbox!" They were rewarded with champagne compliments of the Xbox team. Soon, much of the restaurant was roaring the same thing. The headwaiter was fuming and kept asking them to quiet down.

"The restaurant people didn't like us much," Blackley said.

The maitre d' tried to explain that he wanted to create a "fine dining" atmosphere at the restaurant. So Jeff Henshaw, executive producer of the Xbox software development kit, went around from table to table asking if he could pick up the tab for any customers who were annoyed. He paid for about ten dinners.

Later, the group continued partying. At Drew Angeloff's urging, everyone squeezed into the elevator. Blackley was the last to get in. He was talking to somebody in the hallway when he noticed the elevator was beginning to go down while the doors were still open. He jumped into the elevator and it started to drop. To Angeloff, whose memory of the event was admittedly foggy, it seemed like the elevator was already sinking as Blackley came running in full bore. "It looked like he was jumping through the closing blast doors in a *Star Wars* movie," he said. "I thought he was going to get decapitated." With Blackley's added weight, the elevator slid down almost four floors. It stopped halfway between floors and the occupants had to pry open the doors and climb out. Horace Luke, the Xbox creative director, shouted, "My leg! My leg!" Luke had a sore knee for about a week. Half the crew wanted to make a getaway, while others asked if they should tell someone the elevator was broken. "You could tell who grew up in bad neighborhoods and good neighborhoods," Blackley said. Questioned about this incident later, Blackley was red-faced but unrepentant. "I believe that a team can't produce a fun product unless you have fun making it," he said.

Bachus, who was also in the elevator, said he counted 24 people in the elevator. From then on, he said, "I paid a lot more attention to the maximum capacity signs."

The party moved to the top of the Fairmont Hotel, where Alan Yu had a penthouse suite. High-profile developers were partying away. They all drank heavily, and company distinctions melted as people from Nintendo, Sony, and Microsoft celebrated. Blackley had a chance to become the center of attention once again as he pulled up to the piano and played classic music.

Then hotel security showed up. Yu emptied out most of the crowd through one door, but he invited half of them back through another door of the suite. The party continued until 3 A.M. or 4 A.M. The team had proven that it was just as cool as anybody else in the games business. Robbie Bach shuddered when he read about the elevator incident later in the *Wall Street Journal*.[1] He tolerated the shenanigans, but warned the team, "Remember, you guys are representing Microsoft."

CHAPTER 20

GATHERING STEAM

ONE CONSEQUENCE OF THE BLITZ of decisions just before the GDC was a management shake-up. Rick Thompson resigned as vice president and general manager in charge of the Xbox, and his boss, Robbie Bach, took over as "chief Xbox officer."

Too many problems had been piling up for Thompson. The Nvidia chips cost more than he wanted to pay, and so did the rest of the box. He lost out on his bids to acquire game publishers. And he had his doubts about whether Microsoft was moving fast enough to come up with its own killer games. He was still convinced that the profit-and-loss picture on the Xbox was weak.

"I wanted Ed [Fries] to figure out how to keep more of the money," Thompson says, referring to the low estimate for the first-party team's share of total revenues.

Ed Fries, on the other hand, stood by his guns and wanted to grow the Xbox business organically, by commissioning in-house teams and signing up more individual game development studios. Fries knew that it was hard to absorb another game publisher unless you had a very good relationship with the talent. He figured that if he doubled the resources going into every one of his studios, they could crank out more games without going through the disruption of an acquisition. Fries wouldn't have minded an alliance with Nintendo, which could focus on kids while he focused on adults. But that deal wasn't happening.

"The surest and easiest way to enter a new business is to buy someone," Fries says. "But I was saying my team can do it."

Thompson, on the other hand, was looking at profit-and-loss statements that showed a loss of $900 million over eight years and perhaps $3.3 billion in the worst case. The only way he saw to avoid that was to move toward Nintendo's model, where 50 percent to 70 percent of the games sold on its platform were internally developed. That would have generated much more profit for Microsoft.

"I said we were not on the right path. I said it 50 times. I was consistent all the way. Steve Ballmer said that I should help them find the right path," Thompson says. "Only by some miracle in the business model for online gaming could I see us making money sooner."

And it was clear that—as with most things on the Internet in the spring of 2000—users firmly believed that games were supposed to be free. Microsoft's Internet Gaming Zone had generated 18 million members, but the fee-based games had few takers. Cameron Ferroni's team was only starting to develop the system software and had not yet formed the online game strategy, so Thompson wasn't confident that the resulting revenues would be enough to offset the projected losses.

"Nobody else cared about profit-and-loss," Thompson says. Others have called him the conscience of the team.

John Connors, the chief financial officer of Microsoft, says that the Xbox represented an investment in the near term for the company. He adds, "When a CFO says *investment,* that means it's not profitable. It will be a big investment for a couple of years. If you don't have hits, it's not a good business." On the other hand, he points out, "When your company is big, if you are going to grow profits, you have to move into significant new markets. The games business is a significant market. We think when you deliver broadband online gaming, it becomes even more pervasive."

Connors also says, "There was a small group of really enthused people who got the Xbox going and convinced Bill and Steve it was the right thing to do to get people excited about a new Microsoft platform. They created a buzz about the Xbox that is huge, especially among gamers. Those users are an important group for Microsoft as influencers of technology buying."

In the meantime, Thompson saw another opportunity. He had made a small investment in an Internet company called Go2Net. As Internet valuations soared, the company became a big hit for early investors. Thompson's net worth, already in the multimillionaire bracket because of his longtime tenure at Microsoft, skyrocketed. Thompson had been offered a board seat at Go2Net, but Microsoft brass decided it was too much of a conflict for Thompson. So he decided to resign and take a job as Go2Net's chief financial officer—just in time for the Internet stock crash. (Thompson left Microsoft on April 11, 2000, and the stock market tanked on April 14.)

The irony was that the business-minded Thompson had made a colossal business blunder, giving up his job at Microsoft for a dot-com that would later implode along with the rest of the overvalued Internet stocks. He couldn't make the numbers work on the Xbox, and yet somehow he thought he could make Go2Net work. He turned into a walking illustration for a new Microsoft slogan: *friends don't let friends go to work at dot-coms.* He set himself up for the ultimate "I told you so."

"It was a terrible move financially," Thompson said later. "I left a lot of money on the table. All that shows was I wasn't very smart. I was impressed with the team at Go2Net and thought they could do a lot more."

By the time Thompson left, the Xbox was becoming a juggernaut. No single person seemed key to the project's survival anymore. Kevin Bachus recalled that he finally considered it to be a legitimate enterprise when he went to a meeting on how to collect royalties and found 50 people from different parts of the company already engaged on the topic.

Fries was promoted to vice president and continued to run the internal games division at Microsoft that would make both Xbox and PC games. Fries had won his arguments with Rick Thompson, but (as often happens) victory turned out to be a beginning and not an end. He thought, "Holy shit! We really have to go and do this now." After Thompson was gone, J Allard carried on the same arguments. Allard and Fries didn't see eye to eye on the pace of game development. Fries was pragmatic. "J is a revolutionary," Fries says.

Robbie Bach now had to step in and fill the gap that Thompson left. He had been doing several jobs at once and relying on Thompson to do the Xbox. Now he decided he would become "the chief Xbox officer." Bach wasn't pleased to see Thompson leave, but he says, "I was glad that he left when he did," meaning it was early enough to recover from a change in leadership.

Allard took on the responsibility for third-party games, becoming Kevin Bachus's boss. They immediately set about defining their policies for third parties and the contracts needed to sign up publishers. Unlike their counterparts at rival console makers, Allard and Bachus wanted to make sure the deals were consistent. They would give no special discounts to the biggest publishers or hit makers. Then they opened the floodgates for publishers and developers to submit proposals to the Star Chamber. Soon enough, the Star Chamber had to learn how to balance its portfolio of games so that not all the games came out at once. It also had to make it clear it would not allow publishers to simply port PC titles to the Xbox and pollute the platform with "shovelware." Bachus felt at times that the Star Chamber was too strict in its role as the standard bearer for quality. Too often the personal tastes of committee members collided with the business interests of publishers.

After the GDC, Blackley formalized his advisory team by appointing Epic's Tim Sweeney, John Carmack of id Software, and a dozen other game development luminaries to a technical advisory board for the Xbox. With Bach in charge, Blackley felt he was appreciated and heard. Bach said he liked Blackley's passion and he tolerated Blackley's indiscretions because his motives were pure. (And some of his indiscretions were really indiscreet. For example, in one interview Blackley said that playing video games was like masturbation. "Everybody does it, but no one wants to admit it," he said. He got a storm of e-mail from Microsoft people who were offended. Human resources executives said they were deeply disappointed in Blackley's comments. Gamers, however, loved the comments.)

Blackley and Angeloff continued to create more demos and Xbox prototypes, which were running at about 10 percent of the graphics capability of the final box. The team took to harassing each other with the model shop tools. One day, a *Time* magazine staff writer—there to talk with Blackley about the Xbox—overheard Rob Wyatt snarl at Angeloff, "Get away from me with that blowtorch, you skinhead." The quote made it into *Time*.

On March 24, Blackley made a trip to Nvidia to participate in its Xbox victory celebration. The Xbox announcement had sent Nvidia's stock soaring above $100 a share. Thanks to some rumormongering and perhaps some insider trading, the stock went from $58.50 a share on Monday, March 6, 2000, to

$100.29 a share on the following Thursday. After the announcement on March 10, the stock closed at $118. That triggered executive whoopla because Nvidia's management team had contemplated the occasion as far back as September 1999, at an executive retreat at Birk's restaurant in Santa Clara. A couple of executives—sales chief Jeff Fisher and software engineering head Dwight Diercks—had a long running pact on what they would do if the stock ever went above $100. Dan Vivoli, vice president of marketing, grabbed pen and paper, wrote down everyone's pledge and had every executive sign it.

Now it was payoff time. In front of the whole company, Huang had to get his ear pierced. To share the pain, Blackley, who already had a stud in his right ear, offered to get his left ear pierced. He took the pain in front of 400 cheering Nvidia employees. Still, Huang grimaced as a trained body-piercing specialist stuck a needle through his left earlobe. Vivoli got an Nvidia logo—a green and blue eye—tattooed on his left shin. Chris Malachowsky, the vice president of hardware engineering, had his head shaved Mohawk-style and dyed his remaining hair green down the middle. John McSorley, the vice president of human resources, got a nipple pierced. David Kirk had his nails painted green. Curtis Priem had his head shaved and got the Nvidia logo tattooed on his head. And Jeff Fisher avoided the shave and got the logo tattooed on his bottom.

Of course, Nvidia's celebrations meant gloom elsewhere. Later that month, Haber decided he wouldn't make it to the IPO anymore. GigaPixel needed a partner, and so he accelerated merger talks. 3Dfx Interactive, a once-hot graphics chip company that was stumbling, agreed to acquire GigaPixel for $186 million in stock. The deal netted Haber $37 million, which was better than the proverbial smack in the face but still not exactly the brass ring. It was the second time that he had to sell out before hitting an IPO, which could have netted him much more money. Of course, he said, it wasn't about the money. It was more about winning and losing and building a great company. Months later, Nvidia bought 3Dfx. Haber had since departed, but GigaPixel engineers like Phil Carmack went along with the deal. There wasn't much bitterness about the fight; besides, Nvidia was just about the only graphics company left standing. Where else could they go?

Nvidia soon got down to work. Shortly after the GDC, the company signed a deal to provide a media and communications processor, dubbed the MCP, for the Xbox. This chip would combine a sound processor with other input-output functions in the "south bridge" of the chipset. Nvidia had never done a sound chip before and had to compete against Analog Devices, Creative Labs, and a bunch of other contenders. However, Nvidia had recruited engineers from Aureal, a company that had blazed trails in 3-D sound before it collapsed. They came up with a winning pitch.

Huang planned to use the $200 million advance on revenues to hire a bunch of new engineers to fully staff the two projects. Malachowsky allocated 120 engineers from the GeForce 3 chip for the PC to adapt the chip to the Xbox. They had to work with another 40 engineers who would take the nForce "north bridge" chip and integrate it with the GeForce 3. Another 40 or so engineers worked on the MCP, and 10 more engineers tied everything together in a system. These engineers worked closely with Microsoft's Todd Holmdahl and his team of hardware engineers on the final specifications. All told, Nvidia had just over a quarter of its staff of 800 working on the Xbox. They had less than a year to finish two chips—a task it usually took about 18 months to finish.

"We redeployed the entire company to do this box," Huang said.

Back at Microsoft, Robbie Bach got down to work. Bach himself wasn't much of a gamer. A 12-year veteran of Microsoft, he had enjoyed great success running the Microsoft Office business software division for more than five years. He was a "shipper"—someone who had established his credibility among Microsoft's top leadership for getting products out the door. He didn't know a ton about the games business, but Bach, who had a background in economics and business administration, was excited about the opportunity to grow a giant new business within Microsoft. His boss, Rick Belluzo, says Bach had a talent for creating teams that were extremely motivated. Bach started out as a business guy among the geeks, but he earned their respect by taking the time to learn the business of games. One of his first jobs after Thompson left was convincing other companies that Microsoft was still committed to the Xbox.

Shortly after the GDC, Bach's growing army began engaging with a horde of game publishers and developers. The Xbox team expanded dramatically, growing to 1,000 employees through the summer. Another 5,000 to 6,000 third-party developers would be working on Xbox games. Fries and others made frequent trips to Japan to court key developers there. Blackley visited Japan once or twice a month, making more than 20 trips before the launch of the Xbox.

Now was the time of guerilla warfare. Microsoft dispatched its emissaries to woo game developers into the Xbox camp, promising them great rewards for defecting from Sony, Nintendo, and Sega. In a sense, the situation favored Microsoft as a new entrant. Sony had messed up its PlayStation 2 launch in a couple of ways. Not only was it short on units for the U.S. launch, it also failed to come up with any first-party (Sony-made) games at the launch. That was because in the year of the launch Sony reorganized its game studios, combining separate groups like its 989 Studios development team with its Sony Computer Entertainment America teams. The chaos caused a lot of churn among the executive and employee ranks. The resulting lack of in-house games meant that Sony's "razor-and-razor-blade" model was a lot duller than the company really needed.

Microsoft was now on the map when it came to video games. Xbox announcement coverage hit the media worldwide.

Two dozen game publishers had good things to say about the Xbox. Larry Probst, chief executive officer of Electronic Arts, said his company was intrigued at the idea of making games for the Xbox. In private negotiations, Probst had told Microsoft officials that he welcomed Microsoft. If Sony had demanded more royalties per game from EA on the PS 2 than it had charged on the original PlayStation, EA would have had no choice but to pay it. EA's investment in Nintendo's N64 had been fairly lackluster. With another player making hardware, Probst would enjoy the fruits of a more competitive market.

"If you provide me with a way to not be so dependent on Sony, I will work with you," Probst told Microsoft.

It wasn't quite a commitment. And Probst said he wasn't going to be Microsoft's "lead horse." But Microsoft's standing shot ahead of Sega's, which had never gotten Electronic Arts to make games for the Dreamcast. That had doomed Dreamcast to failure.

In various follow-up meetings, EA executives wanted a lot of answers, like whether Thompson's departure meant that Microsoft wasn't committed to the business, if Microsoft would buy Square, or whether they would receive competing game console pitches from WebTV. Kevin Bachus and J Allard met repeatedly to deliver updates and assure EA that Microsoft was going to be in the business for a long time. Probst asked whether EA could get special discounts on royalties, but Microsoft stood its ground on that. It was, however, willing to offer marketing funds, allow EA to make its own games, and make special arrangements to deliver large numbers of development kits to EA.

Microsoft made its appearance at the Tokyo Game Show in late March 2000. This twice-yearly venue provides an opportunity to pitch Japanese consumers. Attendees get discounts if they show up dressed as their favorite game characters, so it's a somewhat wackier place than its U.S. counterparts. This time, plenty of exotic dancers graced the booths at the show. Women showed up in leather *anime* character outfits—based on the style of cartoon animation that is popular in Japan—and posed for a huge crew of paparazzi.

As the show was ending, the Xbox team found itself hopping from bar to bar in Roppongi, a nightclub district in Tokyo where American expatriates mingled with other international travelers. They were accompanied by Hisashi Suzuki, president of Square, one of Sony's most prominent game publishers and the maker of the *Final Fantasy* series, which sold in the millions with every new game. Blackley and Bachus urged James Spahn, Microsoft's Xbox contact for games in Japan, to call Ken Kutaragi, the head of Sony's game division. Spahn had Kutaragi's number on his cell phone, but he resisted because it was 11 at night. Finally, Blackley got Spahn to dial the number. He apologized for calling so late. Kutaragi was polite. Spahn asked him what he thought of the Xbox. Kutaragi offered some congratulations. Blackley and Bachus were laughing away, but Suzuki was dead serious when he insisted that Spahn not mention that he was with the Xbox team.

"The Japanese guys were always especially nervous. Their relationship with Sony was like the worst rumors you heard about Microsoft and its relations with Windows developers in the antitrust case," Bachus said. "We heard rumors that Sony would take reprisals against game developers who weren't loyal. Japanese publishers were concerned that they might be the only ones sticking their necks out and supporting us, and we had to reassure them that was not the case." Sony's Kazuo Hirai, chief operating officer in the U.S. games unit, said this fear of retaliation by Sony was ludicrous.

One of the risks in Japan was that Sony was also the distributor of games made by Japanese third-party publishers. That meant they had to maintain good relations with Sony or risk their distribution.

Toying with their more powerful adversary, the Xbox team continued their fraternity pranks in Japan. Bachus suggested the team visit a bunch of Tokyo landmarks, including Sony Computer Entertainment, the games division run by Kutaragi, in the Aoyama district of Tokyo near the emperor's palace. There, Bachus and Blackley and others took their Xbox prototype with them and placed it atop the Sony logo on the building's sign. And they snapped a bunch of pictures.

The main battleground for the hearts of publishers and the press was the Electronic Entertainment Expo (E3) show in May 2000. Based in Los Angeles's sprawling convention center, hundreds of publishers set up booths full of cacophonous gaming machines and staffed by "booth bunnies" from the pages of *Playboy* magazine. Each year, the publishers hold lavish parties or build exotic booths to win the hearts of retailers and the press. Since more than 2,000 games are shown each year, the glitziest titles stand to receive the bulk of the attention.

Just before E3, Microsoft hosted about 60 Japanese game developers and publishers at Club Cha Cha in Los Angeles, where the executives and their bar hostesses consumed more than $30,000 in alcohol, from the finest $3,000 bottle of Petrus Pomerol to an $80 bottle of Chivas Regal scotch. The point was to make the Japanese feel comfortable with the Xbox crew, but it definitely made some of the Microsoft brass feel uncomfortable.

Microsoft's rivals took their chance to seize the spotlight and cast aspersions on their new rival. Nintendo was silent about its GameCube console, then code-named "Dolphin," and instead talked about how this was "harvest time" as it made tons of money from Pokemon and other titles for its old systems. As a joke, Nintendo officials handed out gift bags with toy foam dolphins, which were dubbed "Dolphin Developer Kits." It was a tacit admission that the tools developers needed to make GameCube games were late.

Kazuo Hirai, president of Sony's U.S. games unit, noted confidently that Microsoft lacked the experience to understand the console games market. The PS 2's Japanese launch was breaking all video game sales records, with nearly 1 million units selling in the first weekend. Hirai pointed to dozens of games on the floor that were being shown for the first time, and he noted that publishers were working on more than 270 games for the PS 2, which was launching in the United States in the fall. The implication: How could Microsoft catch up? Yet some game developers at the show, like Lorne Lanning, creative director at Oddworld Inhabitants in San Luis Obispo, California, complained to the media about how hard it was to write games for the PS 2. The PS 2 development system—which every game developer had to buy to program games—cost a hefty $25,000. And it was a bear to work with. These sore points would eventually give Microsoft an inroad into key developers.

Peter Moore, president of Sega of America, pressed Microsoft to name the titles or brands that would carry it to greatness. Minoru Arakawa, president of Nintendo's United States games unit, was also skeptical. "Microsoft? They are a great company. I don't know how much they know about video games. It's a little surprising."

Some publishers were also predicting difficulties for Microsoft. "They will have a challenging time entering the console business," said Bobby Kotick, CEO of Activision, one of the largest and oldest game publishers. "Things like the controller are critical. Nintendo spends so much time figuring out the controller, and Microsoft just doesn't have the experience."

Blackley demoed the sound capabilities of the Xbox, which would allow games to dynamically generate sound effects. So if the gamer was in a tense part of the action, the music would accelerate its pace, or it might play spooky music as the gamer was exploring a scary scene. It was these kinds of special audio effects that Chanel Summers had been laboring to create while working for Blackley's Advanced Technology Group.

Although there wasn't much to show at E3, Microsoft did stage a public relations event. The marketing department polled fan Web sites like Msxbox.com and staged a contest to see who could come up with the best name for Blur Studio's animated female martial artist, who would become the Xbox's mascot character. The winning fan came up with Raven, named after the character's dark skin. Microsoft hired a sleek woman with intimidating muscles to make an appearance at E3. She carried a big package into the convention center with lots of TV news cameras following her. She cracked open the box and revealed a gigantic chrome X.

Rumors had surfaced that Sony would respond to Xbox's more advanced hardware by announcing a separate hard disk drive that gamers could purchase for the PS 2. But Bach pooh-poohed that idea, saying that developers would never make games that would make use of that hard drive because they could never be certain that all gamers would have it. That would automatically cut the potential customer base. And Bach took his potshots at Sony.

"Our Japanese garden demo requires more texture memory than the PS 2 has in its entire box," he said. "Sony is good at what they do. Are they unassailable? No. It's all about execution."

By the summer of 2000, Microsoft completed its initial software development kits for the Xbox. That helped the company gain credibility with developers. The company's launch was about 18 months away, and here it was already arming developers with the tools they needed to create games. These kits were plentiful, and they were as simple to use as PC game development kits. By comparison, Nintendo had only a few game development kits ready in late 2000, and it would be much later—in early 2001—before more advanced kits were ready. But, as usual, Nintendo's handpicked stable of internal developers and trusted outsiders received information about making games for the GameCube much earlier. That made it plausible for Nintendo to claim it would launch its GameCube console at the same time as the Xbox.

Sony gave Japanese developers barely nine months to get their titles out from the time they received their tools. It was no surprise that the Japanese PS 2 games were initially weak.

Around this time, Blackley decided that he needed to give a little morale boost to the troops. He called Tim Miller at Blur Studios again and asked him to rush out a new animation in two weeks. The demo—dubbed *Survival of the Fittest*—was a deep secret, and the public never got to see it. It showed Microsoft's Raven and Rex characters (the woman with the Xbox tattoo on her belly and the giant robot) at a shooting range. One by one, targets moved into their view. First came Sega's Sonic character, gagged and bound to a post. Raven and Rex shot at Sonic, and he disintegrated into red chunks. Next came Nintendo's Mario, who also exploded. Last came Sony's Crash Bandicoot, who got cut down by a laser. Blackley showed it to about 200 members of the Xbox team and the word quietly spread. On another occasion, the team held a small contest to figure out the best way to "kill the PS 2." One of the team members brought in a heavy-caliber automatic weapon and fired a huge round into a Sony machine. As always, Blackley acted first and asked forgiveness later.

On June 19, 2000, Fries announced the acquisition of Bungie Software, a game development house in Chicago. Though it had been around for a decade, Bungie was a small shop that had not yet had a hit that sold more than 200,000 units; as such, it wasn't too expensive for the budget-minded Ed Fries. Bungie was working on a hot PC title called *Halo,* a sci-fi shooting game that was so beautifully rendered that graphics chip makers used it to show off their latest chips. *Halo* was one of the potential mega-hits that Fries believed might inspire people to choose the Xbox over other consoles. *Halo*'s designers were shooting for the pinnacle of graphics in their design. They wanted players to be able to gaze at spectacular sunsets, star-strewn skies, and mist-shrouded waterfalls. Bungie had had hits before, but Fries had a chance to catch them before *Halo* put them into the unreachable orbit of overpriced stars. The deal was complicated since another publisher owned part of Bungie, but Fries's busy lieutenants figured out a way to acquire Bungie and make the other publisher happy too.

Unfortunately for Fries, Bungie happened to be one of the premiere companies that created games for Apple Computer's Macintosh machines. Bungie's programmers had even demoed *Halo* for the Mac crowd at the Macworld show in January. So after the announcement, Steve Ballmer got a surprise phone call from Steve Jobs, the brash and mercurial CEO of Apple. Ballmer passed it on to Robbie Bach, who passed it on to Ed Fries. Fries called back. Jobs screamed at Fries for a while. To smooth things over, Fries arranged to set up a new company that would take some of Bungie's titles and publish them for the Macintosh. Plus, Fries made an appearance at the next Macworld trade show to pledge that Microsoft, through the newly created company, would continue making games for Apple's machines.

Jason Jones, Bungie's technical lead on *Halo,* was jazzed about the Xbox because in the ten years that the company had been making games it had never had a game ready at the launch of a new console. This time, Jones was willing to bet big on the Xbox, even though that meant the company would have to rewrite most of the game that it had been working on for two years. Because there was so little time, Jones' team decided to focus on a single-player experience. Before, they had been contemplating a role-playing game where thousands of players could wander through the world of *Halo.* After the team moved to Redmond in the fall of 2000, they started tossing out ideas that wouldn't work.

"A lot of us were skeptical about doing a first-person shooter on a console instead of a PC," Jones said. "We believed we could make it work."

There was little more than a year to go before the game had to be finished. No one believed it yet, but Fries felt that he had secured a crucial game for the launch of the Xbox.

Bungie was just one of many deals that Fries had in the works. Sherry McKenna and Lorne Lanning of Oddworld Inhabitants were also attractive targets, but the courtship lasted a long time and it involved a series of chance events. McKenna and Lanning had formed Oddworld Inhabitants in 1994 in downtown San Luis Obispo, a small college town on the California coast. They convinced an investment banker to give them $3.5 million in venture capital, which allowed them to escape their jobs (working on Hollywood commercials and theme parks) and apply their special effects and computer animation skills to their own stories.

Lanning was an old arcade hound whose father worked at Colecovision. He saw games as a new medium where he could create characters and stories that could eventually be built into a movie franchise. McKenna, who had created theme park rides at Universal Studios Florida and worked on many films, was skeptical. Lanning convinced her to make games based around a set of five stories in the Oddworld Universe. The stories involved empathic little alien characters who had their own personalities, unlike most action-oriented video games. The game was laced with political messages pointing out the horrors of toxic waste, global warming, consumerism, exploitation of the poor, and animal testing. Always "embarrassed by shallow stories," Lanning felt that using the game's environment and story as a vehicle for a political statement could carry games to a new intellectual level without sacrificing a sense of irony and humor.

"I sat down with Sherry and said let me tell this story," Lanning says. "I said this was our most logical path on the road to making movies. I believed the games would catch up with the movies in terms of graphics resolution."

"I fell for it," says McKenna.

Abe's Oddysee and the sequel *Abe's Exxodus* were hits, selling more than 3 million units on the Sony PlayStation. But Oddworld's publisher, New York-based GT Interactive Software, began to implode in the late 1990s. McKenna went shopping for a publisher. In the back of her head, she fondly remembered her meetings with Steve Schreck when he was working at Broderbund Software before moving on to become a planner at Microsoft.

McKenna met Ed Fries for the first time at a restaurant in the middle of the Game Developers Conference in March 1999, shortly after the Xbox announcement. Fries was having dinner with another game executive. He came over to McKenna, who was dining with a Sony official. Fries pulled up a chair as if he and McKenna went way back and mentioned how much he admired Oddworld's games.

"You know each other," the Sony official asked, slightly suspiciously.

"We're old friends," Fries said.

McKenna played along but inside she was thinking, "Sony thinks I'm talking to Microsoft. This is the most uncomfortable conversation on the planet."

Meanwhile, Lanning and his crew of technicians were trying to figure out how to do their next game on the Sony PlayStation 2. They couldn't make it work. They were upset with the hassles of the system. They discovered problems like how they would have to create their own software for anti-aliasing—a technique for smoothing out the jagged lines of polygons in round animated objects—which they had expected the hardware to handle on its own.

They wanted a lot of action on the screen, but most of all they cared about facial expressions and eyes on the characters.

"A lot of game developers don't care about the eyes," McKenna said. "But we come from making motion pictures. We care about our characters more and much of the emotion and empathy starts with the eyes."

Lanning and McKenna had started hearing about Microsoft's Xbox project in the summer of 1999. Lanning liked what he heard. He wasn't happy with the lack of communication from

Sony about how to make the process of programming games for the PS 2 easier. Fries and Blackley sent emissaries to solicit their feedback.

"Microsoft did something very uncommon and asked us what we wanted in a console system," Lanning said.

At the E3 trade show in May 2000, McKenna was indeed talking to Microsoft again. Lanning was showing the art from the third installment of the Oddworld series to Steve Schreck. Then Bruno Bonnell, CEO of Infogrames, which had purchased Oddworld's publisher (GT) in 1999, walked in during the middle of the demo.

"We're busted," McKenna thought.

"I just smiled," Bonnell recalled. "I thought we could all be friendly here and work something out."

The talks continued through the summer. Microsoft's game managers told McKenna about the Xbox and their plans for it. Lanning was getting excited about its capabilities. He had switched from the PlayStation 2 to the PC. But now he was prepared to switch once again.

When Lanning began communicating with Blackley on technical details in the fall of 2000, he was impressed with Blackley's brilliance. But he did grow tired of how long it was taking Microsoft to make up its mind about the hardware.

In one early conversation, Lanning decided to exaggerate what he needed in his game so he could really figure out what the Xbox was capable of. He said he wanted the ability to put four dozen characters on the screen at the same time, with all sorts of lighting and shading effects and a huge landscape with 400 trees in the background and clouds passing overhead casting shadows.

"With the Xbox this should be a breeze, right?" Lanning asked.

He waited for Blackley's reaction.

"Dude!" Blackley yelled. "You're fucking high!"

Lanning admitted he was kidding, but only a little. His game was going to be ambitious, and he already knew that the

PlayStation 2 wasn't good enough to do what he had described. McKenna decided to hitch the company's fate to the Xbox, and she later cut a deal at an opportune moment.

Not every courtship was as long in the making. During the summer of 1999, Fries quietly hired Toshiyuki Miyata as the top Xbox game studio chief in Japan. He was the No. 2 man in Sony's games unit, but he wanted a chance to have more control. Microsoft's Japanese executives found him through a headhunter.

Miyata assembled a team of 100 game developers and quickly got them working on several big projects. He also signed up numerous companies to make third-party games for the Japanese Xbox market. Sony officials downplayed Miyata's importance, but it was one of a few blows that Microsoft would quietly deal to Sony in the guerilla action before the launch of the real war.

A DINNER BREAK IN KIRKLAND

In mid-July 2000, the Xbox team and its facilities in Redmond weren't that impressive. They were still in a remote part of the Microsoft campus, just across the street from Nintendo's U.S. headquarters. Nintendo staffers commonly came over to have lunch with their friends at Microsoft, and to hear gossip about the Xbox.

In the warren of offices, the Xbox team members were all squished into small cubicle-size rooms, but everybody had a door that would close for privacy. Preparations were under way to move the team to its new offices in another part of Redmond, where the team could gather in Horace Luke's custom-designed "war room," splashed with the green colors that adorned the Xbox logo. But for the present the effort looked just like any other part of the Microsoft empire, except for the workshop of Horace Luke, who was like a proud father when he showed off his still-secret design for the Xbox. His office was decked with hundreds of drawings of Xbox prototypes and pictures of inspirational consumer electronics products like audio amplifiers.

That evening, the leaders of the Xbox project dined with a journalist from the *Red Herring* magazine at the Yarrow Bay Grill, a seafood restaurant at Carrillon Point, an upscale district along the shores of Lake Washington. Ed Fries pointed out the general direction of Bill Gates's mammoth 40,000-square-foot home on the shores of the lake, as well as the abodes of various other Microsoft executives.

J Allard and Seamus Blackley consumed a considerable amount of wine, and Allard wasn't pleased with his meal and said so to the waiter. The group was the loudest in the restaurant, even though it had quiet folks in it like Kevin Bachus and Ed Fries. Over the course of the dinner, the crew contemplated why games weren't bigger than movies yet. The conversation jumped around the table, with lots of interruptions. Everyone spoke rapid-fire, in one-liners, just to steal the stage for a moment.

Blackley was characteristically the first to chime in, noting how gaming in Japan and Korea was massive. In England, he noted, TV shows about video games aired during prime time. Bachus said the U.S. demographics for gaming were too narrow, with males between 16 and 26 accounting for the lion's share of the market. Carrie Cowan, from the public relations department, said that the media hadn't caught on yet, noting that game reviews still weren't appearing in many mainstream publications. Allard said, "There are no stars, no heroes, no Tom Cruises, no Steven Spielbergs."

Fries piped in, breaking through his louder compatriots with some difficulty, to say, "We have not made something that I could put in front of Mom and Dad. It's about accessibility. There is a pessimistic view: We have to wait for all those people who don't play games to die. Then the younger audience will become more mature."

Allard noted how there were no heroes in games like Microsoft's *Age of Empires,* and the creators of the games weren't viewed as rock stars. Fries shot back, "There is no point in trying to make the authors of movies famous, like the people who write the screenplays. Lara Croft (the digital vixen character of *Tomb Raider*) is famous, and that's how it should be."

Blackley noted how so many of the veterans of the games industry had started when it was a hobbyist market, and they were still making games that appealed to narrow audiences. Looking Glass, he noted, wanted to make the "literature of the games business." Meanwhile, the moviemakers had tried their hand at games in the early 1990s and failed miserably with games that were spliced with too much video that left the player bored and inactive.

The lessons of 3DO? "Duh, the price can't be $700. It has to be right for the consumer market," Blackley said. Bachus stopped the table chatter cold when he asked, "What is Jumbo the Elephant?"

No one answered until Fries piped in and said, "Emotion. Sony used that word to describe their console's processor. Games just don't make you cry like a movie."

Blackley went on a roll, talking about how games had no formal theory behind them, no common language, as he had often heard Doug Church of Looking Glass say. The reporter asked if anyone could write a book called *Understanding Games* as an analogue to *Understanding Comics,* a seminal 1993 book by Scott McCloud, who described how comics had evolved into a unique art form.[1]

Several chimed in and said not so far, as long as the technology kept changing so fast that programmers dominated game creation, as opposed to artists. The reporter doubted that games could ever catch up.

But Blackley said, "We are going after TV. Why is Microsoft in this business? To kill TV."

Fries added, "Games can be more compelling. I have to just build the right product."

Blackley said, "Games are interactive. They have the twitch factor that makes us like games."

Bachus said, "I think eBay is the most popular game on the Internet. . . ."

He couldn't finish that thought, since Allard said, "Nasdaq is a fucking game, duh."

The conversation went on like that for a while. The wine was plentiful. The reporter asked about the Japanese and the opportunity for the Xbox. Was it limited by a fear of Microsoft?

Bachus said, "I talk to the third-party software publishers and they aren't afraid of us taking over the entire business on our console as they are with Nintendo. But they do worry if we'll give an unfair advantage to their competitors."

Could Xbox be the console that favors American game developers, the same way it was perceived that Sony and Nintendo favored the Japanese developers?

"No," Allard stated flatly. "It's a worldwide business."

"All of us spend more time in Japan and Europe than we do here," Blackley said.

Yes, these dudes had come a long way since Project Midway. They didn't just want to defeat the Japanese. They wanted to rule the world.

21

MOMENTUM

NEWS ON THE XBOX WAS SPARSE in the summer of 2000. In an update for a key vendor, Microsoft said it expected to sell 100 million Xbox consoles over four years. The company had wildly optimistic expectations that Nvidia would finish a preliminary version of its graphics chip design by September 29, barely six months after the contract was signed. The first sample chips were scheduled to emerge from a factory in Taiwan on October 30. Production silicon was expected to begin shipping on February 7, 2001. After months of testing, production of the systems was expected to start on June 15, 2001. And by October 12, 2001, Microsoft expected to have

1 million Xbox units on store shelves. Needless to say, the company didn't keep this schedule. Todd Holmdahl, Microsoft's hardware chief, always knew that the schedule was too aggressive. But his team was figuring out contingencies for what would happen if key projects slipped.

In one sense, doing the Xbox graphics chip was an easier task than working on a graphics chip from scratch. The Xbox would combine the GeForce 3 graphics with other components from the nForce integrated chipset. About 90 percent of the components of the Xbox graphics chip could be borrowed from the already finished chips. But stitching the two chips together was no easy task, and Nvidia had to create new components such as a more efficient memory management unit. The chips would rely on hardware from AMD: the hypertransport data pathway that would connect the Intel microprocessor with the rest of the system. That was the one piece that AMD was able to contribute to the box.

In early August, Robbie Bach said in a speech at the Ziff Davis Games Summit that his team had just approved 20 game proposals that week. He had invited 300 game developers to attend Xfest—a developers' conference in Seattle—and it was clear that everyone now saw they needed to create original titles for the Xbox, not just refashion previously created PC games. Microsoft's Japan group was starting to make headway with Japanese developers.

The Japanese Xbox team scored a deal with Tecmo Ltd., the publisher that made the *Dead or Alive* series of fighting games. Blackley took a crew to show off Xbox demos at the company's headquarters in Tokyo. He met Tomonobu Itagaki, the leader of the company's Team Ninja studio that created the series. Itagaki was one of the most open-minded of the Japanese developers. If the Xbox could do the job, he would make his next game, *Dead or Alive 3,* for that machine. Blackley was a big fan of *Dead or Alive* and was pumped to meet Itagaki. After coming out of the meeting, Blackley hugged his fellow presenters. It was one of their first big successes in Japan. Itagaki and Blackley clicked despite the language barrier, and Itagaki trusted Blackley. Much of Tecmo's communication with Microsoft went through Blackley after that meeting. Tecmo was an underdog compared to Japan's other big publishers, and so Itagaki felt a kinship with the underdogs at Microsoft. He even invited Blackley over to his apartment for dinner, which other Tecmo friends saw as a rare honor. Eventually, Itagaki liked the performance of the Xbox so much that Tecmo made *DOA 3* an Xbox exclusive for a limited time period.

Shortly after the Ziff Davis Summit, Nintendo announced the details of its GameCube console at its Tokyo Space World conference. The box was going to be a tiny machine, only six inches by six inches by five inches. It was powered by an IBM Power PC Gekko microprocessor and a Flipper graphics chip created by the ArtX subsidiary of ATI Technologies. The machine didn't have a hard drive, and it had smaller memory storage than the Xbox. Nintendo was shooting for a much lower-cost system than either Sony or Microsoft. The system also had a different kind of DVD disc, a smaller one that stored less data yet couldn't be copied as easily by pirates. Hence, the GameCube wouldn't play DVD movies, in contrast to the Xbox and PS 2. That smaller disc might also be used one day in a portable device.

The company showed in demos that it was taking its classic Zelda franchise into the age of dazzling 3-D graphics. Game news Web sites posted videos of the demos, and they created a download mania. Yet Nintendo showed so little else that game reviewers were skeptical that it would be able to meet its goal of shipping systems by the fall of 2001. After all, the game development kits that developers needed were still nowhere in sight. Microsoft still seemed to have a head start.

Then again, everyone knew that Nintendo focused on its internal development studios rather than on third-party publishers. No doubt, those teams had been engaged in making new games for a long time. Julian Eggebrecht, president of Factor 5, a game developer in San Rafael, California, had access to early GameCube information. But that was because his company's previous big game, *Star Wars: Rogue Squadron* (developed for LucasArts Entertainment), had been a huge hit on the Nintendo 64. Eggebrecht's company had contributed research on sound libraries and for the sound chip on the GameCube, which also gave the company advance information. Mostly, the efforts of Nintendo's internal studios remained a mystery. Thus Nintendo inadvertently caused a mad rush to develop games for the Xbox.

Not only did Horace Luke get passionate about designing the box, he felt the team had to have its own distinct place. He nicknamed his work space Area Xbox. Then he helped design the permanent home of the Xbox team. Most Microsoft teams didn't have real identities of their own in Microsoft's sprawling headquarters. But the Xbox team was able to commandeer a three-story office building in the Millennium office park across town from the main campus. Luke designed the lobby and the main meeting room. In the lobby, the trademark glowing green and white colors of the box were splashed everywhere. An Xbox logo hung above the main desk. Upstairs, the conference room was similarly washed in green. It had a wall of storyboards for meetings and a DVD player with a big-screen projector. The meeting room and the lobby communicated that the Xbox was special and it was here to stay, Luke said. As a reward for his relentless work on the Xbox designs, Luke earned a permanent job in the middle of 2001. He later shifted out of the project to redesign one of the crown jewels of Microsoft, the Windows logo.

In September 2000, the Xbox team moved into its own headquarters at last. Blackley lobbied heavily to get the Advanced Technology Group into a section of the building that could be separated by locked doors. He saw them as symbols of fairness. "I didn't want the risk of having a Microsoft first-party guy come into our offices and then see descriptions of games or actual game code being created by the third-party game developers," Blackley said. He succeeded for a time but then lost the locked doors as Microsoft shuffled people around. Avril Daly put signs on the doors that said "electrical closet," and that helped keep unwelcome visitors out. A sign on one office said, "Our confidential materials are larger than your confidential materials." J Allard said he took the division so seriously that game proposals for first-party games were printed on green paper and those for third-party games were printed on purple paper. "If we saw any green paper in the third-party offices, we knew it didn't belong there," Allard said.

Now it was Microsoft's turn to strike back with some news. On September 1, 2000, the company announced it had made alliances with 17 game developers to make first-party games: that is, games that would be published under Microsoft's brand name. In addition to building up its internal game studios, Microsoft was relying on the common industry practice of outsourcing much of its game development to the geniuses who preferred to run their own companies. It seeded the companies with lots of money and computers, and in return the companies would spend their time making Xbox exclusive games.

The star of the group was the legendary Peter Molyneux, whose Lionhead Studios was working on a mammoth PC game, *Black and White,* that promised to be a runaway bestseller. A so-called god game, it allowed players to become gods with the power to create and lord over their very own world, full of subjects who prayed for mercy. The players could be as good or as cruel to those subjects as they wanted. A similar Molyneux title, *Populous,* had much cruder graphics when it debuted more than a decade earlier, yet it sold more than 4 million copies worldwide. Now Molyneux said that after he finished *Black and White,* he would embark upon making games for the Xbox, mainly because it had the technology to finally make his decade-old visions real.

Microsoft scored a few of Sony's developers, like sports game producer Stormfront Studios and Universal Interactive Studios. Yet most of the developers had backgrounds in the PC industry, leading critics to wonder if Microsoft truly understood the challenge of making games for a console. Included in the group was Pipeworks Software, the friends of Blackley who had done the demos for the Xbox debut. And Fries had packed his in-house development ranks with lots of veterans who came from Sierra Studios, which was also based in Seattle, as well as Dynamix, a company that Sierra's new owner, Vivendi Universal, had shut down.

At the ECTS trade show where the announcements were made, the Xbox team joined together in a drunken revel in London with Peter Molyneux, who had created seven No. 1 hits in his 41-year lifetime. Inside the Pharmacy restaurant and bar, Blackley started lighting absinthes on fire. Blackley and Molyneux debated each other on who was more pathetic. They ordered three bottles of absinthe—a strong liqueur banned in many countries but once popular among artists like van Gogh for its hallucinatory effects—and drank them all. During the revelry they came close to burning Molyneux's eyebrows off. Allard joined them. They moved on to another party. Then they went outside and tried to hijack a garbage truck. They couldn't get the truck started and were chased away by the annoyed truck driver.

Then, on September 20, 2000, the Xbox team unveiled its third-party publishers. A week before the event, Kevin Bachus was calling up all of the game publishers. He said that Microsoft would be announcing its third-party partners. Would they sign on? The first list in the draft press release had 75 companies. But, by the time the release went out, more than 150 third-party game publishers and developers had signed up to make Xbox games. Fries expected them to account for at least two-thirds of all sales on the Xbox.

Included were hotshot Japanese companies like Konami, which planned to move its top PlayStation franchises, *Metal*

Gear and *Silent Hill,* to the Xbox. Other big names included Activision (however skeptical its CEO Bobby Kotick was), Capcom Ltd., Eidos, Hasbro Interactive, Havas Interactive, Infogrames Entertainment, Midway Games, and THQ. Against the odds and despite suspected pressure from Sony and Nintendo, Kevin Bachus's team had convinced many of the best Sony and Nintendo developers to make games for the Xbox.

When Microsoft unveiled the list in San Francisco, J Allard reeled off all the names as fast as he could. After the press event, game developers talked about how easy it was to do Xbox games. Brian Upton, director of development at Red Storm Entertainment, said it was much harder to start from scratch on PS 2 games than to take the code for a PC game and tailor it to the Xbox. He noted that, a month from the launch of the PS 2 in the United States, he had no clue how to write a networked game for Sony's machine. But, because of the PC-based standards, his team already knew how to make a networked game for the Xbox.

Microsoft had pretty much made a clean sweep in rounding up support worldwide for the Xbox. Kevin Bachus negotiated and signed lots of contracts during this time. Inside Sega, there were rumblings. Peter Moore, president of Sega of America, started making contingency plans on whether Sega should get out of the hardware business because of sagging sales of the Dreamcast. In the fall of 2000, Sega quietly accepted its first development kits for the PlayStation 2, and it was in talks with both Nintendo and Microsoft about acquiring development kits for their systems too. Sega was taking baby steps toward abandoning its hardware and focusing on software.

Still, at the Xbox press conference, Sega was nowhere to be found. And there were a couple of key publishers missing. Where, everyone asked, were Electronic Arts and Square?

EA's CEO, Larry Probst, had suggested he would make games for the Xbox, but no deal had been struck yet. Square also appeared to be lagging in its talks with Microsoft. Numerous efforts by Fries didn't pan out. The Xbox team met with Visual

Concepts, a sports game studio in Northern California that made the top-selling football and basketball games for Sega's Dreamcast. Microsoft tried to steal away the team, but they were happy with Sega. As a result, Fries commissioned Microsoft's own sports game studio to start work on Xbox games.

Fries made a bid to get the game rights to the tremendously popular *Harry Potter* series. Fries had even invested time by reading all of J. K. Rowling's books. This license had the potential to give Microsoft a sentence huge "mascot" character for its game console, and the Potter series had been specifically named by Rick Thompson in December 1999 as one of the key properties that could get the Xbox off the ground. But Electronic Arts outbid Fries, spending tens of millions of dollars on the license. Fries feared he lost because of an alliance: The books' publisher was part of AOL Time Warner. And EA had a deal to publish games on America Online. It was all in the same mass media family, and one of the rare times when Microsoft was on the losing side of a set of alliances. In addition, EA could offer a better deal to Rowling because it could sell its games across a variety of console platforms, not just the Xbox.

In addition, Fries had a chance to court Naughty Dog, the Santa Monica, California, game development studio that had created Sony's spectacular hit, *Crash Bandicoot. Crash* was one of those rare franchise games that sold well in Europe, Japan, and the United States—more than 22 million copies worldwide.

Jason Rubin and Andy Gavin created Naughty Dog as a couple of 16-year-olds in 1986. They went on to minor successes in console games until they came up with *Crash Bandicoot,* a quirky marsupial character who became Sony's answer to Nintendo's Mario and Sega's Sonic. The game was an instant hit on the PlayStation and it led to three sequels. In the fall of 2000, Naughty Dog was at a crossroads. Some programmers had heard about the Xbox and wanted to switch to the new machine.

Rubin called Ed Fries at Microsoft and asked him to visit the company in Santa Monica. Fries went down and gave Rubin the pitch. But Rubin and Gavin didn't buy it. They felt at the time that Microsoft wouldn't come up with the kind of performance it was promising. Fries felt like it was fruitless to make a bid for Naughty Dog. He said he didn't want to get in a bidding war with Sony over the company if Rubin was so happy with Sony. Rubin said he didn't mind the programming challenge of the PlayStation 2. So they parted ways. At the end of 2000, Sony agreed to buy Naughty Dog and bring it into the fold.

Finally, there was one more setback. David Wu of Pseudo Interactive suffered another heartbreaker. Wu had previously had his cartoon-based car combat PC game canceled by Microsoft because it was too console-like. He then received a $3 million advance from Microsoft to work it up for the Xbox. Ed Fries called Wu on Christmas Day, 2000. Fries told Wu politely that he had decided to cancel his game once again. After running some focus tests, the Microsoft marketing department couldn't figure out how to sell such an unusual game. And upon reviewing it, Fries decided that it would do OK but wouldn't be a top seller. On top of that, Wu's game hadn't shown much progress on the art. At first, the cartoon characters in the game had been targeted to younger children. But as the mission of the Xbox morphed to focus on 16- to 26-year-old males, Wu's artists were asked to focus on cooler characters that could appeal to teens and adults. That put the artists behind schedule.

Wu was thunderstruck at his bad luck. It was a depressing Christmas. He thought about shutting down his company, which had 18 employees. Blackley disagreed and clashed with Fries over it, to no avail. Wu shopped the title around again, with some assistance from Microsoft. After talking to 20 different people among game publishers, he finally landed one. Electronic Arts agreed to publish *Cel Damage,* and it planned to make it one of its first titles for the Xbox. Microsoft's loss, however small given the limited potential of the game to be a runaway hit, was EA's gain.

CHAPTER 22

SETTING RECORDS, MISSING EXPECTATIONS

SONY MADE BIG NEWS in October 2000. The company scaled back its forecast of PlayStation 2 sales from 10 million to 9 million boxes, and it pushed back its launch date in Europe so it could ship more boxes to the United States. That was because it fouled up manufacturing of its graphics chips. The delays alienated retailers and software developers who were counting on brisk PS 2 sales for the Christmas season. Now, only 500,000 units would be available at the U.S. launch, not 1 million as promised.

In Japan, the launch had gone well. Even though Sega had launched Dreamcast earlier, for most observers, the inauguration of the "next generation" began with the launch of the PlayStation 2 in Japan on March 4, 2000. Nearly a million units sold in the first weekend. One poor kid lost his newly purchased machine when two muggers knocked him off his bike and stole the briefcase-size blue box from him. But a few months into Japanese sales, retailers were griping that nobody was buying games. It turned out that Sony had walked straight into a market anomaly. In Japan, consumers were just warming up to digital video disc players, which replaced analog VCRs, but the players were still expensive—well over $400. Since Sony's machine included a DVD player for free and cost only $360, many consumers bought the machines so they could watch movies—they didn't care about games.

Next came the U.S. launch. For Sony, this debut on October 26, 2000, wasn't just another new toy for Christmas. Together with the Japan launch, the event marked the beginning of the game trade's most ambitious assault on the broader entertainment market.

On October 17, Microsoft announced to retailers that it had snared Oddworld Inhabitants as a developer. Lorne Lanning and Sherry McKenna would now make the third game in the Oddworld series, *Munch's Oddyssee,* as an exclusive first-party Microsoft title for the Xbox. The deal was complex because Oddworld was under contract for the game with the French publisher, Infogrames. But one of Fries's aggressive product planners, Steve Schreck, had known Oddworld's CEO, Sherry McKenna, from past attempts to recruit her, and Kevin Bachus had steered Fries to Oddworld because he knew that Infogrames was willing to entertain a joint publishing deal.

Schreck and McKenna and Infogrames, as well as lawyers from both sides, worked 36 hours straight to finish the deal by October 17. In what McKenna called one of the "nightmares of my life," they cut an elaborate deal and signed the papers with minutes to spare. Fries had two copies of his speech ready. As his aide told him about the signing, he went with the first speech and told the retailers he had just signed one of Sony's developers. Bruno Bonnell of Infogrames was growing more excited about the Xbox. His teams had decided to do 10 games for the Xbox, and soon Bonnell would increase that to 25 games. "The more we looked at the machine, the more comfortable we were," he said.

In San Francisco, Sony staged the launch at its entertainment mall, the Metreon, a complex full of movie theaters, arcades, restaurants, and its own PlayStation store. The midnight scene was like a movie premiere, with searchlights, big blue signs, executives in limousines, camera crews with obnoxious young reporters—and a line of die-hard fans who had waited overnight to purchase the units for $299 each.

Scarcity had made the machines more valuable in the eyes of fans. The young crowd at the front of the line regarded their mission as attaining a status symbol of modern society. They wanted to be the first to experience the next wave of coolness.

Paul Krivda, a 23-year-old Lenscrafters lab technician, didn't really care about the clash between Sony and Microsoft. All he knew was that he was the lucky man who got the first PS 2 just a little after midnight. He walked into the Sony store amid a crowd of cheering onlookers shouting "PS 2! PS 2! PS 2!" and the bright lights of four TV cameras. By that time, he had been interviewed several dozen times by reporters. After buying the console, Krivda held it above his head like a trophy, and began to high-five his friends—and the complete strangers who had bonded with him during the wait.

It was just like the launch of the Sega Dreamcast a year earlier, but no one stopped to think that the Dreamcast was already forgotten. Next in line at the Metreon was Nathaniel Sinlao, a 24-year-old student at San Francisco State University. He said, "This is just like waiting for *Episode I*," referring to the experience of waiting for the latest *Star Wars* movie. "This," he said, "is my 15 minutes of fame." Further down the line, Darryl Evans, a 29-year-old chauffeur, said, "It's a wonderful experience, it's a once-in-a-lifetime experience."

Despite the lack of first-party titles and the chip shortage, it was a good enough start. Unit sales were taking off three times faster than the original PlayStation. It was scary enough for Microsoft. By the time the Xbox launched, Sony might easily have 20 million PS 2s in the market. Kunitake Ando, president of Sony, admitted during a dinner at the Comdex computer trade show in Las Vegas in November that his company had been very worried about Microsoft when they first announced the Xbox.

"But now that we have launched the PS 2, we are not so worried anymore," he said.

Still, the shortage took its toll. Toysrus.com sold out of its allocation to online customers within 23 seconds. So customers had to cruise the auction Web site eBay and pay enormous markups if they wanted to get a PS 2 by Christmas. Sony's officials said they were unsure when they would catch up to demand. Retailers started taking pre-orders for the Xbox, and they were doubly upset at Sony when it asked them to take down the Xbox signs in their stores. Although stories circulated on the Net that the Babbage's chain faced pressure, Sony denied that it was threatening to withhold supplies of PS 2 hardware and software from retailers who didn't comply.

Perhaps the most damaging to Sony was the cost among publishers who now felt they had to diversify to other platforms. Software publishers like Electronic Arts were reporting unexpected earnings shortfalls because they had been counting on bigger sales of PS 2 software in the fourth quarter. Electronic Arts showed up at the Xbox party with its own press announcement in December 2000. The company committed its 12 internal studios to fully support the Xbox. EA said it planned to launch 10 titles in the Xbox's first six months on the market. It had ordered more than 500 software development kits from Microsoft. That effort was only somewhat smaller than the 15 games it had committed to do during the first six months of the PS 2.

In December 2000, Microsoft announced that it would postpone its European launch until 2002. Robbie Bach had watched Sony's launch hardships, and he was determined to have enough machines on hand for the key U.S. and Japanese markets. He also announced within Microsoft that he had pushed back the date of the U.S. launch from October 10, 2001—known internally as X/X/01—until sometime in November 2001. Internally, the optimistic schedules were falling apart. Nvidia was running behind schedule; it would have its first sample of its graphics chip done on January 22, 2001, rather than October 30, 2000. The sample availability of Nvidia's second chip, the media and communications processor, had also slipped, from August 15 to December 22, 2000. Nonetheless, the company still had bright expectations for beginning Xbox console production on June 15, 2001.

Around this time, Robbie Bach and the executive team adopted a five-year plan for their "purpose and principles." They laid down a bunch of ground rules that expressed their mission. It included goals such as making sure that the Xbox would contribute to Microsoft's bottom line. The Xbox had to beat the PlayStation 2 as the No. 1 game console: "Being a good No. 2 is not acceptable." It said that the Xbox would use Microsoft technology where appropriate, but it would not be compelled to use every company technology. The document was a road map for resolving strategy conflicts with other parts of Microsoft and for emphasizing the mission to deliver the best gaming experience.

Microsoft announced that Singapore-based contract manufacturer Flextronics International Ltd. would manufacture the Xbox at factories in Hungary and Mexico. Flextronics would make 957,000 Xbox machines in the second quarter of 2001. It would make 2.27 million in the third quarter of 2001. And it would make another 1.7 million in the fourth quarter of 2001, for a grand total of 4.93 million by the end of 2001. With such big numbers projected, Microsoft still believed it would be able to launch in the United States and Japan in October 2001. It would even be able to supply Europe. But it was too risky to expect that the supply chain would work perfectly.

Microsoft would also put off the launch of the online games for the Xbox until about six months after the launch in the United States. Now that much of the work on the operating system for the Xbox was done, Cameron Ferroni took about a dozen people and formed a group to focus on online games.

They faced tough questions, since the openness of the PC allowed for a free-wheeling online games environment. Developers often released tools that enabled players to create their own custom battlefields to extend the games they bought on store shelves. But Ferroni's team foresaw that the console needed to be bullet-proof in terms of security from hackers and viruses. That meant that Xbox players couldn't play against PC players.

Over the next year, they began developing policies to govern how online games would work. Everywhere they ran into tough choices. On the PC, many games sent players directly to online portals such as Microsoft's MSN Gaming Zone. Because so much traffic concentrated at these sites, they became magnets for online advertising. But the Internet bubble was deflating and online ads were losing their appeal. Plus, online portals took away from the gaming experience. Ferroni wanted Xbox players to launch their games, go online, and find others to fight. They didn't need to waste time outside the game at portals. The problem here was that it eliminated a big source of revenue in terms of lost advertising.

Microsoft had to limit the ability to download new content to stop viruses and other security problems. That angered PC developers such as Richard Garriott, developer of the *Ultima Online* series, who wanted more freedom. Electronic Arts was annoyed that Ferroni decided to require players to visit Microsoft servers first for authentication, saying that they didn't want anyone between the publisher and the customers. But Ferroni said that Microsoft could quickly hand off players to servers operated by game publishers after authentication. They also had to make sure that any new content developed for a game by players had to be tested first either by Microsoft or by publishers. Tim Sweeney of Epic felt that process would be too bureaucratic to allow a community of player-creators to flower. But he still decided to focus on making *Unreal Championship* into one of the first major multiplayer games for the Xbox.

"We decided we couldn't violate the rules of being a console, like how things always have to work no matter what," Ferroni said. "You certify people to make console games, so the same should be true certifying people in making online console games."

Fleshing out all these details would take dozens more employees and months of work, so it only made sense to postpone the online game launches until after Microsoft successfully established the Xbox in the market. And Microsoft was working hard with developers like Sega Sports, but it also had to make sure that there would be enough online games available when the service launched. Ferroni wanted to open a Disney World for gamers, but first he had to build the ticket booths and parking lots.

Blackley and Bachus continued their worldwide tour. On a visit to Japan in December 2000, they had a hard time because many of the Japanese publishers wanted special deals that would allow them to pay lower royalties on games. To Microsoft, this smacked of the favoritism that Sony and Nintendo were known for. But to the Japanese, it was a matter of respect. Microsoft should recognize the value that their key partners would bring to the Xbox. Many still wanted lower royalties even though Microsoft offered marketing dollars that might have been even more valuable. They were only somewhat mollified when Microsoft said it would provide a rebate for any third-party partner whose games sold above a certain number of units, akin to earning free rewards in a frequent flyer program.

In their last meeting in Japan, they discussed the Xbox plans with Shinji Mikami, head of development at Japan's Capcom and creator of the *Resident Evil* game series. The Japanese Xbox crew talked in Japanese with Mikami, and it was clear something was wrong. Bachus passed notes to his colleagues saying they should just end the meeting, but they ignored him. Mikami kept asking what was the vision of the Xbox team. The meeting ended, but Bachus kept trying to figure out what Mikami wanted to know, since much of the time the meeting was conducted in Japanese and he couldn't understand it. After the meeting, a translator said that Nintendo's Shigeru Miyamoto had argued that "game is toy" was his company's vision. Ken Kutaragi had argued that "game is entertainment." Mikami had asked, "What was Microsoft's vision?" Bachus answered, "Game is art." Too bad Mikami didn't get to hear that, the translator said. Bachus slapped his forehead since he and Blackley had been using that phrase countless times with Western developers. Bachus later dispatched the top Japanese Xbox officers to meet with Mikami, but it was too late. Capcom would later announce that it would make *Resident Evil* exclusive to the Nintendo GameCube. Another game, *Devil May Cry,* was too far along to be moved off the PlayStation 2. In spite of Bachus's clever pitch, Capcom had lost much faith in Microsoft. It would be some time before it came back.

CHAPTER 23

THE SOUL OF A BAD-ASS MACHINE

A YEAR EARLIER, BILL GATES had to keep quiet about the Xbox when he made a speech at the Consumer Electronics Show in Las Vegas. But now, in the first week of January 2001, everyone knew what was coming. A line of fans snaked through the Hilton hotel casino, waiting to get into Gates's keynote speech.

Almost everyone in the theater had come to see the Xbox. So, of course, the Xbox was the last thing Gates talked about. He meandered through his speech, mentioning the next version of Windows software, the new Ultimate TV product coming from WebTV, and a bunch of little handheld

PocketPC machines. When his employees came on stage to demo the products, Gates was lifeless. He asked few questions and, after one demo, he said quietly "Super." Then he became more animated and gave a big smile when he started talking about the Xbox.

"Well, digital electronics in the home isn't complete without talking about video games," he began his real pitch. Games, he said, were ready for some breakthroughs in hardware and software.

"So a few years ago we were sitting around talking about, how could we help make this happen? And some of the really hardcore gamers at Microsoft said, well, we could just do it. And the first time they said that it sounded pretty crazy, but they kept coming back."

The end result of that, he said, was the machine under that black drape. Gates unveiled it, and the crowd broke into applause. This machine had gone through a complete redesign since Horace Luke had created the chrome-finished X-shaped showpiece. Now it was black, with a silver X across its top, and the green-jeweled X logo emblazoned on it like a coat of arms. This was the design, one of more than 100 Luke had created, that made it to the finish line.

It was sleek and functional, able to start games in 11 seconds after the player pressed the start button. The box, Gates proclaimed, would support high-definition television displays and have a connector to hook up to high-speed Internet connections through phone or cable TV systems.

To demo the box, Gates invited Blackley out on the stage. Blackley came out and got a good laugh because he sported some enormous red hiking boots. The inside nerd's joke was that the boots were colored "illegal red," the color that developers knew they couldn't use in games because it showed up as green on TV monitors. Blackley wanted game developers to know that Microsoft understood them.

"Hi Bill. So, it's good to see you, Bill," Blackley said.

Then Blackley launched into a couple of demos. One was Lorne Lanning's creation, *Munch's Oddyssee,* a spectacular 3-D game that featured goofy-looking alien creatures whose faces reflected detail down to the glint of reflections in their eyes. Blackley noted that this game had been liberated from the developers' imagination by the technological power of the Xbox. The characters looked real enough to tug at the audience's heartstrings, even though the demo was only running at a fifth of the Xbox's actual speed.

"One of the basic premises of the Xbox is to put power in the hands of the artists," Blackley said.

Next, Blackley showed a demo of *Malice,* in which a little girl with a big hammer goes around smashing cockroaches. He pointed out that the visual richness of the game matched the best that was achieved in the animated film *Toy Story,* which for years had been hailed as a breakthrough in computer animation. Looking at the 3-D images on the screen, everyone could see that it wasn't an exaggeration. The developer, Jez San's Argonaut, had pulled off some tricks that no one had been able to do yet. As Blackley handled the controller, the little girl smashed bugs. "That is one bad-ass little girl," he said, drawing laughs and winning a bet that he could work "bad-ass" into his demonstration, as he had a year earlier at GDC. Blackley maneuvered the little girl into a room with a giant robot. As the girl moved, the robot mimicked her actions. The girl jumped up in the air, and the robot jumped too. The robot's head crashed through the ceiling and got stuck. The robot was just hanging in the air, and the audience was cracking up as Blackley ended the demo.

Then Gates got cool. Blackley left the stage and Gates was joined by "the Rock," a staple on the World Wrestling Federation and a hero to gamers—who bought wrestling video games by the millions. The pair got into a comedy routine, with the Rock saying, "At first glance, to the untrained eye it might appear that the Rock and Bill Gates don't have a heck of a lot in common. Well, the Rock is here to say that can't be farther from the truth. . . . Both the Rock and Bill Gates stand at the top of their industries. Both the Rock and Bill Gates are best-selling authors. And both the Rock and Bill Gates are known worldwide for their vast array of catch phrases. For example, the Rock has, know your role and shut your mouth . . . and, of course, the world renowned, if you smell what the Rock is cooking. And Bill Gates, you have some pretty cool catch phrases as well. . . ."

"My favorite is probably writing hardcore C to create slick, tight code," Gates said.

The routine went on and, at one point, Gates interrupted and said, "Well I think that. . . ."

Then the Rock interjected, "It doesn't matter what you think, Bill!" That drew a roar of laughter, and the Rock feigned an apology. "It's a force of habit," he said. The Rock gave his endorsement, and since wrestling had become a huge genre in games, that meant a lot.

After the Rock left the stage, a beaming Gates and a reawakened audience walked out. Blackley began giving hugs to members of his team. The Xbox was the talk of the show. One game publisher was disappointed. The Rock made his appearance at the special request of THQ, which published games based on the WWF license. But Gates forgot to mention THQ during the speech. "I scratched their back and mine is still itching," said Brian Farrell, CEO of THQ in Calabasas, California. "They still owe me one."

That evening, Blackley and the Xbox team gathered for a dinner with the press at the Rum Jungle, a tony restaurant at the sprawling Mandalay Bay Hotel. Asked where his red boots were, Blackley replied, "We're back down to DefCon 1," meaning things were back to normal and he didn't need his boots anymore. (In the Pentagon's jargon, DefCon 5 refers to an active nuclear war, and the numbers lower to increasingly calm conditions. It was the sort of military nerd-speak that endeared him to the developers.)

Blackley bounced around from table to table, charming the press. The dinner gave way to a big Microsoft party. But not everyone had a great time. Kevin Bachus and Chanel Summers had trouble getting past the bouncers at the Rum Jungle. Microsoft had failed to make provisions for everyone to get inside. One bouncer motioned for Summers to proceed, but another stopped her and pressed his hand to her chest. She knocked away his hand and the bouncer told her to step out of the line. Bachus hopped over a rope to come to her assistance, and the bouncers got angrier. They told the couple they could either leave the hotel or be arrested. Bachus said they were staying at the hotel, so the bouncers now said they had to go up to their room and stay there. Bachus and Summers did so and called the hotel manager. The hotel manager apologized, took them down to the Rum Jungle, and tried to get them inside. But the bar manager stood by his bouncers and refused to let them in. Blackley came out and claimed he was a vice president at Microsoft. He insisted that he needed Summers inside immediately because an MTV film crew wanted to interview her. Only then did the bouncers relent.

NVIDIA CRANKS OUT ITS CHIPS

The Xbox love fest continued on February 14, 2001. A year after the St. Valentine's Day Massacre, Nvidia announced that it had released to manufacturing both the Xbox Graphics Processing Unit (XGPU) and the Media Communications Processor (MCP). It was a triumph for Nvidia's engineers, many of whom had joined the company in December when it acquired the assets of 3Dfx Interactive. (Among the 120 engineers Nvidia picked up in that deal was Rami Friedlander, who'd been GigaPixel's chief of engineering, so he at least brought a GigaPixel presence to the Xbox.)

Wall Street welcomed the news that the chip designs had been completed because it was a big milestone. If Nvidia was finished with the design of the chips more than seven months before the launch of the Xbox, the odds were good that Nvidia's chip production would be smooth, in contrast to the tough launch that Sony had. Later events showed this reaction was misplaced, but it made the investors happy at the time.

The final XGPU wasn't as fast as Microsoft originally promised. Nvidia had expected it to run at 300 megahertz and hit a peak theoretical performance of 150 million polygons per second, compared to 66 million polygons per second for the PlayStation 2 and an estimated 48 million polygons per second on the GameCube. But when the GeForce 3 and nForce graphics chips came back from the factory, Nvidia had to downshift the speed of the XGPU. The circuits in the predecessor chips could not run at 300 megahertz, so Nvidia would have to scale the XGPU back to 250 megahertz. Mike Abrash, the graphics expert at Microsoft, wasn't as upset about the change as he might have been. The memory chips weren't fast enough to keep up anyway, so the ultimate hit to performance was only about 5 percent.

Even with the lower numbers, many expected the Xbox games to look much better than PS 2 games because the Xbox had shortcuts built into the way it depicted pixels on the screen. It could apply more details to individual pixels in a single pass, or one tick of the clock, whereas the GameCube and PS 2 often required multiple passes to achieve the same sort of effects.

Behind the scenes, it was no easy task for the engineers. They worked day and night to get the job done. Nvidia had mastered chip design tools and could reuse whole chip components from the predecessor chips, along with the same driver software they'd already tested out on the PC. They worked on a hierarchical flow: Chip architects would design the chip on a conceptual level at the outset. Once they finished, they handed the design over to logic designers, who translated the architecture into an electrically accurate design. Then they gave it to the layout engineers, who decided exactly where to place the components of the design on a chip.

The first prototype that came back from the factory in March had a flaw in a tricky portion of the chip that contained analog features, dubbed the phase lock loop. The engineers debugged the chip and sent the revised design back to the factory. Once it was fixed, it went off to manufacturing. Now the prototypes came back and worked. Once again, Nvidia had to downshift the speed of the chip—this time from 250 megahertz to 233 megahertz—so the circuits wouldn't overheat. That meant the chip would only process 116 million polygons per second, instead of the original goal of 150 million. It also meant that Intel would have to redesign the main system board of the Xbox to accommodate the new speed. Game developers were disappointed that the original promise of higher performance hadn't been met. The Xbox wouldn't be as superior to the PlayStation 2 as Microsoft had originally expected. However, it would still blow the other systems away. The Xbox had 21.6 gigaflops of computing power, or the equivalent of 58 Cray YMP supercomputers circa 1988.

"They started out with unrealistic expectations, but the final result was still incredibly fast," said Tim Sweeney, the developer at Epic Games who was now working on *Unreal Championship*, a multiplayer shooting game for the Xbox.

While everyone was relieved that the chip was done, nobody had time to celebrate. Nvidia had missed a crucial deadline. The final graphics chips were supposed to be part of a new software development kit and sent out to game developers weeks before the E3 show in May. But the chips were so late that developers decided to show their games on the older development systems at the show. This meant that many of the games would run about 50 percent slower than intended.

Microsoft would surely take a hit in the press relative to the final GameCube hardware. The press wouldn't notice any improvement in the Xbox titles that they saw at Gamestock.

Malachowsky's team soldered the first finished chip into a system board and shipped it to Todd Holmdahl at Microsoft. By this time, Huang and his colleagues had come to regard Holmdahl as "Commander Data from *Star Trek: Next Generation,* without the emotion chip." He was all business. "What did Todd say to us when he got the chip," Huang said. "It was something like, 'when are you going to send the next ten?'" Once the chips arrived, Microsoft was able to create another version of its software development kits that it could send to game creators.

There would be many months ahead to wrangle over the production of the graphics chips and the Xbox. But Huang was very proud of what his team had accomplished. He wanted to make sure the magnitude of the feat was understood.

"We made it possible for Microsoft to catch up," he said. "Nintendo started making their new console two years before Microsoft did, yet they're coming out at the same time."

Not everyone felt that Microsoft was running on time. Julian Eggebrecht, president of Factor 5, ran the team that had created a big hit for the Nintendo 64 with its *Star Wars: Rogue Squadron* title. He was looking for a platform for a sequel, dubbed *Star Wars: Rogue Squadron II: Rogue Leader.* This game would allow players to relive the experience of the original *Star Wars* trilogy, putting them into the cockpit as pilots attacking the Death Star or protecting the rebel base on the ice planet Hoth from Imperial invasion. The technology had moved so far ahead, Eggebrecht felt, that it could deliver a movie-like feel.

LucasArts had the rights to the *Star Wars* property, but Eggebrecht was in the driver's seat since his last game had done so well. He met with both the Xbox and GameCube representatives in January 2001. At the time, Nintendo had all of its ducks lined up. From Eggebrecht's view, the Xbox didn't. Final Xbox hardware wasn't available, although earlier generations of Nvidia chips were ready so that developers could at least get started.

"We had this description from the Xbox people on paper," Eggebrecht said. "We had to ask if they would really come through with that."

To Microsoft, it seemed that Eggebrecht was just biased toward the GameCube. Eggebrecht believed the Nintendo box had a certain beauty because it had been under design since 1998. Nintendo's engineers had applied all of their energy to removing bottlenecks from the processing of 3-D images. They had figured out where clever combinations of memory, graphics processing, and bandwidth could overcome brute-force solutions. By contrast, Eggebrecht said the Xbox had a logjam because there were too many things like graphics and sound contending for the available memory at the same time. There were bottlenecks in memory and data pathways, and the estimates from Nvidia on performance were overly optimistic. Eggebrecht's team wanted to create translucent images, such as see-through explosions, but the Xbox seemed slow on this feature.

"We had more time to approach the problem from scratch," said Greg Buchner, vice president of engineering at ATI Technologies, whose acquired ArtX unit created the graphics chip design for Nintendo.

Kevin Bachus met with Eggebrecht's team to pitch them on the Xbox and he almost snared them. "But they kept throwing up these obstacles and that told me they really wanted to work on the GameCube," Bachus said.

Eggebrecht contended that he made a fair-minded choice in sticking with the GameCube. This turned out to be a devastating loss to the Xbox—months later game reviewers named Eggebrecht's game the killer application for the GameCube.

While Huang's team at Nvidia had finished their chip in record time, it was off schedule and it wasn't early enough to steal Factor 5 away from Nintendo. Yet the vast majority of Xbox developers rolled with the punches as Nvidia revised its specifications for the graphics chip. They said they kept on working because they had never worked on a console that was easier to develop for.

"In that respect, Microsoft lived up to its promises," Sweeney says. "It's been totally smooth."

CHAPTER 24

PRELIMINARIES

ON FEBRUARY 28, 2001, Trip Hawkins, CEO of 3DO, a die-hard PlayStation 2 devotee, was giving a pitch to license his top franchises to the Xbox team, in part because his company didn't have the resources to develop games for the Xbox. They met in the main conference room of the Xbox headquarters. Suddenly, the walls and floors started shaking. Seattle had been hit by a devastating earthquake. Damage in the building was minimal, but everyone dove under the table. Robbie Bach said, "I hope that's not a comment on our plans." The shaking didn't persuade Hawkins to change his ground, at any rate; he still remained skeptical about the Xbox and went on to publicly criticize it.

GAMESTOCK

Fortunately, the quake didn't throw anyone off schedule. That was good, because the season of big events had come. In early March came Gamestock. Game journalists were arriving by the busload. Microsoft had rented one of Seattle's newest museums—the Experience Music Project, the latest largesse from Microsoft co-founder Paul Allen, who was a devoted Jimi Hendrix fan and an amateur guitarist himself. Located in Seattle Center north of downtown and just a stone's throw from Seattle's famed Space Needle, the 140,000-square-foot museum, which looked like a piece of chewed-up gum, was the latest tourist attraction.

But the party on the eve of Gamestock, Microsoft's annual showcase for the game press, showed how clueless the company could be at times and how its roots in nerdy PC games could come back to haunt it. The museum had just opened and it boasted 80,000 artifacts from the history of music, including Allen's personal collection of Jimi Hendrix memorabilia. It was a cool place to hang out. And of course, Microsoft's game geeks did not take advantage of the setting at all. The 170 game journalists from around the world didn't get to see the museum or hear much music. They were ushered into a room filled with tables and offered hors d'oeuvres and beer. They heard a comic monologue from Chris Taylor, a game developer at Gas-Powered Games, and then had to sit through 90 minutes of a game trivia contest. Somehow, in the midst of one of the hippest and potentially loudest museums in the world, Microsoft managed to bore just about everyone.

Gamestock was Ed Fries's event, and he thought the trivia contest was fun. The next morning, the contemplative Fries took the stage. It wasn't the biggest venue, but Fries was about to have his moment in the spotlight.

Standing up on stage before the crowd of journalists, Fries noted how it was a special time for him. He had run the games division at Microsoft for five years. He had worked at Microsoft for 15 years. And it had been 20 years since he made his first game, the clone of *Frogger,* which Fries proudly demonstrated to the laughing audience.

"I wanted to set the bar so low that everything else we show today will just blow you away," Fries joked. "It is amazing to think how far we've come since then. An Xbox DVD has 2 million times more storage than this game. But the thing that scares me and worries me is that for a large part of the population this [the old *Frogger* game] is what they think of as a video game," Fries said, his voice fully serious now.

He found it exciting that there was a huge section of the population that really didn't know games as they had evolved. The potential audience was much bigger than the target 16- to 26-year-old male population. Fries said he believed that in the next five years the games industry would break out to capture the true mass market. Game designers had come a long way, mastering 3-D graphics and learning techniques to make games more accessible. Well-developed characters who were part of strong stories were now built into many of the more serious games.

"The thing that is happening with technology that is so exciting to me is we are finally ready to leave the cartoon world behind," Fries said. "For the last 20 years in games, because of the technical limitations of the machine, the best that we could do was make fancy cartoons, animated cartoons, 3-D cartoons. And as long as the things we made looked like cartoons, that set in people's minds so many expectations about what this game is, who it's for, what the audience is."

Fries noted that one of the hottest Sony games, *Metal Gear Solid,* had characters with no eyes because the technology was too primitive to make the eyes work persuasively. Fries wanted games with fully animated faces that could communicate emotions to the audience. The industry also needed some competitive grist to move upward and onward.

"Take the example of when we first went to the moon," he said. "It wasn't just because it was possible, because it was there; it was because there was a race, a competition with the U.S. and the Soviets trying to get there first. As soon as that competition and push went away, we haven't been back since. We have that push today. We have an epic battle. You've got the world's largest software company fighting the world's largest consumer electronics company and arguably the world's biggest toy company and they're all investing billions of dollars to push this business forward. That kind of a battle is going to drive innovation in this business."

The next thing that needs to happen, Fries said, was for game makers to aspire to a higher goal than mindless entertainment.

"A great book, a great movie, a great play, they are about more than just killing time," he said. "We need to reach out to our audience. We need to create things that are relevant to them. We need to change how they view the world. We ask the wrong questions. What kind of game is this? We should be starting to ask, What are you trying to say with this game? What do you want it to mean to the people who play it? What I'm saying is we need to not create just entertainment. We need to create art. I think that is the goal of all the other forms of media. It's really the only way to advance to where we want to get. If we take that seriously, if we focus on making art, not just entertainment, then I think for the first time we'll deserve to speak to the mass audience and inherit our rightful place as the future of all entertainment."

It was a mesmerizing speech, but the halo it created around the Xbox slowly evaporated as Microsoft showed its games off one by one. As excited as Fries was about the potential of Xbox games, his first four presenters were PC developers who touted the wonders of what they could do with the latest computers. Fries said these first-party, in-house Microsoft developers had to set the bar for what was possible on the platforms. These were his rock stars. They had been toiling in secret for months, and now they had their first chance for recognition on a stage. It was left to Lorne Lanning, founder of Oddworld Inhabitants, to wow the crowd with the first Xbox demo. Unfortunately, he had shown his game at the CES show, so it wasn't all that surprising—even though he really could deploy dozens of little characters on the screen and display a vast landscape at the same time. It was just the kind of scene he had described to Blackley months ago in jest, only now it was real on the Xbox.

"We've been awaiting a time when hardware is not the issue," he said. "The Xbox is allowing us to do what we always wanted to do. This is a sense of the world we've always been after and wanted to create."

"These are stories that we want to tell. These are about characters that have dilemmas. Our characters aren't about the superheroes that we want to be. Our characters are the poor sad schmucks that we really are. That's important to us to empower these characters and bring them to life and make you feel compassion toward them."

As Lanning piloted the demo, the Xbox rendered an incredible scene, and it was only running at half the speed of the final Xbox hardware. It had realistic landscapes, big cliffs, reflective streams, trees that looked like they swayed in the wind—the whole works that was necessary to construct an illusory world. He said, "The problems we have today with the Xbox are not like walking through minefields of obscure technology. It's making things simpler. I'd rather do it the easy way."

The only thing wrong with Lanning's pitch was that people had heard it before. Microsoft had tipped its hand on *Munch's Oddyssee* already, and the novelty had worn off.

Fries also disclosed that he had recruited Toshiyuki Miyata, a star developer at Sony's Japanese games division. He promised that Miyata's team had a big fighting game under way, but he didn't show any games from the Japanese group. He also showed Microsoft's football game, *NFL Fever 2002,* which looked reasonably good and was proof that the company was paying attention to the all-important sports category. Then came a racing game called *Project Gotham.* The cars looked cool down to the headlights, showing that Microsoft had another crucial genre covered.

The crowd livened up when Fries introduced Jason Jones and Joe Staten, the founders of Bungie, the Chicago-based company that Microsoft had acquired nine months earlier. They brought with them *Halo,* a stunning first-person shooting game with heart-pounding music with a thundering drum beat. *Halo* had been one of the best games at the prior E3 trade show, and now Microsoft had shifted it from the PC to the Xbox for its debut. Jones had been moving at a frenetic pace. He had gotten reinforcements in December 2000 after one of his teams finished up a PC game and then moved up to Redmond, nearly doubling the size of his staff. In Redmond, everyone sat in the same room with no office doors separating them; they could communicate quickly and intensely, just the way they liked it. The *Halo* team had ditched the multiplayer Internet version of the game in favor of a single-player game with a story about humans fighting aliens. They spent time building up the story, but they also concentrated on the seemingly minute decisions of game play. They had studied the Xbox controller and figured out a way to map the controls of a PC shooting game onto the two-handed controller. Since it was harder to aim with a thumb stick on a controller in comparison to a mouse, the team built in a little cheating that helped the cross-hairs stay on a target for a split second longer than normal; but they didn't resort to the automatic aiming that made it too easy for veteran gamers to target enemies. They also made it easy to throw grenades by putting the control for that function on the easily-pulled left-hand trigger. The team had also worked hard on artificial intelligence that made the enemies seem smart; they would dodge grenades or sometimes charge in a suicidal rage. Further, while the team gave players a wide variety of weapons, they decided to force the player to make tough choices by giving them limited ammo and the ability to carry only a couple of weapons. Those watching at Gamestock didn't get to hear about these nuances, but they would prove crucial to how the game ultimately played. As the curtain came down on *Halo,* it was clear that it was Microsoft's bet that it would be the killer Xbox application. Bungie had created a game with amazing graphics, such as a rocket taking off and leaving a snaky contrail in its wake. It was stunning.

At least that was what the Microsoft pitch was. It had shown six Xbox games during the presentations and two more in a demo room. That was less than a fifth of the Xbox games in active development. A dozen projects were under way in Japan, but the lack of Japanese examples prompted the game press to print rumors that the Japanese launch of the Xbox might be in trouble. Fries disclosed that the Xbox was going to target 16- to 26-year-old males first, and it would fill in the gaps later. There were no real kids' titles in the works at the moment. Jez San's *Malice* wasn't ready to be shown. In other words, it was going to take a while for the art to materialize.

"We're not there yet," Fries confided offstage, noting it might be five years before the artistry of games became clear. He had drawn the map, but nobody was there yet.

As the journalists boarded buses and hailed cabs at the end of the day, the question about whether Microsoft's games were really going to set it apart was still lingering. Blackley had wanted to attend Gamestock but he was asked to stay clear because he was getting too much press. Others wanted to get some publicity too.

The Xbox represented an opportunity for developers to fulfill all of their dreams. But game development was still a tough business. Fries wasn't necessarily Mr. Money Bags, and he wound up canceling another project that was as dear to Blackley's heart as David Wu's cartoon car game. After doing the demo for Blackley, Pipeworks lobbied Ed Fries, whose producers signed Pipeworks to do an Xbox title based on the Raven and Rex (woman and giant robot) characters from the original GDC demo. But in March, Fries talked to Dan Duncalf, head of Pipeworks. He told them that Microsoft had to cancel the title that he had started. Duncalf understood that Fries was a smart man, but he didn't understand why he had to cancel his game. Fries said the cancellation was just like any other failed project; he had looked at its progress and decided it wasn't worth the risk. He also said he had never counted on the Raven character to be used in a mascot game. Blackley argued the Pipeworks case to no avail.

"Seamus did more than he should have on our behalf," Duncalf said.

Allard and Blackley held a rally to thank Fries's group for knocking everyone dead at Gamestock. Blackley hired a couple of models, who dressed up in suggestive nurse's outfits and walked up on stage with the two men in front of the group. They served shots of alcohol with green Jell-O and green beer. The scene wasn't particularly funny, and it once again landed Blackley in hot water. "I'm going to get fired," Blackley confided to Drew Angeloff. But he said this so often that Angeloff stopped taking it seriously.

Allard, who engaged in plenty of his own antics, says it never got to the point where he had to tell Blackley, "One more time and you're fired." Blackley simply thought he was doing something that other game developers would have loved, but he didn't think enough about how far Microsoft's company culture could be from his usual circles. Allard felt that crazy antics motivated teams to do impossible things. After all, Bill Gates had had milk dumped on his head at charity events and Steve Ballmer jumped in a lake after Microsoft met a big sales goal.

"Sometimes things went too far and you get in trouble, but teams desire leaders who are human," Allard says. "I never felt I had to explain myself to anyone. I could be stoic and lead a team with a very dry approach, but I don't think I'd get a very motivated team."

Secretly, Blackley relished being the crazy guy, except when it meant people wouldn't take him seriously. Kevin Bachus says, "Seamus is a big bottle of nitroglycerin. When you need to blow something up, you use it. But you feel very uncomfortable about having it on your shelf every day."

BACK TO GDC

In March 2001 it was time for the Game Developers Conference in San Jose again. A whole year had passed and Microsoft still didn't have a game console on the market. That was the plan, but it still made people nervous. During that year, Sony had sold 10 million PlayStation 2 consoles. But no one was calling the system a success just yet. Sony's stumbles on the U.S. launch had alienated retailers, developers, and publishers. No publisher had yet launched a game that sold a million units. Artists liked the Xbox message. At this year's GDC, Seamus Blackley himself was going to be the star attraction.

Once again, Blackley set up a command post on the 20th floor of the Fairmont Hotel. His support team had shipped an entire network of computers down to run demonstrations for developers and was on hand to help them with any technical questions they had. While other developers were going to seminars and visiting the exhibit floor of the conference, Blackley was stuck in the hotel suite with about 20 other people, talking with developers and working on his keynote speech. Kevin Bachus helped spruce up Blackley's presentation.

"Your problem, Kevin, is you enjoy PowerPoint," Blackley said, sipping on a diet Coke and tapping away on his laptop computer.

Meanwhile, at an old theater down the street, one of the GDC parties was banging away. A huge crowd had gathered for free drinks and food to hear the video game industry's latest attempt at respectability: the awards ceremony of the Academy of Interactive Arts and Sciences. This event was supposed to be the game industry's version of the Oscars. Everyone cheered as their favorite video and PC games won awards. Microsoft was notably absent among the winners, while Nintendo scooped up a number of wins for its *Legend of Zelda: Majora's Mask* game. When it came time for the top honors, Square's Hironobu Sakaguchi gave the Hall of Fame award to id Software's John Carmack, cocreator of the *Doom* and *Quake* series of games and one of the world's greatest programmers. A videotape from Bill Gates—which Blackley had arranged—offered Microsoft's congratulations to Carmack.

"I want you to know that I can still write slicker and tighter code than John," Gates quipped, triggering an eruption of laughter in the theater.

The next day, Blackley himself got to hog the stage for a keynote speech at the GDC. He was supposed to appear jointly with J Allard, his boss. But Blackley arranged it so that Allard stayed behind since the event was for developers, not publishers. Blackley held out a big picture of Allard pasted on a placard and said Allard was there in spirit. But of course, Blackley was the best speaker for this gig because he was in front of his peers. Other game developers who wanted to change the world just as much as he did were crowding the auditorium, the same one where Blackley had joined Gates a year before to announce the Xbox. This time, Blackley had the newest prototype of the Xbox and some technical demos, but he admitted off the bat that he had no finished hardware or new games to show.

"My job is to be the guy who gets fired if the Xbox games suck," Blackley said. "Save my job. You guys will make Xbox work or not. I'm here to talk developer to developer." His aim, he said, was to tell as much of the "inside scoop as I can tell you without getting fired."

Blackley said his favorite book was *A Soldier's Story,* which chronicled General Omar Bradley's command decisions during World War II.[1] He liked the book because the general knew that soldiers on the front lines often didn't understand the strategy behind the sacrifices that they made. Bradley wrote the book so they would understand the decisions of the generals. Likewise, Blackley knew that game developers didn't always understand the decisions Microsoft was making on the strategic level as it created the Xbox, so Blackley wanted to explain why Microsoft acted as it did. He noted, "There is not a single thing on the box that has not been modified as a result of developer feedback." There were, Blackley said, three stages on every big project: "insane idea, frenzied research, and ruthless execution." (Apparently, no one warned Blackley here about words to avoid in light of antitrust troubles.)

He proceeded to dispel a bunch of rumors that had arisen because of Microsoft's long silence on its progress. Then he disclosed a few new things:

- Microsoft had made six different releases of its Xbox development kit during the past year and the company was not playing favorites by giving them out early to certain developers. More than 2,250 XDKs had been given out to more than 165 companies.
- A mobile Xbox marketing campaign would hit 50 cities before the launch to let gamers see and try out games. U.S. retailers would have more than 10,000 demo stations to show off the games.
- About 12 to 20 games would be released at launch. The games would focus on sports, wrestling, fighting, and action games. The next wave of games would hit before Christmas. Japan would launch for sure this year, and Blackley said he had been to Japan 18 times in the past year just to make sure that it would happen on time.

"We are on track for a fall 2001 launch. We really are. Really."

Since Blackley didn't have any games to show off, he used some Xbox demos from Microsoft's research department. Jed Lengyel, a 3-D graphics researcher, had been dreaming up some ways to make everyday scenes more realistic. He came up with techniques to show blades of grass, leaves, fabric, fur, and fuzz. Blackley showed off a little bunny rabbit whose fur flattened when he turned on a blow-dryer effect. Blackley promised developers would get final hardware before the E3 show in Los Angeles in May.

Xbox.com, a promotional Web site, had gone live and had received 7.7 million hits from 530,000 unique visitors. He noted the Xbox online strategy was on track, despite rumors to the contrary.

His favorite rumors: The green jewel in the Xbox design was a camera. The Xbox would have a Nintendo 64 machine or Sega Dreamcast in it. The Xbox is just a PC. The Xbox would make your TV go blue screen, or crash. The Xbox would never ship on time. The retailers would never support Microsoft. Publishers like Electronic Arts would never support the Xbox. At the end of the speech, Blackley displayed a document from Nintendo's executive vice president, Peter Main, who was criticizing retailers for showing off displays for a new console and hurting sales of current product. The hidden message, Blackley joked, was "All your base are belong to us." It was a reference to a Japanese game called *Zero Wing* that had such an awful translation that it had become the butt of jokes on the Internet. Very insiderish stuff. And the game developers loved it. The message they got was that people like Blackley understood what made them laugh. Still, they were sore that Blackley had no news.

After the speech, Blackley had a chance to relax. He and Bachus hit the parties, including a shindig at the Agenda Bar and Restaurant in the redeveloped section of downtown San Jose. Once again, Blackley's buddy Alan Yu, an organizer of the GDC, threw an exclusive invitation-only party for the top media and game developers.

Yu was frustrated with Blackley because the speech was so "content free." Blackley had promised more earlier, and he had even planned to talk about online games on the Xbox. With no content to show, Blackley had to resort to a funny speech. But Blackley had said that Microsoft had decided to release more information at the E3 show, which for Yu made the developers seem even less important. Blackley was sympathetic and noted he didn't agree with everything the marketing department did.

At the Agenda Bar party, Blackley floated from conversation to conversation. He looked at his friend David Wu, who had a kid's face and a muscular bodybuilder's physique. His game had been canceled by Microsoft but rescued by Electronic Arts. Blackley disagreed with the Microsoft decision, and he joked, "Dude, you are so buffed. I'm intimidated. You're like going to the gym and thinking 'I hate Microsoft.'" The ever polite Wu smiled and said he was just glad that another company had picked up his game.

About this time, Ted Hase and Otto Berkes resurfaced. Since their decision not to join the Xbox team, they had never given up on their dream to create a Windows entertainment platform. Now they tried to pitch an idea they called "HomeStation." Hase said it was their attempt "to revive the original WEP vision." In the form that they pitched it, HomeStation was a Windows PC that was bigger than the Xbox. It was like a digital entertainment tool that could fit in any room of the house. It would play PC games, but it would also play MP3 music files, connect to the Internet, play broadcast TV, and record television shows onto a hard disk drive. The ideal targets were college dorm rooms, kids' bedrooms, or small apartments and condos where space was precious. The box would not run Xbox games, but some in the media thought it was meant to compete with the vision for the Xbox.

Hase felt the box was complementary and it was filling a hole in the PC product line. It used a low-end microprocessor with a high-end graphics chip, much like the Xbox. Unlike a computer, it would be noiseless and occupy about as much space as a boom box. The costs were expected to be higher, with the final box selling for about $500. But Gates and the top executives didn't necessarily buy the pitch. Instead, Hase and Berkes handed the work over to Will Poole, who headed the eHome division of Microsoft. There, the idea might possibly be used in future products. A Web site and a British magazine broke news about the HomeStation, but Microsoft officials said that there was no such project in the works anymore.

INTERLUDE IN TOKYO

The next important event was the Tokyo Game Show at the end of March in 2001. This show highlighted the upcoming hot titles for Japan and so it was a crucial test of the viability of the American-made Xbox in the world's most competitive video game market. This was another show where attendees typically showed up in costumes of their favorite game characters, with hair painted and skin tattooed. It was Japan's version of Wrestlemania.

Bill Gates got up on stage and delivered a keynote address. His presence was another message that the Xbox was a key business for Microsoft and that the entire corporation was behind it. He announced that Microsoft would set up a partnership with NTT, Japan's telecommunications company, to develop an online gaming network for the Xbox in Japan. Sega officials announced that they were going to do 11 games for the Xbox.

Gates also watched the ribbon-cutting ceremonies, standing next to Robbie Bach. He asked Bach about a group of "booth babes"—and whether there were any at the Microsoft booth. Bach squirmed a little and said he didn't think so. Later, Gates walked over to the Microsoft booth and was greeted by a host of dancing girls, some sliding up and down brass pipes like strippers.

"That was the fastest strategy change I've ever seen," Gates said to Bach.

Blackley found a quiet moment of reflection with Kevin Bachus. As he sat and looked at all the games at the Tokyo

Game Show, he couldn't believe how far the Xbox had come. The demos on display were the direct result of Blackley's evangelism. He remembered when developers feared that either Sony or Nintendo would find out that they were preparing to make games for the Xbox.

Overcome briefly, he shed a few tears. He had had so many moments like this that it seemed he was too gentle a character to be at Microsoft, where ruthless execution was the name of the game.

CHAPTER 25

MIDWAY OR PEARL HARBOR AT E3?

IF THE GDC WAS THE SHOW for developer togetherness and for enemies to party together, E3 was the show for publishers and console makers to launch their wars.

At Microsoft, preparations for the show were frenzied. Microsoft's booth wasn't very large—only 20,000 square feet—and it had to show off both PC games and Xbox games. In Solomonic fashion, Robbie Bach decided to carve the booth in half between the platforms. After Sega pulled out of hardware, it offered to give Microsoft its much larger booth. But it was too late. The Nvidia chips were running late, and game publishers were told to display their games on the slower Xbox development kits. Microsoft put out calls to all publishers for games to be displayed at the show. Dozens of game demos came back, and it took time to whittle down the numbers.

Ed Fries wanted to show all the games from Gamestock; he didn't want anyone to wonder why anything disappeared from the line-up. One of the best-looking games was Tecmo's *Dead or Alive 3,* but Kevin Bachus and the Xbox Japan representatives couldn't talk the company into showing it as a playable game. Tomonobu Itagaki, the perfectionist leader of Tecmo's Team Ninja, worried that the game play wasn't polished enough yet.

The fireworks went off on Wednesday, May 15, 2001. It was the day before the exhibit floors opened, and traditionally the day when the hardware makers held press conferences to announce their news.

Microsoft used the same soundstage at the Los Angeles Entertainment Center, a cavernous concrete nightclub that Sega had used a year before to launch its first Internet games. That event was Sega's last hurrah before it canceled the Dreamcast. Sega's bad luck was about to rub off on Microsoft.

When the press conference got started, the house was packed with international journalists, Microsoft PR people, and industry VIPs. Acid-green light bathed the room. A swirling Xbox logo created a surreal effect. Dance music pounded. The lights zeroed in on a chair on the stage, the music faded out, and Lorne Lanning of Oddworld Inhabitants came out with his long ponytail. He repeated his familiar message about how the Xbox was for the artists, and that game developers could now show off their talents as storytellers. Geoff Keighley, editor-in-chief of the game Web site GameSlice, called this the "PlayStation 2 didn't let me be the artist I can be" routine.[1] Sitting on a big stool, Lanning showed off *Munch's Oddyssee.* But to the jaded press that had viewed the demo twice before, this was old news.

Next, Lanning introduced Robbie Bach, who came out on stage with his characteristic exuberance and golf shirt. Bach said the Xbox would be available in the United States on November 8, 2001, for the price of $299, the same amount Sony charged. Bach promised the company would ship 600,000 to 800,000 units for the launch, and the total would reach 1 million to 1.5 million units by December 31, 2001. Those numbers were modest, but they would be good enough to beat Sony's numbers on the PS 2 launch. He didn't say anything about the planned simultaneous launch in Japan. Bach added his usual cliché, which he believed with all his heart: "It's not really about the console, it's about the games."

Bach's first demo was simply to show the final Xbox prototype being turned on. A live video feed was supposed to show the machine powering up. "Let's get that video up," Bach said. He said it again. Had it worked, the crowd would have seen the machine turn itself on. Then it would have shown the familiar ping-pong ball demo from Pipeworks, but this time with 1,000 more ping-pong balls and a ceiling fan that sucked the balls into a vortex. Thanks to an ill-informed video director, nothing happened, so Bach moved on to his announcements. It was every speaker's nightmare, and it foreshadowed bad things to come. Bach went on to say that 15 to 20 spectacular games would be ready at the launch. He then introduced Bungie's Joe Staten to demo the now-familiar *Halo* game. The game looked beautiful, but those who saw it later close-up would complain that it was too slow. Nvidia had been so late with the chips that nobody had final Xbox consoles. Because there was no final hardware at the show, *Halo* only ran at a third of the speed intended for it. Jason Jones knew that the game would be criticized for its slow speed, but he wasn't about to waste time creating a special demo just for E3. His team was hard at work on making the game playable. They had tested the first level of the game—which was key because it trained the player how to shoot with the controller—with game testers four different times with slightly different versions. But feedback from the trade show they ignored.

"I knew we had a product to build and it wasn't done," Jones says.

Bach said that 200 third-party developers and publishers were working on Xbox games in all the major genres. About 80 titles were going to be Xbox exclusives, half of those from third parties. Bach then introduced several developers who demoed more third-party games. Electronic Arts, the largest independent game publisher, reiterated its commitment to producing 10 Xbox titles, though it only showed a somewhat wanting *Pirates of Skull Cove* being developed by EA's Westwood Studios division. The Westwood title was a last-minute addition to the lineup, and apparently a bad one.

Then, Tomonobu Itagaki of Tecmo introduced a filmed demo of *Dead or Alive 3,* arguably the most impressive game in the works for the Xbox. The game art featured crystalline waterfalls, leaves and dust being kicked up in a forest, flocks of birds in flight—all of it rendered as smoothly as a movie. And yet, the game was disappointing in the sense that the superior artistry was simply the backdrop for yet another punching and kicking game. (Tecmo's insistence on not showing a playable *Dead or Alive 3* to journalists resulted in its disqualification from the Best of E3 awards.)

More announcements droned on. Most significant was Bach's statement that 27 online games were in development for the Xbox. In contrast to the other consoles, Microsoft would pioneer online gaming on a console much as Sega had tried to do with its Dreamcast. So optimistic was Microsoft that it would even start selling a microphone headset so players could talk to each other as they played Internet-based games. Bach promised that online games could introduce "episodic content" like a TV show, so players could download a new episode of the game every week or every month.

Peter Moore, president of Sega of America, then walked on stage—the same one where he had proclaimed Sega's greatness in online gaming a year before. He said that Sega would make software for the Xbox, including online versions of its football and basketball games. The press conference closed on time. Microsoft dominated the news on television channels such as CNN. But it wouldn't be the lead story for very long.

"Solid, but unspectacular," wrote Geoff Keighley, of Game-Slice, as he summarized the Microsoft press conference.[2]

NINTENDO STRIKES BACK

Nintendo was up next. The seasoned Japanese company showed its E3 savvy by having buses available to take reporters over to the Biltmore Hotel about six blocks away. In the cavernous Biltmore Bowl in the basement of the hotel, there was an even bigger crowd than at the Microsoft event. It appeared that Nintendo had stacked the crowd with a lot of its own employees.

"This is an extremely exciting day in the history of video games, and Nintendo says that with 20 years of experience," boomed the baritone voice of Peter Main, executive vice president of marketing at Nintendo of America. "Nintendo is absolutely assured that GameCube and GameBoy Advance will be successes no matter what other manufacturers may plan to do."

Main said that the GameBoy Advance handheld would sell an estimated 24 million units in its first 12 months on the market. Portable game players were Nintendo's stronghold. While Sony suffered a decline in sales in 2000, Nintendo was able to demonstrate solid growth thanks to continuing sales of its GameBoys. Satoru Iwata, a member of Nintendo's board of directors, joined Main on stage to talk about the "pure magic" of the GameCube console. In halting English, he took one of what would be many jabs at his rivals that day, saying, "We consider ourselves a game-based entertainment company. We see other people see themselves first as technology companies. This is an important distinction."

Iwata complained that games all looked too similar. Developers were spending millions of dollars on the best 3-D graphics, and, if they scored a hit, they'd make sequels. Competitors would copy the hits.

"This is dangerous to our industry," Iwata said. "If they become too bored, they will go away."

Nintendo's aging chairman, Hiroshi Yamauchi, had of course commissioned his game designers to be different, Iwata said. To do games that were full of surprise, freshness, and joy. This tried-and-true method allowed Nintendo to make the most popular games, even though it didn't make the most games. And it would rely on franchise characters like Mario, *Zelda's* Link, Donkey Kong, and Pokemon. (Of course, since the games weren't boring, players didn't tire of the sequels.) Then Iwata introduced the game designer responsible for most of those hits, Shigeru Miyamoto, the living legend of Nintendo.

"Let me introduce our new baby," Miyamoto said. "Like all babies, it is small. But it will make a lot of noise."

Then Nintendo rolled a video with sequences from all of its upcoming GameCube titles. In contrast to the Microsoft press conference, the crowd actually cheered as they saw their favorite characters cavort across the screen, from *Mario* to *Yoshi*. Whether it was the Nintendo employees who started the screaming wasn't clear. But the enthusiasm in the audience was infectious. Miyamoto used a slick wireless controller to demonstrate *Luigi's Mansion,* a ghost-hunting game. In the game, players controlled Luigi, who sucks ghosts into a vacuum cleaner. (Upon hearing this, Microsoft had to change one of its own games that had a vacuum-wielding character.) Heading off questions, Iwata said that Nintendo had high-quality 3-D, but other companies were promoting fast 3-D performance even though they had other bottlenecks in systems, whereas Nintendo had built a balanced system.

But none of that mattered compared to the rabbit that Miyamoto pulled out of his hat. He showed off a game dubbed *Pikmin,* which he had been inspired to create by looking at the ants in the elaborate gardens at his home in Kyoto. The cute little Pikmin creatures moved around at Miyamoto's command like little herds of sheep. They were cute, funny, and absolutely Nintendo. When Miyamoto was done, the stunned crowd let loose a thunder of applause. He had done it again. Main announced that the GameCube would launch in Japan on September 14, in the United States on November 5, and in Europe sometime in 2002. Pricing wouldn't come until a week later. Nintendo later announced it would sell the machine for $199, a discount of $100 versus its rivals. In an interview later, Minoru Arakawa said that Nintendo was not going to lose a great deal of money on its hardware, confirming analysts' speculation that Nintendo's machine was designed to cost much less than its rivals.

Main said that Nintendo would launch the GameCube with only six to eight titles, compared to Microsoft's 15 to 20. That was in keeping with its style. He noted that Nintendo published 225 titles on its prior platform, while Sony had 1,100 titles. But Nintendo always sold more copies of hit games than its rivals to make up for the difference. One of the most eagerly anticipated titles was coming from Julian Eggebrecht's Factor 5 and LucasArts. They were introducing *Star Wars: Rogue Squadron II: Rogue Leader* as an exclusive on the GameCube at launch.

SONY SHOWS ITS CLOUT

Sony's press conference was just a few blocks away in a huge complex of soundstages, the same place it had used a year earlier. It provided a sumptuous lunch for the press, with lots of open bars to cool everyone off in the simmering Los Angeles heat. The stage was ringed with rows of concert lights and two giant video screens.

"Despite the current economy, the interactive entertainment industry has remained very healthy," said Kazuo Hirai, president of Sony Computer Entertainment America, in his booming voice. He noted that Sony had the two top-selling consoles with the PlayStation 2 and the original PlayStation, which was still selling briskly. With 60 percent of the overall market, Hirai said, "the real question for 2001 is who will be in the No. 2 spot."

Jack Tretton, senior vice president for sales in the United States, reviewed the past year of the crusade. Sony's PlayStation 2 sold 500,000 units the first day in both North America and Europe. Across the world, it had sold 10 million units since March 2000, a sales rate that was three times the rate of the PlayStation. To date, 82 million PlayStation machines had been sold. The production rate for the PS 2 was 1.5 million a month, and it would hit 2 million units a month by the fall. About 300 game developers were working on titles. About 50 games were available within the first three months. Eighty games were available as of the E3 show, and Tretton expected 200 more games by the end of 2001. In the fiscal year ending in March 2002, Sony expected to sell 20 million more units. The age demographics were all over the map, from 8 years on up past 54.

Of course, even with its record sales, Sony had botched part of its launch. It was only beginning to ship big titles from in-house divisions. Traditionally, Sony had 30 percent of all titles on its platform. Now the figure was much lower. That meant Sony had not yet turned a profit on its game sales.

Acknowledging that Sony's internal studios were offtrack at the PlayStation 2 launch, he noted that seven of them were now rededicated to games for the PS 2. Titles like *Dark Cloud, Twisted Metal Black,* and *Gran Turismo 3: A-Spec* were about to hit the U.S. market. In Japan, *Gran Turismo 3: A-Spec* sold a million units in its first day. Jason Rubin and Andy Gavin, co-presidents of Sony's recently acquired Naughty Dog studio, showed off a new game called *Jak and Daxter,* a game that Ed Fries had once hoped to snare.

Next, Andrew House, senior vice president of marketing, noted that Sony still had 55.7 percent of the unit share in the United States, compared to 33.8 percent for Nintendo and 10.6 percent for Sega's dying Dreamcast. He said Sony would make new peripherals available in the fall, including a liquid crystal display for the PS One, which was the smaller version of the original PlayStation. He said Sony would spend $250 million in the U.S. marketing effort in 2001. Most of the press didn't realize this was more money than Microsoft planned to spend. Bach had said that Microsoft was spending $500 million worldwide over 18 months. That translated only to $111 million in the United States in a year. Unfortunately for Sony, most of the press thought Microsoft was going to outspend Sony.

Hirai returned to the stage and noted that Square's games remained exclusive for the PlayStation 2. That was a blow to the Xbox in that Square had been the kingmaker that had crowned Sony over Nintendo in the last round. Square's *Final Fantasy X* game would launch on the PlayStation 2 later in the year. Sony would also have *Final Fantasy XI,* an online game, because Square didn't like Microsoft's plan for online games, which required that gamers go online through a Microsoft portal.

Hirai described more exclusive games, then, running out of time, he hurriedly disclosed Sony's online plans. Hirai said AOL Time Warner's America Online would be the feature online service for the PS 2 and that a combination broadband Ethernet and ordinary phone modem would go on sale in the fall. Sony consumers could also buy a hard disk drive to attach to the PS 2 to aid their online game playing as well.

Most people just saw the new peripherals as something for the hardcore gamers to buy in case they were feeling a bit like spending their money on the Xbox. Sony was just making a feint in Microsoft's direction, but everyone knew that it was betting most of its future on good old-fashioned PS 2 games that had big followings, like the *Metal Gear Solid 2.* It was games like those that would keep PS 2 sales going strong as better technologies hit the market.

After the show, Hirai said that Nintendo had indeed surprised everyone with its readiness. But "I think people expected more from the folks in Washington State," he said.

ANOTHER MUSKETEER DEPARTS

That evening, the press and industry luminaries attended Nintendo's E3 soiree, which featured sumptuous food and drink in the art deco lobby of the Biltmore Hotel.

In the posh surroundings, Kevin Bachus circulated in his trademark buttoned shirt and jeans. He began admitting to others that he had left Microsoft about two weeks before the E3 show. There was now only one Musketeer left. Bachus explained that he had grown weary at Microsoft. He had enjoyed the part about starting a dream project. But it was a pressure cooker. He encountered friction along the way. It wasn't fun anymore. There were a few people he didn't get along with, and his interviews with the press were being reassigned to others. So it was time to go. He had also felt that his job in rounding up third-party game publishers was done.

Bachus said he felt like he needed to return to the business of making games himself. He had helped conceive this great platform for games, but now it was time to use that platform to make games. As Bachus circulated around the parties at E3, he saw the rumor mill in action.

"I've heard that I have a terminal disease, that my wife had a terminal disease, that I got fired for failing to come up with great games, that I got fired because I didn't sign up Square, and that I disagreed about the E3 booth and quit," he said. "Sometimes the truth is really boring." He echoed the explanations of so many others before him. "I've been at Microsoft since 1997 and accomplished far more than I ever hoped I could. Microsoft is not an easy place to work and I really wanted to get back to the heart of the games industry. I guess you could say my job wasn't as much fun anymore and I wanted to start having fun again."

Chanel Summers, Bachus's wife, agreed with Bachus that it was a good time for him to leave. She offered her support and told him she expected him to move on to another kind of start-up project. The hardest thing to watch, however, was how much Bachus missed his own employees and the rest of the Xbox team. This was the kind of thing that the taciturn Bachus left unsaid but which couldn't escape his wife.

"Not seeing them on a daily basis, that was hard for him," Summers says.

As word spread, many wondered whether Bachus's departure was a sign of bad things to come for the Xbox. Even though he was gone from Microsoft, he was still one of its biggest cheerleaders. He brushed off notions that Microsoft was in trouble because of Nintendo's rich showing. He noted how remarkable it was that Microsoft had made as much progress as it had.

"People went bananas last year when we showed them a bunch of ping-pong balls bouncing around on mouse traps," Bachus said. "Our success depends on ruthless execution."

Upon hearing this, Activision CEO Bobby Kotick said, "Who are they going to execute?"

Robbie Bach said Bachus's departure was sad but added, "Nobody is irreplaceable, including myself. We had a replacement [George Peckham] in the bull pen and Kevin himself had built a very strong team."

The Xbox project did take a huge toll on the mind. Those who dropped out early found they were forgotten when it came to getting credit. Those who toiled onward found the work debilitating. J Allard never really confessed to these difficulties, but his close friend Jeff Henshaw says, "I've seen him brilliant or inspired and on top of everything, and so under water I thought he was going to lose it. I don't think he had any idea this would bleed the life out of him, nor did anyone else. It has been a pleasure to watch him struggle because he has grown from it. Everyone has been stretched in many ways."

Allard admitted that taking on Rick Thompson's job had stretched him thin. He relied heavily on Bachus to make the transition but now was glad that Bachus had put such a good team in place. Blackley missed his buddy Bachus, and for a time Blackley wondered if he should resign as well. When game developers began hearing about Bachus's resignation, they almost went into a panic. Many came up to Blackley and said, "You can't leave too. You're the only one who understands us at Microsoft."

Blackley had the same ups and downs, but he did enjoy the contact with game developers that the job afforded him. A case in point was a meeting at E3 with Warren Spector, the veteran PC game designer he had known at Looking Glass and who was now heading game development at Ion Storm in Austin, Texas.

Spector went to the booth at the appointed time and had to wait half an hour for Blackley to show up. Blackley arrived and before Spector could say a word, Blackley grabbed him by the shoulders, stuck his face about three inches from Spector's, and said, "Look me in the eye and tell me you're going to make *Deus Ex* and *Thief* console games," referring to Spector's top PC game franchises.

"I'm going to make them console games," Spector replied. "Now, what do I have to do to get them officially approved as Xbox titles?"

Blackley said, "You're approved." He turned on his heels, strode over to a nearby Xbox and started playing an Xbox game with an almost maniacal glee. Spector realized he still had to take his proposal through the formal channels, but he knew that Blackley would go to the mat for him.

The two men chatted for a while and Spector asked a question that hit a nerve: "What are you doing at Microsoft? When are you going to get back to making games?" Blackley didn't have an answer. He thought he was making his mark on the industry, but he also wanted to make games. He still had interesting work to do on his job, in contrast to Bachus. But he sorely missed his friend, and that put him in a dark mood for much of the trade show.

IT GETS WORSE

Bad karma was in the air for Microsoft. And the next day, it got a little worse. Doug Lowenstein, president of the Interactive Digital Software Association opened the show with yet another barn-burner speech on the pervasiveness of games. He said analysts predicted that the next generation of video games would make their way into 70 million households by 2005, making it one of the most successful consumer electronics products in history. The demographics of gaming had expanded beyond teenage boys, with 56 percent of the video gaming audience above 18. The road to overtaking movies and music was just a mop-up operation.

"Games are as important a part of culture as movies and books," Lowenstein said. "Video games aren't child's play. They're becoming a dominant medium."

Having heard the same victory speech for four years in a row, it was easy for some in the crowd to be skeptical. And it still seemed a little early to declare victory. Many in the audience were converts. But why did the game industry shrink in 2000? True, it was a transition year. There was also the matter of Sony's game and console shortages at the launch of the PlayStation 2. The game developers said they needed a little practice programming that weird Sony machine, so it would take another year or so to produce that ultimate game, the one that would make everyone cry. The rest of the U.S. economy was collapsing. The Internet bubble had burst. Maybe the Xbox and the GameCube would change everything and get the revolution back on track. Or maybe there was no revolution?

To answer such doubts, the true believers walked onto a stage bathed in red light. John Taylor, an analyst at investment research firm Arcadia Research, introduced his panelists. Peter Main, the executive vice president of Nintendo of America and longtime chief of its sales and marketing, seemed like everyone's favorite uncle. Kazuo Hirai, president of Sony of America, sat in the middle seat. He was flanked by Robbie Bach, the chief Xbox officer. Taylor began lobbing out his softballs for this well-rehearsed debate.

Main put on his thick reading glasses and began ticking off statistics. He contended that the console technologies were all the same (even though most people felt the Xbox had the edge). But Nintendo, as he said the day before, was unique because of its lock on the content that young gamers loved. He said that Sony was a world-class manufacturer, and Microsoft was a world-class software company, but "Nintendo aspires to be neither. We're an entertainment company." Nintendo had sold 200 million pieces of hardware and 1.5 billion pieces of software.

Hirai noted that Sony met its promise to deliver 10 million PlayStation 2s in the past year and, despite its manufacturing hiccups, met that promise. He noted hot new games coming out like *Gran Turismo 3*. The real question "is who will be in the No. 2 position," he said again. He had such a smug smile on his face as he said this that he drew chuckles from the crowd, which included many journalists who heard him say the same thing the day before.

Bach started out humble. He said it was an honor for him to be there among people who had created an amazing industry and great games. He said that Microsoft started out by following the muses. It listened to game developers, retailers, and gamers so it could deliver a console they wanted. The focus now was all about gaming.

He said the 200 developers working with Microsoft would ensure coverage of all the main genres. He talked of how the hardware would enable virtual worlds that people had never seen before, allowing games to reach a new level. He also said Xbox alone had focused on providing everything from the ground up for the online space.

"The key question isn't who will be No. 1 or No. 2 this year," he said. "It's, as we look over the next five years, who is going to have the secrets to success, and who is going to drive the industry forward."

Taylor led the panelists through some questions where they talked again about product details and how much they focused on great games. They skirmished on the importance of online games and hard disk drives. Main said that Nintendo wasn't going to cram unnecessary hardware down anyone's throat based on speculation that people wanted to play online games. He warned that online business models hadn't been proven yet. He noted that Nintendo could do a better job embracing third-party game developers now that the GameCube offered a new disk-based medium for games instead of the cartridges of the past. These disks were lower cost and could be ordered in mass quantities more quickly. Hirai said that Sony would deploy online games as early as the fall of 2001. Bach said that Microsoft had 80 exclusive titles in the works, about half from third parties. About 30 percent of Microsoft's game sales would likely come from first-party developers and 70 percent from third parties, the same ratio as Sony's.

"Kaz and I would agree," Bach said.

"Follow our lead, follow our lead," Hirai said, a little mockingly.

Main chimed in, "Kaz hit a very interesting notion, called profitability."

Main said that there were 1,300 titles published in the last round of the video game cycle. About 70 percent sold less than 300,000 units each. The new break-even point, he said, was sales of about 350,000 to 400,000 units. He suggested developers do fewer titles better. It was an implicit criticism of Microsoft's and Sony's plans, which Main suggested would lead to a lot of red ink.

"We don't need 12 games in every genre," Main said. "There has been an absolute bloodbath among game developers in the last two years."

Bach said there were elements to Microsoft's plan that suggested new ways to make money. For instance, developers could engage in episodic games, which could be released one by one much like soap operas. Players would pay to download additional episodes, and the developer could cut its losses if the title wasn't popular.

"It could be much more like producing a show than it is a game," he said.

Bach also said that technology for transmitting voice over the Internet—fairly common among PC gamers—would add new dimensions to multiplayer games. That was why Microsoft planned to sell a microphone headset too.

Hirai talked about Sony's plan to target the "imaginators," or the 18- to 34-year-old males who adopted quickly. From there, Sony planned to spread out from the hard core to new demographics and capture a true mass market. Bach said Microsoft's strategy was similar, targeting the "enthusiast" group first and then expanding outward to include mainstream consumers.

"Was that the Sony strategy?" Hirai said smugly. "Sounds like my answer." That provoked an overly testy "I don't think so" from Bach. He was wound a little too tight and failed to crack a joke in response. Bach didn't realize it, but people expected a knock-out rhetorical blow from the newcomer. And he didn't deliver it. His closer: "We'll spend the money we need to enter into the marketplace."

That night it was Microsoft's turn to spend some money. In keeping with E3 tradition, it held an invitation-only party at the Hollywood Palladium on Sunset Boulevard, a palatial ballroom with two levels overlooking a giant stage. The food, barbecue chicken and beans, was terrible and overcooked. Most people didn't seem to mind as they wolfed down free booze and eyed the night club dancers grinding away. The crowd was filled with executives and journalists. They cheered as a couple of popular rock bands, Blink 182 and Third Eye Blind, hit the stage and made a deafening noise so that many of the older executives retreated to the quiet areas near the exit to chat. The party at the Palladium had its pluses. Dave Riola, the old WebTV opponent who had fought against the Xbox team for months, had changed his mind. He congratulated both Bachus and Blackley, shaking their hands and saying he was surprised at how well the Xbox had turned out.

The only thing bad about the Microsoft party, other than the food, was that a spectacular Sony party again overshadowed it the next evening. Returning to the downtown soundstages where it held its press conference, Sony threw a party that spilled across several gigantic buildings. It featured much better food, multiple bars, star sightings from Sony's stable of movie and music talent, and hordes of people. It had its own popular bands and no doubt a much higher budget. Microsoft had been trumped once again.

In conversation after conversation during and after E3, it was clear that the influential members of the press had fallen in love with Nintendo's GameCube. Microsoft was losing out in the perception war. The tide of sentiment, fairly or unfairly, had turned against Microsoft.

Trip Hawkins, CEO of 3DO, said that he could easily see Microsoft's board of directors meeting a few years from now. "We're losing how much money, and it's going to take this much more investment?" Then the board would vote to pull the plug on the Xbox, Hawkins said. He pointed out that Sony had to succeed because it had invested $1 billion and more in its own manufacturing capacity, while Microsoft's bet was limited to hiring contract manufacturers.

Consumers shared similar feelings. At Gamespot, a news industry Web site, interest in the GameCube console shot up sixfold in the month after E3, based on how often site surfers asked for GameCube stories and information. Interest in the Xbox had increased only about 25 percent, though it was still leading overall interest in the GameCube. And interest in the PlayStation 2 remained about four times higher than interest in the Xbox.

Every journalist and analyst following the games industry noted that Nintendo's established branded characters would be back.

"Nintendo definitely stole the buzz," said Tom Ham, a freelancer who wrote for everyone from *Newsweek* to the *Washington Post*. "None of the games from Microsoft were must-haves."

Steven L. Kent, a freelancer (the one who penned the questions for the disastrous trivia game at the earlier Microsoft party) who wrote for *USA Today* and MSNBC, knew spades about the industry because he had covered it since 1993 and had just finished a book on the topic.[3] He believed that E3 had been abysmal for Microsoft. Afterward, he offered to tell Fries everything that Microsoft had done wrong. His list included highlighting *Halo* and *Munch's Odyssee* when they'd already been seen. Microsoft should have put more of its resources into a launch in Europe instead of Japan, where he didn't think it had much chance. Above all, Kent said Microsoft's big error was failing to show more playable games. If none of the games were far enough along, well, Kent said, why weren't they? Fries didn't take Kent up on his offer. Instead, Kent delivered his criticisms to the top person at Microsoft's PR agency.

"It took an hour and a half, and by the end of it she was pretty tired of me," he says.

It wasn't just the media people who were excited about Nintendo. Electronic Arts also made a big decision after E3. The company decided to shift more of its resources into games for the GameCube.

"Nintendo always focuses on fewer titles and more in-house titles," said Peter Moore of Sega. "And it never hurts them." And, though he sang Microsoft's praises for raising the competition, Activision's Kotick agreed that Microsoft now seemed positioned to be the No. 3 player in the market.

Among the Microsoft loyalists, E3 was a bitter pill to swallow. "E3 broke my heart," says Sherry McKenna.

CHAPTER 26

LAUNCHING

KEVIN BACHUS BRIEFLY EXPLORED a number of options, including starting a new company, taking time off, or joining a game publisher. But after E3, he decided to go full circle instead, taking a job as senior director of marketing at Wild-Tangent. He was once again working for Alex St. John, the cocreator of DirectX and the man who had recruited Bachus into Microsoft.

In contrast to Bachus, who felt he had little more to do on the Xbox, Blackley was busy assisting key developers with their work. So he stayed on board so the developers could get their games launched. But he was furious at the outcome at E3. He'd wanted Microsoft to make a big deal of David Wu's *Cel Damage* car combat game at the Microsoft booth. But Fries's game division raised objections since it was no longer an official Microsoft title (it was from Electronic Arts), and so it was relegated to just one kiosk in a corner. Just a few days before the show, Wu finalized papers with EA. He was able to display the game on one machine in the EA booth, with no fanfare or marketing. Even so, *Cel Damage* gathered small crowds of influential game critics. Word of mouth spread that it was good. To Wu, seeing his game at the booth brought some satisfaction that he might finally realize his vision of showing that physics can be fun. It was the same vision that Blackley had on *Trespasser.*

Ed Fries, who got the blame for the lackluster showing compared to Nintendo, told Seamus and others to calm down. He said that the change in perceptions wouldn't matter in the long run.

"We showed a half-built house in terms of the games we had on display," he says. "Nintendo showed one very nice room in a half-built house."

Fries told everyone that his teams would come through.

"In games, my job is to believe," Fries says. "Believe in people and projects. Sometimes it pays off in spades. A lot of times I get challenged on a decision to invest in a game, and all I can say is I believe in them."

Blackley and Fries had been at odds on occasion. But they were very close by this time because they were the last two original Xbox advocates left out of the group that had attended the first games strategy meeting with Bill Gates in May 1999. They had a dinner to talk things over. Each honestly told the other what they didn't like about the other. Fries believed he had a stellar lineup and he created it the smart way. He kept faith that the developers would come through with great games and needed no midcourse interference to meet their targets. Fries said he still believed in his teams. Fries wondered why Blackley dumped so much criticism his way, but Blackley explained that he didn't always mean to be on the attack.

"Later on, I understood what Ed was doing a lot better, and I think he pulled it off," Blackley says.

Blackley was upset because he believed that Xbox had the superior product compared to Nintendo, but Nintendo stole E3 because of superior presentation. With every failure, he felt part of his original dream slipping away. He yelled at Robbie Bach that the company had to do something to turn around the perception that the Xbox wasn't as cool as the GameCube. "We've lost our way," Blackley said. Bach and the entire team called a huddle. They went into radio silence again and stayed quiet until they had some better games to talk about. The company's own surveys showed that while it scored well with consumers, it had lost big at E3 versus Nintendo with the analysts and the gaming press. In the weeks afterward, the news got worse as rumors of production delays arose. Bachus felt that Microsoft was going through a process that every new product endures: hype, backlash, and finally acceptance.

"I said it's done," says Bach. "We accomplished what we wanted by showing we had made progress, but on the outside it didn't meet expectations. From then on, we weren't going to be public until we could show the goods."

Robbie Bach realized that E3 could have gone much better, but he felt there was a difference between what Microsoft needed to accomplish and what people expected. Others expected hot games they hadn't seen before, but only Nintendo delivered that. Brian Farrell, CEO of THQ, said to Bach, "You said it was all about the games, then you showed a bunch of crap."

Strangely enough, and to his credit, Bach responded to Blackley's rant positively. He told Blackley that his developer support group was working pretty well. It would do fine without him because of the team he assembled. Bach said, "OK, if we have a problem, you solve it." He told Blackley to create a new job for himself. Instead of just helping developers with games, Blackley would be more aggressive about helping developers produce games that showed how much better the Xbox was. Part of this task was simply collecting the evidence among third-party developers that their games would look far better on the Xbox. He would identify the games that had the most promise and give the developers everything they needed to make sure the games were ready for launch.

"We needed someone to go out and evangelize the games, get people excited about them again," says Blackley's new supervisor: John O'Rourke, the Xbox sales and marketing director.

Blackley became an externally focused game producer. But his new title was *game otaku,* which is Japanese for an absolutely crazed video game fan. Blackley started his job on July 25, the same day he gave a demo in Redmond to the financial analysts. He showed a demo of *Shrek,* a game based on the hot animated movie of the summer. He showed the financial analysts how much fun it was to get the main character of the game to light his farts. The press quoted him heavily on it, including his comment that the game was a "freak-out experience" for gamers.

On July 9, Ed Fries and the first-party team gathered for one of the meetings where they passed judgment on one of the titles they would ship at the launch of the Xbox. The whole point, Fries said, was to "look someone in the eye and ask them if this team is going to make it or not." They were deciding whether or not the games had made the appropriate progress to deserve their slot in the launch. Wave One titles were going to appear at the launch. Wave Two would appear by the end of 2001. Wave Three would appear in the first six months of 2002. And Wave Four would appear by the end of 2002. Sherry McKenna and Lorne Lanning knew that this meeting was a "go or no-go" meeting for their game.

"We were terrified and felt like throwing up all day," McKenna said.

But they got the go-ahead. They had had more than a year to work on their game and had built up a staff of 60 people whose livelihoods depended on it. Now they entered crunch mode, roaring past each milestone.

PRODUCTION DELAYS

In late August, Microsoft finally had a lucky break. Nintendo held its Space World trade show in Japan. It announced at the show that it would postpone the launch of the GameCube console in the United States by 10 days or so to November 18, just before the busy Thanksgiving holiday season. Peter Main, executive vice president of Nintendo of America, said that production wasn't fast enough to stock up enough machines for the scheduled November 5 launch, so Nintendo delayed. He said it wasn't a big setback, but it would allow Microsoft to launch the Xbox without being harried by the competition. It was a big psychological relief to the Xbox team.

A few days after Nintendo dropped the ball, Microsoft stumbled again. It announced it would push the launch in Japan back from November to February 2002. Nintendo would have more than five months to consolidate its lead on the Xbox, giving it a chance to sell millions of units.

Inside Microsoft, team members had been worried for months. Nvidia's chips were coming back from the factory and the picture wasn't pretty. It took longer to get reliable chips than expected, even though Nvidia had apparently finished the job back in February. The first prototypes arrived in March and Nvidia's engineers began the debugging process. The chips were passing all tests, but when Nvidia's systems engineers plugged them into evaluation boards with the other components for the Xbox, bad things started to happen.

The evaluation units could deal with one of Microsoft's test programs easily. The program, which showed a dolphin swimming in the ocean, ran flawlessly for weeks at a time. But when any other application was loaded, it crashed. Some programs failed after a few seconds, some after 20 minutes. There seemed to be no pattern to the failures. More revised chips were coming back from the factory, and a process of elimination showed there was no flaw with the graphics chip. The teams revised the evaluation boards a half-dozen times, to no avail. The complete system was still unstable. The June 15 production start that had been in place in the unrealistic schedules came and went. Todd Holmdahl, Microsoft's hardware chief, was getting very nervous. Starting in April, he had to start placing orders for millions of components. He was forking over huge amounts of cash, but he still hadn't seen a working system.

By July, everyone at Microsoft and Nvidia was in a state of panic. Rami Friedlander, head of the systems engineering on the project at Nvidia, had a vacation coming up, but he expected he would have to cancel it.

Then one night near midnight a cheer went up from Nvidia's engineering department. A team of debuggers who had been working for months had figured out the flaw. A power supply had been improperly designed. Someone had incorrectly typed a specification for the electrical tolerance of the power supply. Whenever electrical usage dropped below a certain level, the power supply sent a wave of electrical feedback into the system. That was causing the failures. Friedlander reported the news to Jen-Hsun Huang the next day. Huang sighed with relief. Once the power supply was corrected, the test applications started running on the evaluation boards.

"A lot of us still have bad dreams about that dolphin," says Holmdahl.

Fortunately for Nvidia, no big changes had to be made in the graphics chips. Nvidia had begun mass producing the graphics chips on the gamble that they were OK. Now it began delivering them by the tens of thousands to Microsoft. But the project had suffered a big delay. Flextronics could start manufacturing test systems, but it needed time to work out its own bugs. Plus, there were no games ready to start testing yet.

"When we started putting together the schedule, it was obvious that silicon chips would be the gating item," said Jim Sacherman of Flextronics. "And among those, it was obvious Nvidia would be the main chip we would wait for. And that's how it turned out. Until the chips were done, there were a lot of things we couldn't do—like testing."

The final approval on working hardware came so late that Flextronics couldn't make up for it. Jen-Hsun Huang, CEO of Nvidia, still believed his company had executed on a superhuman effort to get the graphics chip done.

"All I know is that it took about 14 months from the time I got a contract to when we shipped a million units," he said.

Microsoft executives fretted that the box was still too expensive. But they had come a long way since Rick Thompson had predicted the costs would hit $425 a box and that the company would lose $125 on each one sold. The business model now called for a much smaller loss than previously expected, thanks to constant revisions in the prices of components. Now the company planned to ship 5 million units in its fiscal year ending June 30, 2002, and about 19 million software units. During that time, it would lose about $87 per box on the hardware. Fewer game sales were needed to break even. Microsoft's new estimates may have been rosy. But an independent consulting firm, Portelligent, estimated that the initial Xbox machines cost $323 to make, not including the cost of shipping, retailer margin, and returns. Portelligent estimated the hard drive cost $55, the DVD drive was $35, the Nvidia graphics chip was $32.48, the Intel chip was $22, and the Nvidia MCP (sound and communications) chip was $8.80.

Microsoft expected to slash the hardware costs in half eventually and sell more than 65 million units. Overall, the company would sell 3 first-party games and 5.7 third-party games per box. By the end of the Xbox's life, Microsoft would have a healthy profit. This was not nearly as dire as Rick Thompson predicted, but it assumed that the Xbox rivals would not slash prices at exceedingly fast rates.

"We found early assumptions weren't right and later felt very good about the business prospects," Bach says. "One of the assumptions that Rick made was that we would launch in all major markets at once. It turns out if you go one market at a time, your costs can be lower."

Microsoft had set up two factories at the start, and it typically took six months to get the factories tooled. Hence, there wasn't time to get more capacity in place. Flextronics brought up its plant in Guadalajara first, with the supervisors from Hungary watching every move. It was a record start for volume manufacturing, but it took time for the factories to reach the expected capacity of 100,000 a week each. Robbie Bach had promised 600,000 to 800,000 machines would be available at the U.S. launch. To get there in time for November 8, Flextronics would have had to start production at full capacity no later than the first of October. Back that up a few weeks for the start-up time and it meant that production should begin in early September. Under the revised schedule, the company needed to start production in August.

But even as Nvidia vanquished its final problems with the graphics chip and the power supply, Flextronics wasn't ready. It had to begin its own internal testing procedures. Some of the parts that came in from suppliers had defects, says Sacherman. At the last minute, Flextronics had to set up a filtering system to sort good parts from bad parts. The company also found that there was too much data associated with the manufacturing of the Xbox for its computers to handle. Flextronics had to beef up the factory's computer system and make sure this communicated correctly with Microsoft's own computerized supply-chain systems. That lost time was small compared to the delays from Nvidia, Sacherman points out.

"They were late for months and months," he says.

Luckily, the launch wasn't going to be a complete disaster. Todd Holmdahl had plenty of contingency plans in place. He worked with the suppliers so they could deal with tasks that didn't have to wait. Work got started in advance throughout the entire chain.

Production didn't get off the ground until a few days before the September 21 announcement, so Bach had no choice but to move the launch back a week. In the long run, it was just a minor adjustment. Microsoft still planned to replenish stores quickly, selling a total of 1 million to 1.5 million in its first season. Unfortunately, that was far short of its original goal (a secret number established more than a year before the launch) of 4.9 million, and, in the war with Sony and Nintendo, it was a big psychological loss. Microsoft was failing to execute again. Paper mailings from Toys 'R Us had already been printed in advance, and, as consumers received them in the mail, they were stamped with the wrong launch date. Still, to those who saw the production in the 300,000-square-foot facility in Mexico, it was a staggering sight. Xbox machines were coming off the line every 20 to 40 seconds. Workers in white lab coats sat in chairs that rolled across the pristine white floors. Supervisors walked around from the dozens of computer-controlled tooling stations. Stacks of machines awaited electrical testing at the end of the assembly points. Trucks carrying 1,400 boxes rolled out of the factory every half-hour. They passed from the manicured lawns of the pristine Flextronics site at Parque Integral de Tecnologia, an industrial park a few miles northwest of Guadalajara. Then they moved on past the impoverished Mexican landscape and across the border. The trucks made their way to a big warehouse in Memphis, Tennessee, and then delivered to stores nationwide.[1]

FINISH LINE FOR GAMES

For Xbox game developers, the months leading up to the launch were sheer hell. Inside Microsoft, the top titles were getting lavished with attention from testers and hardware support. Jason Jones was running ragged. His team kept an internal Web site showing the total number of bugs found, the number of bugs still active, and the number fixed. Through the summer, the number of active bugs was well above 400.

"The number of bugs just kept going up," he said. "Then we finally began to close the gap."

For those who weren't at the Redmond headquarters, the feedback on testing took longer. When Oddworld submitted its first version of *Munch's Oddysee* to Microsoft's testing department, the testers reported more than a thousand bugs.

"It was horrible," McKenna said.

Lanning's group had to finish their content for the game by the second week of August; after that, they could no longer change the art. Then they hit a feature deadline, freezing any changes to the game's features. Then they got their final debugging kits, which had arrived late because Microsoft conceived them late in the game. These kits, cheap machines that could only test content, not create it, were intended to be used by armies of testers in comparison to the more expensive development kits. Line by line, the entire company began looking for the biggest bugs—the No. 1, or crash, bugs that stopped the game from working altogether. In early September, they hit their first zero bug release. But soon enough, the testers found another 50 bugs.

They were due to hit zero bugs on September 11, 2001. But, like everyone else in the country, the team had been jarred by the terrorist attacks in New York and Washington. The attacks grounded air traffic and halted shipments of parts to Flextronics's factories for days.

Blackley's constant travel had taken him to New York in early September, and he was actually in a plane over Manhattan at the time of the attack on the World Trade Center. He looked out the window and couldn't understand why there was so much smoke over the city. He and other passengers turned on the satellite TV screens on the backs of their seats. They listened to CNN anchors talk about a plane hitting the World Trade Center. Blackley looked out the window and saw the smoke from another explosion as another plane hurtled into the second building.

"Not fun to watch outside of the window of a jetliner," he says. "There was just this stunned silence."

The pilot diverted Blackley's plane to Buffalo, New York. There he had to sit out the crisis as the nation's air fleet was grounded. Canadian air space opened first so Blackley flew to Toronto. Then he caught a plane to Vancouver and Kevin Bachus drove to pick him up. Robbie Bach had been on the ground in New York; he had to drive a car home across country, a trip that took 54 hours. But, as the dust settled, Bush asked the nation to get back to normal while he worked on plans for retaliation. Economists predicted that the direct losses to the economy from the attacks added up to $70 billion, while the harm to consumer and business confidence was so great that it was likely to push the United States into a recession. Against this world backdrop, Microsoft's problems seemed puny. But the company, already stressed out by the launch, had to scramble to adapt. It canceled a press event scheduled for Tunisia, where the team planned to shine green lights on some ancient ruins. Instead, it moved the event to the south of France. And it renamed the launch events in New York and Los Angeles—"Ground Zero" just didn't work anymore.

Blackley agreed about getting back to normal. He hated the terrorists as much as anyone else, and he insisted on flying to visit people who would no longer get on an airplane to visit his team in Redmond.

"You can think of the Xbox as research into human happiness," he says. "You don't want those guys to stop you from doing things that make people happy."

The hardware production schedule was upset once again by the absence of air freight for a whole week in the wake of the terrorist attacks. Some team members were afraid of flying commercial airlines, so Todd Holmdahl secured private jets for anyone who wanted one, and he moved to enhance Microsoft's videoconferencing usage.

Munch's Odyssee finally got to zero bugs later in the week. Microsoft started telling retailers that it expected Oddworld's game to sell to about 40 percent of the installed base of users in the first season. That was second to *Halo,* which was expected to sell to 80 percent, but better than other titles like Microsoft's football game, which was projected at 20 percent.

Everyone took time out to watch the launch of the Nintendo GameCube in Japan on September 14. The craze over the new console was muted. A few long lines did form at stores in Tokyo's Shinjuku district, but the city's famed Akihabara district was relatively deserted. Everyone knew that Japanese consumers were in shock over the terrorist attacks in the United States as well, but no one expected such a poor showing. Nintendo had 500,000 machines ready at the launch, expecting to sell out almost at once. After the first few days, however, it still had over 100,000 left in stock. The machines were priced at 25,000 yen, or 10,000 yen lower than the Sony PlayStation 2. But the problem was the same one that dogged Nintendo on the previous console generation: There weren't enough games. Only three titles were ready at launch. Still, Nintendo had months to go before the Xbox launched in Japan in February. That was a long head start.

At Flextronics, the company was rolling into action. The test systems were finally working, and components were rolling into the factory. In Guadalajara, they flipped the on-switch and began working like mad.

When Microsoft said it would delay the U.S. launch by a week, the move sparked mixed reactions. Some didn't mind the wait, but others thought it said something about Microsoft's incompetence as a newcomer. Microsoft didn't explain its reasons, but many speculated that it needed more breathing room on manufacturing the boxes. Others thought it wanted to put more distance between it and the terrorist attacks.

"Microsoft is not ready for war," wrote Telly O'Neill, a gamer who posted comments on the Gamespot Web site. "They are trying to be like Nintendo and are actually planning things out. Nintendo has been in the game longer, so they know the deal. Take notes, Microsoft." An anonymous poster said, "Nintendo handed Microsoft a window of opportunity to get some sales in, and Microsoft is blowing it. When it comes to consoles, Microsoft is as green as the Xbox logo."

But in the weeks after manufacturing started, Flextronics put the pedal to the metal. Holmdahl had expected it to take three months for the factory to reach full capacity. But Flextronics hit full production in a little over a month. Moreover, the Flextronics team from Sarvar, Hungary—who had watched the Mexicans start the first plant—were able to get their plant to full capacity in just three weeks. Both factories were soon producing 175,000 units a week, more than the original expected capacity. Production looked like it would fall short of the 600,000 to 800,000 that Bach had promised for the first day. But the available amount was respectable in part because the replenishment rate was better now.

"The retailers cared a lot more about how soon we could replenish the stores and what our schedule was for doing so," Robbie Bach says. It didn't matter if they didn't have quite so many boxes on the shelves the first day as long as they could order more quickly.

Blackley was traveling everywhere trying to tell people how cool the Xbox was. Fighting the negative perceptions of the press and developers, he was trying to hold the launch together.

At one point, he said, "I was really upset that we had lost our way at E3."

Soon enough, he picked up a fresh dose of pep. Bach had decided that Blackley was such an enthusiastic spokesman that he sent him around to do all the major press interviews with news outlets including *Time* and *Newsweek*. During mid-October, he traveled to Japan and Europe to show off games to the press on a nonstop schedule. Sony's PR department actually kept a file on Blackley and it fretted that Sony didn't really have anyone as articulate as Blackley to counter him on the rhetoric. The interviews made him feel important again and he enjoyed delivering the message repeatedly until the interviewers understood it.

"It's frustrating to not do anything anymore," he said. "I talk and I travel. I shouldn't just be demoing a game like *Halo*. I should be working on a game like that."

The deadline for final debugging for Xbox launch titles was October 10, and the deadline for release to manufacturing was October 17. It was a race to the wire to finish everything on time.

Game reviewers started getting their final Xbox consoles ahead of the launch during the week of October 23. The reviews started coming in. John Davison, editorial director of the Ziff Davis Media Game Group, which published the *Official PlayStation* magazine and *Electronic Gaming Monthly,* said he was astonished at how much progress the Xbox had made. The editors of *EGM* had voted 6 to 5 that the Xbox was a better machine than the GameCube, particularly if gamers only had enough money to buy one console during the holidays.

"The launch games are better, simple as that," said Dan Hsu, editor-in-chief of *EGM*.

Of the launch titles, Microsoft had managed to have 5 out of 19 produced under its own name. So it had a good chance of making the business model requirement that it produce 33 percent of the revenues for games on its console. And the results coming back on *Halo* from the game reviewers were huge. *EGM* and *Edge* magazines gave it a 10 out of 10, a rare accolade. Even though it carried a "mature" rating—the first time that Microsoft had ever shipped a game intended only for adults—it was the flagship. Reviews were also astonishing for Microsoft's *NFL Fever* football game, and for *Project Gotham Racing.*

One of the minor hits among the reviewers was David Wu's *Cel Damage.* His team had finished on schedule, at the beginning of September. He gave them a much-needed vacation and holed up in his studio in Toronto. His publisher, Electronic Arts, had asked him to strongly consider adapting his game to run on the Nintendo GameCube. He felt some loyalty to Blackley and wondered if it would hurt their friendship. But the business case was compelling. Microsoft hadn't paid any money to make the game exclusive, and it had even had the gall to cancel the game. *Cel Damage* was the very first game to be finished and so it was useful in working out all of the kinks in the certification process. Wu had enough time, so in the next three weeks he locked himself in a room and adapted the game run on the GameCube. That hurt Microsoft, but Blackley said he wasn't angry. He knew that Wu had to make a business decision and that it wasn't a make-or-break game for the Xbox anyway.

Ed Fries didn't sweat the *Cel Damage* news. *Halo* was finished. Jason Jones had stayed until 4 A.M. one night with the testers and they finally put it to bed. There had been more than 10,000 bugs in the code. Most had been fixed. A few remained but the game worked without crashing. That was good enough to ship, and Jones wasn't about to experiment more with stable code. At 11 A.M. the next day, it went off to manufacturing.

"It was beautiful," Jones says. "It was great. I went home and finally got to see what my house looked like. I had never really moved in. I still had my license plates from Chicago."

By this time, Blackley had plenty of other things to celebrate. His new girlfriend, Van Burnham, shared his passion for video games. She was a journalist and had written a book on classic video games. They agreed to draw a line between their professional and private worlds, but she accompanied him on the biggest events of his life. At the same time, they could talk about shared passions like their love for the classic arcade game *Robotron: 2084*. Blackley had a *Robotron* machine in his home and the two enjoyed playing it on the "super mega bad-ass difficulty, or level 10," Burnham says.

"I met a girl who makes me happy," he says.

As the good news rolled in, Blackley calmed down. His fury at E3 had been replaced by self-confidence and surprise at how Ed Fries's teams and the third parties had come through at the end with finished games.

"I've become numb to the good news now," he says. "It's nuts."

During October, he shared his enthusiasm with journalists all over the country, adding to the nearly 900,000 frequent flyer miles he had accumulated during the project. He was excited that even the game enthusiasts in Japan were starting to favor the Xbox as sales of the GameCube floundered for lack of games. Over time, he believed that "creative exclusives" would emerge that would be available only on Xbox because it was the only machine capable of running them. Companies were beginning to say they were doubling or tripling their Xbox development budgets.

"We've lit the fuse," he said at a promotional event for game players in Los Angeles at the Universal Studios CityWalk entertainment complex. "It's waterproof and it's going to happen. It made me proud. It's a testament to our vision."

Fans were going bananas. Many waited for half a day in lines just to make sure they could compete in the Xbox Unleashed events in Los Angeles and New York. Hideo Okada, another self-described *otaku*, or game freak, flew from Japan for the Los Angeles event with nothing but some money and his passport. He had to buy a sweatshirt to keep warm, but he wasn't disappointed in the games.

"I wanted to test my endurance," said Okada, who stayed up all night waiting in lines and taking his turns during the Xbox tournament competition.

As players gathered around the machines at the events, they noticed that a good thing had happened in the six months since the E3 show. The games were done, and there were a lot of them. Microsoft and its allies had finished 19 games for the launch day, living up to the promise made months earlier that 15 to 20 games would be available on day one. None of the major titles had slipped. When Nvidia cut the speed of its graphics chip from 250 megahertz to 233 megahertz, that was a setback for teams such as the one making *NFL Fever,* a fast-action football game that had to run at a very high speed. But Blackley's old team at the Advanced Technology Group worked closely with the football game programmers to help them hit their target.

Microsoft's top games had all hit gold in the weeks leading up to the mid-October deadlines. By comparison, Nintendo was still only ready to launch seven or eight games, and Shigeru Miyamoto's big hit from E3, *Pikmin,* looked like it wasn't going to show until December. It could have just been luck, but Microsoft believed it had beaten Nintendo to the finish line on games because of a combination of superior development tools and an enormous emphasis on testing—something that had come from Microsoft's deep experience in shipping software. (Most people still make fun of buggy Microsoft programs, but few know how serious it is about testing.) And since the launch titles were all that mattered at first, Microsoft threw its resources into making sure that all 19 titles slated for the launch received the fastest possible turnaround on final certification.

"I know for a fact that we spend more resources on testing than any other company," Fries said.

Brian Farrell of THQ was surprised at how much the final games had improved since the poor showing at E3. "It looked like everything was going wrong, but my hat's off to them."

The power of Microsoft's $500 million marketing campaign was finally hitting. This budgeted amount impressed everyone, especially since it matched the amount spent on the launch of Microsoft's Windows XP operating system in the last week of October. The XP launch went well, but it wasn't enough to pump sales for personal computers in the midst of an unprecedented recession. But the enthusiasm for games seemed to be hotter than ever.

"You won't be able to escape the damn green X," said John Davison, editorial director at the Ziff Davis Media Game Group.

Microsoft had the No. 2 brand in the world, according to a survey in the summer of 2001 by Interbrand, Citigroup, and *Business Week*. Sony ranked No. 20, while Nintendo was 29. But Microsoft's brand had a lot less power in the gaming market. That was why Microsoft had to make its marketing dollars go further. The company hired the ad firm McKann-Erickson WorldGroup (a unit of Interpublic Group) to make its ad campaign. TV commercials aired on the World Series and on channels like MTV and ESPN to reach young audiences. Teaser ads featured a big glowing green orb with voice-over narration saying, "The hair looks like real hair. The clothes move like real clothes. The sweat drips like real sweat. Pity those who play to escape reality." Other ads focused on game play. That stemmed from John O'Rourke's core strategy: You can't fool gamers, so just show them the games. Microsoft also struck a promotional deal with Taco Bell, which began giving away 6,800 Xboxes to customers. Taco Bell was the favorite restaurant of hardcore gamers, and it saw its year-over-year sales rise as a result of the promotion.

"It legitimizes the product if Taco Bell thinks it's great," says Don Coyner, an Xbox marketing director.

The company installed 11,000 Xbox prototypes in stores across the United States, but it found that some of the machines (enclosed in glass cases) overheated and that some retailers had failed to install them correctly. Marketing had to dispatch troops to fix them. With all the new marketing people and the growing games division, there were now 1,500 people working on the Xbox, which made it the biggest start-up in Microsoft's history.

Peter Main, executive vice president of marketing at Nintendo of America, didn't think Microsoft would get much bang out of its ad budget. Even with the spend, he said, Microsoft would wind up with only about 7 percent of the console market at year end, even though it would account for 30 percent of the spending.

"They're spending money against no sales on machines that may sell out anyway," Main said. On November 2, 2001, Microsoft got another lucky break. The company and the Justice Department announced they had reached a settlement in the long-running antitrust case. The state attorneys general didn't go along, but it was a sign that Bill Gates's long legal nightmare was ending. Xbox ads began to debut on TV.

Blackley was booked to speak on stage with Bill Gates at the Comdex computer trade show in Las Vegas on November 11. Although Comdex itself typically drew about 200,000 attendees during one week, only 130,000 were expected this time because of security fears. Gates's keynote would probably draw its usual full house of thousands anyway, but Blackley was no longer nervous about going on stage in front of big crowds.

As the big night came, Bill Gates opened to the expected crowd under the klieg lights at the MGM Grand Hotel's theater. He noted that the disaster of September 11 wouldn't hold down the technology industry for long. He showed the notorious Monkey Boy video clip of CEO Steve Ballmer jumping up and down at a Microsoft rally in a ridiculous show of corporate enthusiasm. Once again he saved the Xbox for last.

Blackley came walking out slowly, holding the Xbox above his head like a gladiator with a trophy. "Xbox!" he shouted to get the crowd going. Blackley handed the box to Gates, saying, "I got a lot of stuff to say to these guys so can you hook this up?"

Gates went over to the TV set and hooked up the machine and its controllers. Blackley deadpanned, "So simple, even Bill Gates can hook it up."

Blackley turned on the Xbox and it booted in the promised 11 seconds, much faster than the other boxes. Blackley showed demos of *NFL Fever.* He received a kickoff and ran it back well to the applause of the crowd. He stopped the action in the football game during a pass and zoomed in on the football itself, revealing the intricate texture of the bumpy surface of the ball. "Don't try that on your PlayStation 2," he said happily, adding, "Our football has more memory in it than the GameCube has video memory." The crowd laughed along. Then Blackley dazzled the crowd with demos of games like Activision's *Wreckless,* which led players on wild car chases through the crowded streets of Hong Kong during rush hour. The chase scenes—with pedestrians scampering out of the path of destruction—were so real they resembled a reality TV show. Blackley closed, saying, "Thank you, Bill, for letting us execute on our vision."

Gates was supposed to say, "So, we're done." To which Blackley would reply, "No, Bill, I don't want to be done." Instead, Gates flubbed his line and said, "So, why don't we give away an Xbox?"

Blackley proceeded to give away four Xboxes by calling out the section, row, and seat number of the winners. The crowd got very excited as some of the winners held their hands up in triumph.

THE LAUNCH

On the night of November 14, New York City's Times Square was bathed in green light. Electronic marquees glowed with the Xbox colors above the four-story, 101,000-square-foot Toys 'R Us store that would be opening for the first time at midnight.

J Allard was standing outside the store with his hair dyed white and a light green shirt. A man in a sweater came up to him and asked if he should get in line to buy an Xbox. Allard assured him that he would be able to get a box if he stood in line and got a wristband.

"Do you know much about the Xbox?" the man asked. Allard looked around and laughed. "Yeah, I do." He proceeded to tell the man why he should buy one.

Hundreds of people were picking up the wristbands. Vendors gave away Krispy Kreme donuts with Xbox green sprinkles on them. Women with green hair handed out glow-in-the-dark necklaces. A bikini-clad model based on a character in the *Dead or Alive 3* game wrapped herself in a body-length sweater to escape the cold air. Most of the men in the line fit the Xbox demographic. They were young males in their twenties who had to own every game console that came out. Dan Zuccarelli, a 24-year-old Web programmer, was visiting from Philadelphia and he decided to line up for an Xbox. He held two jobs but still found time to play games about 20 hours a week. Only a year ago he had waited in line to get a PlayStation 2.

José David, a 21-year-old butcher from the Bronx, waited for more than six hours in the line. He was going to shell out $299 for the system and more for an extra controller, *Munch's Odyssee, Halo,* and *Dead or Alive 3.*

"I think the Xbox is the best system out there," he said. "I want to be telling my friends I have the Xbox before they do. I have a PS 2. Too boring. I believe Bill Gates knows what he is doing."

As he said so, the security noticeably thickened. A contingent of plainclothes officers and New York's finest shielded the richest man in the world as he approached the line. Gates shook hands as TV cameras and photographers flashed bright lights at him. Hussein Chahin, a 19-year-old student from Brooklyn, shook Gates's hand as he passed by. Gates went into the store and the security guards sealed off the access. Inside, TV cameras angled for position. A few minutes earlier, Gates had walked into the headquarters of the World Wrestling Federation, based on the other side of Times Square, and faced off with his old friend, the Rock. The wrestling champion played *Dead or Alive 3* with Gates. The Rock won two out of three rounds.

Inside Toys 'R Us, almost all of the high-level Xbox team was waiting for the doors to open: Robbie Bach, John O'Rourke, J Allard, Ed Fries, Don Coyner, and Seamus Blackley, who smiled and said, "I'm feeling very proud." Back in Redmond, Jeff Henshaw, Mark Thomas, and Avril Daly were celebrating by driving through the Microsoft campus in a Ford Expedition armed with a powerful spotlight that they beamed into all the offices, much to the consternation of Microsoft's security department. A big white searchlight with the green X in the middle lit up three stories of a building just across from Nintendo's headquarters. Kevin Bachus was in Seattle watching at a local game store. He called Blackley on the cell phone and said, "I feel like my baby is going out into the world and strange men are putting their hands all over her." In the days before the launch, the Xbox finally seemed real to Bachus because now there were real Xbox games and soon gamers would be playing those games on their machines. Up to that point, he had always thought about Xbox games being in development with a long way to go.

Just before midnight in New York, Gates walked into the labyrinth of the store and played to the TV cameras. He pulled the first customer out of the line and began playing against him at an Xbox terminal. Edward Glucksman, a 20-year-old from Keansburg, New Jersey, had gotten his place in line by waiting 12 hours. He played Gates at *Fusion Frenzy,* a party game, and crushed Gates.

"I'm very excited," he said. "Bill Gates is god. Ever since I was young I told people I wanted to be like Gates. I told him that and he just smiled."

Allard said the launch had "absolutely exceeded my expectations." Flextronics was now churning out 120,000 boxes a week, more than its expected capacity. He saw before him a cross section of society, with young people from all walks of life. He didn't mind at all that Sony had more than 20 million PS 2s in the market already.

"I think there is room for all three consoles," he said. "Could we have come out sooner? Sure. It's always scary to do a razor-and-razor-blades business model. But I think tonight we are showing that we have the right blades."

The crowd erupted as Gates stepped up to a microphone. "Bill, Bill, Bill," they chanted. John Eyler, CEO of Toys 'R Us, welcomed the crowd to the store, which he said was twice as big as the next-biggest toy store in the world. Gates said the Xbox team had been working furiously for the past 18 months since the go-ahead announcement at the Game Developers Conference.

"Amazingly, it all came together," he said. He noted the company would keep restocking Xboxes until it sold 1.5 million units by the end of December.

"At the end of the day, it's all about having fun," he said in closing. "Come on in and let's have some fun."

As midnight struck, Bill Gates handed over the first Xbox to Glucksman.

Robbie Bach was beaming as the first machines went on sale and the crowds started pouring through.

"Welcome to the starting line," he said to Blackley, who was standing nearby with his girlfriend.

"Fuck off," Blackley said. They both laughed and high-fived each other.

A little later, Blackley and his girlfriend walked to a remote part of the store where Gates had moved. Gates turned to Blackley, saying, "Big night, don't you think?"

Blackley replied, "Pretty cool, very very cool."

Pointing to Burnham, Gates said, "She seems very nice."

Blackley said, "She's a pretty good one, yeah."

Gates said, "You know Seamus, I think she could help you get your act together."

"You think so? Something has to," Blackley said.

"You ought to marry her," Gates said.

"You think so?" Blackley replied.

"Yeah, absolutely," Gates said. "Here's a ring," handing Blackley a ring with a square-shaped diamond with a couple of baguettes on each side in a 1920s-style platinum setting.

"I'll give it a shot, OK, cool," Blackley said. He got down on one knee. "Vanessa, will you marry me?"

She laughed and said, "Yes."

"Thank you," Blackley said.

Blackley rose, and they kissed. Everyone in the store applauded. Blackley put the ring on Burnham's finger. They kissed again and Burnham displayed the ring. John Eyler, CEO of Toys 'R Us, presented a giant stuffed unicorn to her. This time Gates got all of his lines right, although he ad-libbed the part about Blackley getting his act together. Kevin Bachus, who had been let in on the secret, agreed to be the best man.

CHAPTER 27

THE FIRST SEASON

THE DAY AFTER THE XBOX LAUNCH, the United States was still abuzz with news. The war in Afghanistan was going well, and—though the rest of the economy was in tatters—video games were still going strong. It faced headwinds as consumers tightened their gift-spending during the recession. John O'Rourke in Xbox marketing believed Xbox sales would be strong because people were staying at home instead of traveling. Even in a tough economy and in the wake of the September 11 attacks, people would want to be entertained. "We are in the business of delivering smiles to people," he said.

Console fans were already coming out in droves. In the first nine months of the year, video game sales were up 34 percent versus the same period in 2000, according to market researcher NPD Funworld. Ziff Davis Media Game Group reported that 42 percent of gamers said they planned to buy a new console starting in the fall.

Nintendo didn't stage a spectacular store event on November 18, but it did hold a party for a select audience of actors and models at its Cube Club in the SoHo district of New York City. To hip-hop dance music, the club-goers played Nintendo's launch titles on more than 50 GameCube consoles. Among the celebrities present were actors John Turturro and Matthew Modine, NBC correspondent Maria Shriver, and rapper Lil Kim. A fair number of the crowd confessed that they weren't game fans, but many brought their kids to check out the hardware. Others just checked out the pretty scenery.

Minoru Arakawa, president of Nintendo of America, said that some of his employees had bought a few Xbox systems and were testing the games. He acknowledged there were a wide variety of titles, but he insisted the quality wasn't there. Arakawa admitted that the buzz about the Xbox was significantly improved since the E3 show, a turnabout that disappointed him. But he felt that once consumers got their hands on the GameCube games, they would change their minds.

"I agree about the change in perception," Arakawa said. "They are doing a great PR job. What counts is how satisfied the consumer is after they bought it."

Now the battle of the press releases and surveys was under way. Nintendo announced that its first-day GameCube system, game, and accessory sales were $98 million, exceeding the $93.5 million for the opening day of the *Harry Potter* movie. Of course, many more people saw the movie with its much lower per-ticket prices. Not to be outdone, Microsoft also said it exceeded the movie launch, though it declined to disclose revenues.

By Thanksgiving weekend, many stores had sold out of both Xboxes and GameCubes. A couple of weeks after the GameCube launch, Nintendo said it would ship 200,000 more units during the Christmas season than expected, giving it a total of 1.3 million units in the United States by year-end. Then, two weeks before Christmas, Microsoft said it had shipped more than 1.1 million units to retailers, a surprise amount considering how short supplies were at the outset. It was on schedule to meet its optimistic target despite the glitches in the months before the launch. Resupply from Mexico, and the fast ramp at the Hungary plant, was saving the day.

Sony noted a survey that showed most people were planning to spend more time viewing home entertainment during the holidays; about 43 percent of the 800 people surveyed said they would spend more time playing video games. Changewave Research, meanwhile, noted in its survey that kids considered the Xbox the No. 1 gift they wanted for Christmas, with the PlayStation 2 a runner-up and the GameCube a distant third. Sony said that it saw a boost in console sales as some big titles—*Metal Gear Solid 2, Devil May Cry, Grand Theft Auto 3, Tony Hawk Pro Skater 3*—hit the market. "We were very happy with our sales in October," said Kunitake Ando, president of Sony.

Sony kept its advertising blitz strong during the holidays. Nobody, it turned out, was a loser during the Christmas season. Console sales had more than tripled during November in the United States compared to the same month a year earlier. Game sales rose 357 percent during the same period. Xbox games were initially outselling GameCube games, a reflection in part on the wider availability of titles on the Xbox, said Richard Ow, analyst for NPD Funworld, a market research firm in Port Washington, New York. The top Xbox title was *Halo,* while the top GameCube title was *Star Wars: Rogue Squadron II: Rogue Leader.* In the first few weeks, *Dead or Alive 3* sales on the Xbox shot past 500,000, surpassing

Tecmo's expectations, said John Inada, director of marketing in Tecmo's U.S. office.

"They all succeeded," Ow said. "Both new consoles are well established now. I believe that what is happening now is an expansion of the market."

In the first season of competition, everyone was a winner. Sales of video game hardware, software, and accessories topped $9 billion in 2001, eclipsing movie box-office receipts and showing a growth rate of more than 40 percent over 2000. Sony had the most plentiful supply and it added another 5 million hardware units to its tally in the fourth quarter of 2001, bringing its worldwide installed base for the PS 2 to 25 million units. Worldwide PS 2 game sales hit 125 million, giving Sony a tie ratio of five games for every box sold. During November and December of 2001, Sony's North American unit said it sold almost 3 million PS 2s, and in December it sold six games for every machine. Of the top 20 titles in December, 14 of them were for the PS 2 or the original PlayStation, according to NPD Funworld. By the end of December, there were 220 PS 2 titles on the market in North America. And Sony hit its numbers without needing to cut its $299 price in the United States. The spike in game sales finally enabled Sony to make an operating profit of $493 million, compared to a loss of $103 million a year earlier. The division had endured six quarters of losses from PS 2 sales before making a profit. There was no sign the Xbox or GameCube had hurt Sony.

But Sony did suffer from some execution problems again. It had promised back in May that it would deliver a hard disk drive and network adapter for the PlayStation 2, but neither product was ready for the holidays. Sony announced late in the season it would launch an online game service in Japan in April and later in the United States and Europe. It also estimated it would sell 18 million PS 2s in the year ending March 31, 2002, not 20 million, because of the need to tighten inventory during the recession.

The Xbox and GameCube both sold out, thanks to hard-core gamers—who number around 9 million in the United States, according to the Ziff Davis Media Game Group. These are people like Steve Simons, a 19-year-old in Westford, Massachusetts, who decided to drop $1,395 to buy the Xbox and the GameCube as well as a boatload of accessories and games. He stood in line a few hours to pick up his pre-ordered Xbox console at an Electronics Boutique store and then returned a couple of days later to wait a couple of hours for a GameCube. Simons owns just about every console ever made, but he keeps buying. He purchased nine Xbox games and four GameCube games right out of the gate. He already had a library of PlayStation 2 and Dreamcast games. But he said, "The Xbox has so much more to offer now and so much more in the future."

The GameCube sold about 2.4 million units worldwide by the end of 2001, a respectable number given the tough market conditions that Nintendo faced. The Japanese launch didn't go as well as expected, and resupply in the North American market was handicapped because it had to ship units in from overseas. In early January, Minoru Arakawa announced he was resigning from the top job at Nintendo of America after 22 years. That wasn't a good omen for sure. On the other hand, *Super Smash Brothers* for the GameCube outsold *Halo* during December, and the GameBoy Advance sold more than 5 million units in the North American market in 2001.

Robbie Bach, meanwhile, announced at the Consumer Electronics Show in early January that Microsoft had met its goal of selling 1.5 million units in the U.S. market. He said the company had sold more than three games for every console, making it the best console launch in history. Microsoft shipped more than a million units of *Halo* into the channel, making it by far the top game on the Xbox. It may have been just a simple first-person shooter game with beautiful graphics and a nice science-fiction story, but it turned out to be the killer game for the Xbox. Ed Fries beamed with pride, saying he had believed in *Halo* for a long time. Jason Jones, relieved after months of nonstop work, said, "We had done what we wanted to do. That was a great feeling." In the fourth quarter of 2001, Microsoft reported earnings of $2.28 billion. The losses from Xbox hardware, no more than $150 million, were partly offset by profits from games. But the overall impact on the company was unnoticeable. Microsoft ended the quarter with cash of $38 billion.

Will Microsoft win? It will be a year or more into Xbox sales before anyone can tell if Microsoft stands a chance of catching up to Sony's installed base. The newcomer still has to gain solid ground in Europe and Japan. Microsoft must successfully launch Xbox online, cut the costs of its hardware, launch more triple-A titles, and deal with marketing the box after it is no longer supply-constrained. In his own message to the Xbox troops, J Allard predicted that the competition would turn up the steam. Sony would cut its price to $199, launch a dozen online games by Christmas 2002, top 20 million consoles in the United States and 500 titles, and launch more exclusive titles. Nintendo would beef up its support from third-party publishers and leverage the success of the GameBoy Advance.

"It looks like it's going to be a three-horse race," said Brian Farrell, CEO of THQ.

Allard wishes that the company had managed to make more machines for the launch and to snag more of the top titles that Nintendo and Sony kept for themselves. With bluster, he says Microsoft won't be satisfied until there is an Xbox next to every TV. So far, it hasn't yet surpassed the achievements of Sega's Dreamcast, which tumbled into defeat after selling 8 million units. On the other hand, in the past 15 years the leadership in the console business has turned over three times. Most said the task of launching a new console was impossible. Nintendo looks vulnerable in the Japanese market, and even after the GameCube launch it appeared that Sony would stay on top there with the PlayStation 2. Later on, as the second Christmas titles begin hitting the market, the competition will likely spread out into visible winners and losers. Nintendo executives remembered well that they didn't lose the previous console war until the second year of competition. Nintendo's games were more expensive, and developers shifted much of their development to the PlayStation. Perhaps with that in mind, Hiroshi Yamauchi sold about 10 percent of his Nintendo stock in November and said he planned to provide collateral-free loans to developers making GameCube games.

For once, all three consoles in the market had considerable developer support. Even Trip Hawkins, CEO of struggling 3DO, had to admit in a conference call with analysts that he might have to make games for the Xbox and the GameCube in addition to the PS 2. While Nintendo courted third-party developers more slowly, those who studied the system decided it was easy to program for. Hence, Nintendo looked like it was on its way to the largest developer support it had ever seen for a console, even as it tried to keep the market from being flooded. Microsoft had hundreds of developers on board, while Sony also had hundreds delivering games. Many expected GameCube sales to get good bumps as Nintendo released its Mario, Zelda, and Pokemon franchises for the GameCube in 2002.

Nintendo had the advantage of having the cheapest hardware, and it expected to drive its costs down quickly. Sony had trouble reducing the cost of its PlayStation 2 but was on track to do better than Microsoft, whose system was the costliest of all. Microsoft could halve its original cost over five years and still be only at Nintendo's starting price. Peter Main of Nintendo said that he expected the GameCube hardware to turn a profit in early 2002. Nintendo and Sony were likely to put pressure on Microsoft by cutting prices on hardware more often. Microsoft might not suffer losses as bad as the ones Rick Thompson originally feared, but the financial picture will still be scary for a few years.

Microsoft had banked heavily on online games for the Xbox by putting the networking technology in the box. But that bet might not pay off because of the slow acceptance of broadband in the home. The restrictions Microsoft put on on-line gaming will protect players from security threats, but they also limit appeal compared to PC games. Sony's policies were expected to be more liberal, and that prompted Square to focus its *Final Fantasy XI* game on the PlayStation 2. Still, Epic Games was making its *Unreal Championship* one of the flag-ship online games for the Xbox, and that was sure to build a lot of enthusiasm. By 2006, Jupiter-Media Metrix expects the number of households with Internet-connected consoles to be 12.6 million, up from 700,000 in 2000.

The upshot of the competition is that analysts believe that Sony will come out ahead of the game. The PlayStation 2 was expected to have 42 percent of the worldwide video game con-sole market in 2004, according to the European Leisure Soft-ware Publishers Association. Nintendo and Microsoft are expected to take about 29 percent of the market each, accord-ing to the forecast. Likewise, Forrester Research predicted that the margin between the winner and the second- and third-place console makers would be much smaller this time than in the previous console war. Microsoft was expected to do best in the United States and Europe, but poorly in Japan. Nintendo, meanwhile, was expected to grab the greatest profits because of its monopoly in portable games.

In Japan, Microsoft expected to launch with 12 games. Hi-rohisa "Pat" Ohura, managing director of Microsoft's Japan subsidiary, said about 80 companies had signed up to make games for the Japanese market, and those companies were working on about 150 titles.[1]

The Xbox remains the underdog. But the very fact that it made it to market was a miracle in itself. The better the games that the artists develop for it, the better its chances for long-term success. Its best hope is that the growing demographics of gaming would make it possible to support three healthy console makers.

Microsoft still has a long way to go before it even catches the market penetration that Sega achieved with its Dreamcast before Sony's PlayStation 2 crushed it. But it seems clear that, if Microsoft keeps its willpower, it has great chances for success. In places like Korea, where Internet gaming on the PC has triumphed over video game consoles, Microsoft has a wide-open market in part because of the enmity Koreans have for Japanese products. And Microsoft is not coming into a weakened industry to clean up the dregs. The games business has never had a better ecosystem. Profits are a little scarce, to be sure, and consolidation will continue. But there are more game publishers who can spread their franchises across multiple platforms now. The creative artists have the freedom to break away to form their own boutique development shops. Start-ups and established companies are pioneering new markets like wireless and online games. Games have enormous momentum in penetrating new demographics. All Microsoft has to do is carve out a role in the ecosystem: predator, prey, or the air itself.

It's fun to wonder what Xbox Next will be. J Allard admits he's already got people working on it. The "emerging efforts" team includes Margaret Johnson, Mike Abrash, and Jeff Henshaw. Microsoft's top dogs have dropped hints here and there. CEO Steve Ballmer said in a speech at an investment conference in November 2001 that the Xbox is part of a broader concept that Microsoft will test in the future.

"We went and said, 'Hey, we have some ideas for an all-purpose box, kind of a PC, kind of a game console, kind of a set-top box," he said. "You know what they said? They said, 'Get outta Dodge, we're not going to write software for that thing.' We came back a year later and said OK, we're going to start by doing the world's greatest video game machine. And they said OK, let's talk. We know we have to succeed, but there is a broader concept there that we will pursue at some point.

You can say this is the end of the road or is there a bigger play? And the answer is yeah, there's a bigger play we hope to get over time."[2]

Gamers can only hope that Microsoft won't try to create a Trojan Horse before its time. They will want an even better game box next time, not something that will turn the room lights on and off or record their favorite TV shows. Convergence will get easier over time, but, in Blackley's words, convergence in the past has only been bullshit. A dedicated game box will be able to deliver the future of gaming much better than an all-in-one box. If Microsoft doesn't build this box, a competitor might do it instead. In any case, everyone knows that Bill Gates isn't going to quit with just the original Xbox.

"This is a business where it takes a while before you get it right," says Bobby Kotick, CEO of Activision and a self-professed fan of Bill Gates. "Microsoft is a version 2.0 company."

CHAPTER 28

THE FUTURE OF GAMES

THE ECONOMIC DOWNTURN didn't hurt the mass market acceptance of the newest video game consoles, and it may even have helped as consumers stayed at home to entertain themselves. But what lies beyond the initial sales numbers? How far will the consoles penetrate into society? Could there one day be as many game consoles in homes as there are video cassette recorders or TV sets?

The beautiful thing about gamers is they can be both the harshest of skeptics and the truest of believers. They've been sold a bill of goods before. Marketing messages lie to them. Sega promised that its Dreamcast was so good as a computer opponent that it seemed like "it's thinking." Sony's PlayStation 9 commercials (used to advertise the PS 2) promise a virtual reality experience in the living room. But the PlayStation 2, while it has some of the best games ever created, is still a long way from virtual reality. The Xbox Web site claims its 19 launch titles will "forever change gaming." Every gamer would like to see games that are truly artistic. But whenever someone says a game is a piece of art, they're usually trying to sell something.

There is no equivalent of the film *Titanic* yet, unless you consider *Pokemon* to be fantastic art. And failing to live up to promises has harsh consequences in the games business. None knows that better than Seamus Blackley, whose *Trespasser* dinosaur shooting game crashed and burned years ago on just that rock. With the Xbox, he set out to transform games into an art form as legitimate as movies. Now it's time to fulfill that pledge, and some games look promising. Peter Molyneux, who has had seven titles that have sold more than a million units, is toiling away on *Project Ego,* a role-playing game for the Xbox that will allow players to make a complete impact on their own virtual worlds. The player will age through the game and so will the environment; a player who chops down a tree among a bunch of saplings can return to the spot 20 years later and find a stump in a forest. Characters will develop wrinkles. If they're wounded, they will have scars that will heal. The world will be real down to the blades of grass, Molyneux says. That's pretty cool, and maybe close to art.

The Xbox can deliver the kind of experience that Molyneux is talking about. It offers the state of the art of what game consoles can deliver. In spite of the marketing statements from Sony and Nintendo, the Xbox hardware should be able to deliver more oomph. It has the programmable pixel shaders of the Nvidia graphics chip that programmers are only beginning to use. The hard disk on the Xbox will pay off in unexpected ways as well. And the built-in networking will make the Xbox a good platform for online games, which—as J Allard says— offer new social dynamics that can widen the appeal of games, even bringing geographically separated families together. These design decisions, while expensive, give the Xbox potential to deliver a better experience in the long run. Gamers will be able to participate in football games where 11 human players square off against 11 human opponents. Broadband has been coming for a long time and in the next decade or so it may finally hit a mass market in the United States. And with broadband will come much better multiplayer games, enabling players to communicate via voice. The chance to wire gamers together gives the Xbox headroom, but it remains to be seen if gamers will pay extra for the headroom when they can get the here and now for $100 less in a GameCube.

Game machines still have a long way to go if reality is the target. The next Xbox will no doubt be more powerful as high-performance components become cheaper. It's a given that graphics will keep getting better and better, and in the process the systems will hook more and more people on games. Alvy Ray Smith, a former Microsoft researcher and pioneer of computer graphics who co-founded Pixar Animation (maker of the animated film *Toy Story*), once noted that to make images that looked real, a computer needed to be able to process about 80 million polygons per frame.[1] At 30 frames per second for fluid animation, that requires performance of about 2.4 billion polygons per second, which is about 20 times more than what the Xbox can deliver. Rick Rashid, vice president of research, believes that it will be possible to re-create reality within the next decade on a game console, and perhaps as soon as the next five years.

"It's easy to see the line between games and life beginning to blur," says Scott McCloud, author of *Understanding Comics*. "Games are capable of completely and seamlessly taking people out of their lives."[2]

Game characters that cry and sweat and "do things that real people do are just around the corner," says David Perry, whose Shiny Entertainment is working on a game based on the film *The Matrix*. But photorealism isn't the end in itself that, once reached, will magically turn games into a universal medium. Shigeru Miyamoto, Nintendo's top game designer, says, "You can create a huge world, but as a game it can still be boring. To me, it's about creating a world that fits the game." Games as they exist now are extremely popular in countries like South Korea and Japan, but in the United States they still have some way to go. To capture more consumers, games will have to follow them wherever they go. For sure, the future of gaming is going to be broader than a single platform.

"There are as many futures as there are people making and playing games," says Warren Spector, a seasoned game designer at Ion Storm in Austin, Texas.

The Xbox alone will not deliver the peak of gaming as an art form. The PC's own capabilities will race ahead of the Xbox within a year of the console's debut. Most new experimentation in gaming usually happens on the PC. Online gaming was born on the PC and it will take time for the consoles to catch up. Many of the stalwart PC developers are sticking with the PC. One of the hottest games of the fall season was *Sid Meier's Civilization III*, a chesslike strategy game published by Infogrames that had almost no chance of being released on a console. Ted Hase and Otto Berkes, ever faithful to the original Xbox vision, are still at Microsoft contemplating strategies to keep games alive on the PC.

Few of the games on the new platforms can be said to be breakaway titles that will appeal to women, girls, and others outside the target demographic. Gaming isn't just about the way bullets interact with objects in the universe.

"I think the industry has been remarkably blind to most of the market," says Brenda Laurel, the founder of Purple Moon, which tried making games for girls on the PC. Nolan Bushnell, the father of video games—he founded Atari and is now CEO of uWink—believes that the future of games will be in multiplayer terminals in public places like airports and bars. Drop a quarter into a machine and play across the Net.

"I think the universal hit is ultimately going to be a simple game that takes a short time and can be played anywhere," says Bushnell. "Don't forget about *Pong* and *Tetris*."

Ed Fries gave a rousing speech at Gamestock in 2001, but he will have a hard time living up to it.

"If we focus on making art, not just entertainment," he said, "then I think for the first time we'll deserve to speak to the mass audience and inherit our rightful place as the future of all entertainment."

John Carmack, whose string of hits from *Doom* to *Quake* qualifies him as one of the industry's artists, feels that art is the wrong word for gaming. (Even though such a declaration would protect him from his censors.)

"That's not what we're doing," he says. "We're doing entertainment. Saying it's art is a kind of sophistry from people who want to aggrandize our industry."

Jason Jones, who is now working on the sequel to *Halo*, agrees. "I don't want games to be taken seriously," he says. "Whatever you call it, turning your brain off and not thinking about the world for a while, ultimately it's just a way to have fun."

Someday someone may prove them wrong. One of these days, as Blackley hopes, someone will put game reviews in the arts section of the *New York Times*. The revolution will come in fits and starts. It probably won't come from giving hardcore gamers more of what they already like. Doing a fighting game with better graphics isn't really a new invention. Yet much of the industry is currently afflicted with the illusion that it is. About 60 percent of the successful games now are either sequels or extensions of brands that exist in another medium. There is a real risk of what the IDSA's Doug Lowenstein calls "creative ennui."

There has to be a killer application out there somewhere— a game that catches on like a virus and appeals to everybody up and down the intellectual spectrum. It's like the *Harry Potter* books that got kids interested in reading. Or the *Lord of the Rings* novels that inspired several generations. The game that is going to sell 100 million video game consoles—it's out there somewhere. The gaming industry has produced cultural icons before, from *Pac Man* to *Pong,* and it will do so again. As every gamer believes, the ideal game isn't here yet. It's just around the corner.

"These games are first-generation on the new consoles," says John Semikian, a 23-year-old college student from San Dimas, California. "Just imagine the future."

CHAPTER 29

EPILOGUE

FOR COMPANY MEN LIKE Robbie Bach, J Allard, and Ed Fries, there was still work to do after the U.S. launch. They had to get the Xbox off the ground in Japan and Europe, and they had to make plans for the online launch, which was pushed back from the summer of 2002 to October. Bach reorganized the management to get ready for year two. Allard expanded his responsibilities after the Xbox launch, taking charge of areas such as Todd Holmdahl's hardware group, which was slated to expand so that Microsoft could find more ways to drive the costs of the Xbox down. Fries, awaiting the birth of his first child, got on with the next slate of Xbox games. In the ultimate admission of defeat, the WebTV group suffered some layoffs thanks to poor sales of UltimateTV and, after a reorganization, some of its people were transferred to the Xbox team. While Jason Jones was the hero of the Xbox launch, others like David Wu were crestfallen as games like *Cel Damage* sold poorly. *Munch's Oddyssee* sold well but it wasn't runaway hit like *Halo*. Nvidia reported record earnings and revenues in the fourth quarter of 2001 and its stock was the best performing on the S&P 500 index. But its record was tarnished as it announced the Securities and Exchange Commission was investigating Nvidia's expense-recording practices. The government agency began the probe when Nvidia turned over internal data to it as part of the insider trading case related to the release of the Xbox news. The company said it was cooperating with the investigation and launching its own internal audit of its books, but the news coming in the wake of the collapse of Enron and its accounted-related woes sent Nvidia's stock into a tumble. Rick Thompson, the former vice president in charge of the Xbox, left his dot-com start-up after a short time and said he was "unemployed, not retired." Nat Brown, meanwhile, was enjoying time off with his wife and toddler son and was toying with the idea of creating new consumer devices with the Linux operating system. Otto Berkes, Ted Hase, and Horace Luke were hard at work figuring out ways to make the PC more like an appliance. PC game advocates were proud to point out that the Nvidia GeForce 4 released in the spring of 2002 made the PC's graphics far superior to the Xbox's.

The launch of the Xbox was a bittersweet moment for everyone on the Xbox project. Drew Angeloff, a member of Blackley's Advanced Technology Group and the man who built the original Xbox prototypes, said, "I don't think there is anything interesting to do anymore. Once you build a game console, there is nothing left to do."

At the same time, some game lovers felt like they had been sitting on the sidelines watching others play. Blackley began to have these feelings as well. In a meeting at E3 in May 2001, Warren Spector, Blackley's former Looking Glass colleague, was one of many people who planted the seed in his mind that he should be making great games. The comments made an impression on Blackley, though at the time he felt the need finish the Xbox job.

Blackley himself began to wonder about how much impact he could have and where he should do it. He had proven himself a great leader. Maybe now it was time for other managers to take over in the classic Microsoft hand-off. Blackley still wasn't rich since his stock options weren't very valuable because of the weak performance of Microsoft's stock. Microsoft also had a policy against giving bonuses to employees who created new businesses. At least he didn't have to worry about having spending money to buy cans of Coke anymore. Blackley wanted to get back on the playing field, which for him meant making a game that the critics and everyone else outside of gaming considers to be genuine art.

In a dinner one evening, Mr. Blackley asked a question that revealed the personal demons that he still hadn't quite exorcised.

"Have I made up for *Trespasser* yet?" he asked.

The answer was all in his mind. He had the soul of a game creator. He and his colleagues had created the artist's palette. The making of the Xbox is linked to the redemption of Seamus Blackley. The story might have ended quietly, like Icarus falling into the sea. But Blackley's tale began as he plunged into the waters and survived the impact. He held his breath, swam to the shore, dragged himself up the beach, found a companion who could help him make a new pair of wings, and then he stepped off the cliff again. He isn't the sole creator of the Xbox or the most important person in the project. But he deserves to soar in the clouds. Of all the Xbox advocates, he lasted the longest.

"I desperately wanted to take games to the next level," Blackley said. "We had to fight every day, and it made me miserable. I'm proud of the fact that I could deal with it."

At the same time, he wasn't superhuman. Nobody on the Xbox team performed to perfection. They were flesh and blood. The Xbox was the product of a chain of flawed individuals, and yet by many small miracles it came into being.

Blackley kept in close touch with Bachus. If they were going to get back to making games, they wanted to do it together. Their friendship had survived all of the hardships of the launch. Unencumbered by his duties on the Xbox, Bachus wasted no time on regrets and set off to find a way to do something equally innovative as the Xbox. He began raising money to start a new kind of game production company, one that focused on working with developers to produce games and offloaded the risk of development from game publishers. He was, he said, so ingrained in the games industry that he was of no use to anybody else. The odds were good that if Blackley didn't find a way to make games at Microsoft, he'd wind up with Bachus again.

Those who left the Xbox project found that they didn't get to take much glory with them. Bachus, Ted Hase, Otto Berkes, Rick Thompson, Bob McBreen, and Nat Brown were not listed in the secret screen of credits of hundreds of Xbox contributors that scrolled by if you pushed the right buttons on the Xbox controller. Microsoft said the omissions may have come from the programmers taking a list of names from an e-mail distribution list, but some people who were no longer working on the project and hadn't for some time were listed. These omissions were unfortunate but typical of the slights that people who dropped out of the Xbox scene had to suffer. The sad thing about the project was that people got chewed up in the pursuit of Sony as if that were the only way to get the job done.

There are many more unsung people who haven't been mentioned in this book. But since this isn't an encyclopedia on all things Xbox, they haven't been mentioned. The Xbox in the end is their reward. If it prevails, they will have succeeded in rewiring the minds of a whole generation.

"In the end the Xbox is excellent," Blackley said after the launch, hoisting sake and sitting in a Japanese restaurant with Bachus and a group of friends. "We had the opportunity to participate in something totally extraordinary."

NOTES

CHAPTER TWO

1. Ken Auletta, *World War 3.0* (New York: Random House, 2001), p. 166.

2. Ibid., p. 162

3. David Kirkpatrick, "Microsoft: Is Your Company Its Next Meal?" *Fortune*, April 27, 1998.

4. Reiji Asakura, *Revolutionaries at Sony* (New York: McGraw-Hill, 2000).

5. Dean Takahashi, "How Four Renegades Persuaded Microsoft to Make a Game Machine," *Wall Street Journal*, March 10, 2000.

6. John Markoff, "Fight of the (Next) Century," *New York Times*, March 7, 1999.

7. David Bank, *Breaking Windows* (New York: Free Press, 2001), p. 124.

8. See original comment in "Microsoft Explores New Territory: Fun," by Chris Gaither, *New York Times*, November 4, 2001.

9. David Bank, *Breaking Windows*, p. 175.

CHAPTER THREE

1. Geoffrey Moore, *Crossing the Chasm* (New York: Harper-Business, 1999).

2. Donald Tapscott, *Growing Up Digital*, (New York: McGraw-Hill, 1999).

3. Henry Jenkins, "Game Theory: It's a Video Game, Certainly, But Is It Art?" *New York Times*, October 14, 2000.

CHAPTER FOUR

1. Van Burnham, *Supercade: A Visual History of the Videogame Age 1971–1984*, (Massachusetts: MIT Press, 2001) p. 317.

2. Dean Takahashi, "Physics' New Frontier: Computer Games," *Wall Street Journal*, May 3, 1999.

CHAPTER FIVE

1. Michael Drummond, *Renegades of the Empire* (New York: Crown Publishing, 1999), p. 3.

CHAPTER SIX

1. Dean Takahashi, "Nvidia's Boss Talked Doom, Demanded Success," *Wall Street Journal*, October, 7, 1999.

CHAPTER SEVEN

1. David Bank, *Breaking Windows*, p. 175.

CHAPTER EIGHT

1. David Bank, *Breaking Windows*, p. 13.

2. Source: Portelligent Inc. consulting firm, Austin, Texas.

CHAPTER ELEVEN

1. Paul Andrews, *How the Web Was Won*, (New York: Broadway Books, 1999), p. 327.

CHAPTER FOURTEEN

1. Jeffrey M. O'Brien, "The Making of the Xbox," *Wired*, November 2001.

CHAPTER NINETEEN

1. Digits, *Wall Street Journal*, March 16, 2000.

CHAPTER TWENTY

1. Scott McCloud, *Understanding Comics* (Northampton, MA: Kitchen Sink Press, 1993).

CHAPTER TWENTY-FOUR

1. Omar Bradley, *A Soldier's Story* (New York: Henry Holt & Co., 1951).

CHAPTER TWENTY-FIVE

1. Geoff Keighley, Gameslice.com.
2. Ibid.
3. Steven L. Kent, *The Ultimate History of Video Games* (Roseville, CA: Prima Publishing, 2001).

CHAPTER TWENTY-SIX

1. Jeffrey M. O'Brien, *Wired,* November 2001.

CHAPTER TWENTY-SEVEN

1. Source: Interview with Steve Mollman on Salon.com.
2. "Ballmer Discusses Xbox's Broader Concept," *Reuters,* November 29, 2001.

CHAPTER TWENTY-EIGHT

1. Mark Pesce, *The Playful World* (New York: Ballantine Books, 2000), p. 208. Note: Wording corrected from the book, which said polygons per second.
2. Scott McCloud, "Outside In," *Computer Gaming World,* December 2001.

INDEX